INSTRUCTIONAL
CONSULTATION TEAMS

The Guilford School Practitioner Series

EDITORS

STEPHEN N. ELLIOTT, Ph.D.   **JOSEPH C. WITT, Ph.D.**
University of Wisconsin—Madison   Louisiana State University, Baton Rouge

Academic Skills Problems: Direct Assessment and Intervention
EDWARD S. SHAPIRO

Curriculum-Based Measurement: Assessing Special Children
MARK R. SHINN (Ed.)

Suicide Intervention in the Schools
SCOTT POLAND

Problems in Written Expression: Assessment and Remediation
SHARON BRADLEY-JOHNSON and JUDI LUCAS-LESIAK

Individual and Group Counseling in Schools
STEWART EHLY and RICHARD DUSTIN

School-Home Notes: Promoting Children's Classroom Success
MARY LOU KELLEY

Childhood Depression: School-Based Intervention
KEVIN D. STARK

Assessment for Early Intervention: Best Practices for Professionals
STEPHEN J. BAGNATO and JOHN T. NEISWORTH

The Clinical Child Interview
JAN N. HUGHES and DAVID B. BAKER

Working with Families in Crisis: School-Based Intervention
WILLIAM STEELE and MELVYN RAIDER

Practitioner's Guide to Dynamic Assessment
CAROL S. LIDZ

Reading Problems: Consultation and Remediation
P. G. AARON and R. MALATESHA JOSHI

Crisis Intervention in the Schools
GAYLE D. PITCHER and SCOTT POLAND

Behavior Change in the Classroom: Self-Management Interventions
EDWARD S. SHAPIRO and CHRISTINE L. COLE

ADHD in the Schools: Assessment and Intervention Strategies
GEORGE J. DuPAUL and GARY STONER

School Interventions for Children of Alcoholics
BONNIE K. NASTASI and DENISE M. DeZOLT

Entry Strategies for School Consultation
EDWARD S. MARKS

Instructional Consultation Teams: Collaborating for Change
SYLVIA A. ROSENFIELD and TODD A. GRAVOIS

INSTRUCTIONAL CONSULTATION TEAMS

Collaborating for Change

SYLVIA A. ROSENFIELD, Ph.D.
TODD A. GRAVOIS, Ph.D.

THE GUILFORD PRESS
New York   London

©1996 The Guilford Press
A Division of Guilford Publications, Inc.
72 Spring Street, New York, NY 10012

Printed in the United States of America

This book is printed on acid-free paper.

Last digit is print number: 9 8 7 6 5 4 3 2 1

Library of Congress Cataloging-in-Publication Data

Rosenfield, Sylvia A.
Instructional consultation teams : collaborating for change
/ Sylvia A. Rosenfield, Todd A. Gravois.
p. cm.—(Guilford school practitioner series)
Includes bibliographical references and index.
ISBN 1-57230-013-2
1. School children—Mental health services. 2. School
children—Counseling of. 3. Psychological consultation.
I. Gravois, Todd A. II. Title.
III. Series.
LB3430.R67 1996
371.7—dc20
95-33486
CIP

In memory of Dr. Jane Ross-Reynolds,
who, in her lifetime, modelled
the art of collaborative practice
and played a key role in bringing about
our professional collaboration

Preface

The practice of consultation in the schools has grown in scope and influence over the past twenty years. Numerous textbooks, research articles, and even a new journal devoted to psychological and educational consultation all give credence to the belief that indirect service delivery has the potential to facilitate the healthy growth and development of students (Zins, Kratochwill, & Elliott, 1994). The actual practice of school consultation, however, appears to have lagged behind its perceived value (Hughes, 1994). Individual practitioners, in general and special education and in school psychology, indicate the difficulty in making the transition to a consultation model. In addition, it is uncommon to find a collaborative school culture in which consultation may thrive (Rosenfield, 1992). Unfortunately, much of the literature focuses on consultation skills and on helping consultees ulitize these skills, rather than on the issues of transition. There is relatively little written about how to support and empower professionals interested in developing consultation services in school settings.

This book addresses this problem by articulating a design for initiating, implementing, and institutionalizing a consultation-based service delivery system. The design is a systematic approach that respects the culture of the school and the process of change as well as the integrity of a particular model of service delivery—Instructional Consultation Teams (IC-Teams). We are writing this book for those who seek to facilitate and participate actively in this change process. This is a handbook for change, written for the school-based professional, or the *change facilitator*, who seeks to implement a particular kind of support services within the schools. It is our conviction that those who seek to implement interdisciplinary consultation services need two different sets of information and skills: (1) a clearly articulated model for school consultation services, and (2) a road map for adapting this model to the ecology of their own particular school setting and culture. Although the literature on school consultation and school change are rarely brought together, the change facilitator needs to be able to integrate information from both fields of study.

Fundamentally, the book focuses on school professionals seeking to change more than simply their own individual role and functioning. Increasingly innovators are taking more holistic, organic, and multilevel approaches so as to avoid the charge of "tinkering" (Fullan, 1991). As Fullan (1991) suggests, "Discussing [the] individual role . . . , while helpful to a point, seems no longer adequate" (p. 81). Rather, in concurrence with current thinking about school reform, we believe that it is critical to have an impact on the school culture and that change must go beyond the individual professional striving single-handedly to function differently from others within the school. Although a practitioner may adopt new methods as part of an initial strategy to develop individual skill or to introduce a new mode of functioning to other key professionals in the school, the school's response to problems and to at-risk youngsters will not change without major alterations in the school culture. Thus, we pursue the institutionalization of the instructional consultation model, reflecting our belief that school restructuring needs to be carried beyond the initiation stage. We also consider the more fundamental question (Miles & Ekholm, 1991): How can we ensure that once new structures and systems are implemented, they will continue to exist and function?

We address the joint issues of consultation and the change process as they relate to a particular innovation package—IC-Teams. The first chapter describes the current context for developing interdisciplinary consultation support services in relationship to school and special education reform. Chapters 2 and 3 outline the essential dimensions of IC-teams, a combined delivery system and consultation process that has evolved as we and our colleagues have collaborated in change efforts in over sixty schools in four states. In Chapter 4 we consider the role of the change facilitator, elaborating on the skills required and struggles encountered when facilitating the transition to a new service delivery system. The design for that transition is the focus of Chapters 5 through 8. Utilizing a stage-based model for innovation design, derived from the work of Fullan (1991) and others, we provide a road map for initiating (Chapter 5), training (Chapter 6), implementing (Chapter 7), and institutionalizing (Chapter 8) IC-Teams. Each chapter includes sections on the dimensions of the stage under discussion, issues and concerns involved in facilitating the transition, and evaluation procedures required. The chapters also include examples taken from our work in the schools. In Chapter 9, we summarize the major issues and themes of this book. The appendices contain a variety of related forms and materials that we have utilized in the schools and that we believe would be useful to facilitators.

The change process delineated here is not for the faint hearted or for those who wait for others to set the course. Nor do we guarantee success for those who faithfully follow the program—the process of change is too unstable for that. Our justification for writing this book arises from two sources: (1) the concepts presented are based on the extensive literature on school and organizational change, and (2) the activities and themes arise from our growing (in every sense) experience with the process. The energy, commitment, risk-taking ability, and courage needed to make change cannot be found in this or any book. Paraphrasing a popular commercial, one principal said about her team, which was finding every reason to resist change, "We just need to do it!" We urge school professionals interested in change to follow her advice.

Acknowledgments

This book represents the accumulated knowledge gleaned from ten years of practice in real schools across multiple sites. Without the enthusiasm, energy, and commitment, as well as questioning and criticism, of the interdisciplinary practitioners with whom we have been privileged to work, this book would not have been possible. Although we risk not mentioning the contribution of some, we feel compelled to acknowledge as many as possible.

In one of the first two settings in which the first author (SR) collaborated on building support teams, the Early Intervention Project, we acknowledge the following individuals: James Tucker and Don Duville, who had the vision to see the possibilities, Ed Gickling, from whom we have learned the CBA model and who continues to contribute to our projects; Florence Rubinson, with whom SR traveled by car, train, and bus to school sites; and the school and district staffs, most especially those in the New Britain Public School District—Marylu Wojtusik, Susana Sikorsky, and Patricia Brown. During the same time period, the development of a team model, the Child Study Team Project, was supported by the Hyde Park School District, most especially Sara (Sally) Kuralt, who would not allow SR to say no to working with the district.

In Pennsylvania, special acknowledgment to all the Project Link participants, who helped clarify the training and process components, but especially, William Wehr, who saw the virtue in collaborating across intermediate units (IU's) and universities; and the four project link facilitators—Judith Iasiello, Alma Miller, Elaine Moe, and Danette Richards. Our gratitude to Rosalind Fudell, who not only drove with SR across the Commonwealth of Pennsylvania to the Project Link sites and training, but who also designed the first edition of the Level of

Implementation Scale. In that same time period, our understanding of the urban school implementation of IC-Teams was enriched by our relationship with the M. Hall Stanton School and its remarkable principal at that time, Deanna Burney. She has provided an indelible image of caring for urban children, in her insistence on providing a culture of intellectual and emotional support for staff and students.

However, this book could not have been written without the collaboration of administrators, psychologists, and educational professionals in the Howard County Public Schools of Maryland, where the version of IC-teams described here was refined and evaluated. Special acknowledgment to James McGowan, Associate Superintendent of Instruction, and Eleonore Krebs, Supervisor of Psychological Services, who for different reasons had the vision to bring the project into being. Among those willing to break the mold, we acknowledge the two principals of the pilot schools, Karen Moore-Roby and Jacqueline Lazarewicz, and the school psychologists who were willing to move away from their safe testing harbor for the high risk facilitator role, first Grace Jones and Jodi Koch, and in the following years, Susan Garner, Susan Bartels, Betty Skirven, John Klyap, Clyde Robinette, Jim Doonan, Tina DeForge, Marla Phillips, Cindi Schulmeyer, Karen Rakshys, and Nancy Enders. To all of the team members in the schools, our debt is inestimable, and it is our hope that the IC-Team experiences have provided each person with value in exchange.

SR also wishes to acknowledge the special contributions of the consultation students whom she has taught in the School Psychology Programs of Fordham University, Temple University, and the University of Maryland at College Park. Teaching is still the best way to learn!

We are in debt to Karen Herring for her editorial assistance during the final revisions of the manuscript.

To Gary and the late Jane Ross-Reynolds, our gratitude for bringing the two authors to the same place, so that our professional collaboration was able to evolve.

To the home team, we owe the most special thanks for giving up the time that could have been spent collaborating on family projects rather than professional ones. Our spouses, Marvin and Lynne, have always been on our side. Finally, a tribute to a very special person, Alicia Marie Gravois, who has developed even more beautifully than the manuscript.

Contents

Chapter 1 The Context for Change   1

The Call for Reform   2
Beliefs and Assumptions of IC-Teams   11
Summary   19

Chapter 2 The Collaborative Consultation Process   21

The Consultation Relationship   23
The Process of Instructional Consultation   26
Summary   37

Chapter 3 The Instructional Consultation Team   38
              Delivery System

Collaborative Teaming   38
Evaluation Design   54
Summary   58

Chapter 4 The Change Facilitator   59

The Process of Change   60
The Change Facilitator   71
Summary   82

Chapter 5 Initiating the Process   83

Considerations in IC-Team Initiation   83
Summary   99

Chapter 6 Professional Development of IC-Team Skills   100

General Considerations in Designing
  and Delivering Training 101
Content of Training 107
Summary 117

Chapter 7 Implementing IC-Teams   118

Facilitating Team Functioning 119
Facilitating Case Manager Functioning 132
Creating a School Environment That Aids
  Implementation 145
Evaluating Implementation 149
Celebration 149
Summary 151

Chapter 8 Institutionalizing IC-Teams   153

What Is Institutionalization and Why Is It Important? 153
Considerations in Institutionalizing IC-Teams 155
Summary 165

Chapter 9 The Future of IC-Teams   166

Future Directions for IC-Teams 167
Conclusion 170

Appendix A IC-Team LOI—Revised   171
Appendix B Sample Contract   192
Appendix C Simulation Case   194
Appendix D Tape Analysis   200

References   205

Index   213

INSTRUCTIONAL
CONSULTATION TEAMS

1

The Context for Change

Change is a part of life, inevitable but not always planned and often not welcome. Schools in particular have "been more subject to pressure for change" (Sarason, 1982, p. 9) than any other major social institution, with evidence of only limited success. It is a truism that planned and structured innovation in schools requires much energy and know-how, and it is not to be undertaken without consideration of the risks involved and resources needed (see, e.g., Fullan, 1991; Sarason, 1982).

This book is about how to introduce a particular type of change into schools, in this case, a complex innovation termed Instructional Consultation Teams (IC-Teams). It is complex because it results in school restructuring, involves multiple individuals and multiple processes, and, perhaps even more importantly, is based on a paradigm of individual differences that is not yet the dominant conception of the etiology of behavioral and academic problems. IC-Teams' service delivery, described in Chapters 2 and 3, is a particular variation of school-based support services, which have become more widely adopted as problems with the current special education service system have become increasingly apparent. In addition, there is a growing research base for this and similar models (for reviews, see, e.g., Fudell, 1992; Nevin & Thousand, 1987; Rosenfield, 1992).

Innovative practices do not readily introduce themselves into the daily lives of practitioners, and the literature on the dissemination of innovations is replete with cautionary tales of failed implementation. However, the research also contains solid information, much of it generated since the 1970s, about how "to become agents, rather than victims, of change" (Fullan, 1993, p. ix). Given the difficulty of implementing change in schools, a compelling reason must exist before school professionals ought to consider a major restructuring in how services are delivered to the most vulnerable students. This may be especially true for school psychologists, special educators, and other resource personnel who are not often addressed in the school reform literature. Being urged to change is uncomfortable, at best, and even more exasperating if the rationale for the change and the particular direction of the change are not clear. Our purpose in this chapter is to discuss the reasons for recommending change and to show how school-based support systems, such as IC-Teams, address the concerns that have been raised.

THE CALL FOR REFORM

Dissatisfaction with Special Education Services

The current state of affairs in schools is not considered satisfactory. American schools are viewed as failing to deliver either excellence or equity, and much has been said about the inability of American schools in general to deliver a quality product over the past 30 years. Reports such as a *Nation at Risk* (National Commission on Excellence in Education, 1983), *Tomorrow's Teachers* (Holmes Group, 1986), and *A Nation Prepared* (Carnegie Forum on Education and the Economy, 1986) have been cited consistently by reformers. In addition to concern about the general status of American schools, over this same period both special education and general education have experienced internal and external criticism about service delivery to students at risk for failure and to those labeled with handicapping conditions.

In the 1970s the Education for Handicapped Children law, P.L. 94-142, was considered a major step toward providing quality education (and in some cases, any education at all) to students with handicapping conditions. However, criticism has escalated as major problems in the delivery of services have become apparent (see, e.g., Gartner & Lipsky, 1987). Specific concerns included the very act of labeling students (Hobbs, 1975), the disproportionate segregation of minority students in special education (Heller, Holtzman, & Messick, 1982), and the entire special education assessment process (e.g., Ysseldyke et al., 1983). In fact, even prior to P.L. 94-142, Dunn (1968) questioned whether special education for the mildly handicapped student was justifiable. In addition, research supported neither the uniqueness of special education instruction nor improved student outcomes in the disjointed categorical programs that developed (Slavin, Madden, & Karweit, 1990). Slavin et al.'s (1990) summary of the research suggested that it was not where services are provided, but the quality of the instruction that made the difference, a point not unlike that made by

Bloom (1976), whose classic work suggested that "variations in learning and the level of learning of students are determined by the students' learning history and the quality of the instruction they receive" (p. 16). In addition, as Brophy (1986) concluded in his summary of research on instruction, although it is clear that some students need more instruction and some need more intensive instruction, there is no evidence that the type of instruction needed is different. Further, a growing body of evidence suggests that "principles of effective instruction and effective schools have demonstrated utility in reducing referral rates of students to special education" (Nevin & Thousand, 1987, p. 281). Not only does good instruction need to be a part of special education, there is evidence that it prevents student failure as well. The critical issue is the adaptability of the instruction to the individual learner.

As discussion of the problems became more heated in the 1980s, a major schism occurred among professionals, advocates, parents, and policy makers about how students with special needs should be served. While some proposed restructuring the current system (Reynolds, Wang, & Walberg, 1987; Rosenfield & Reynolds, 1990; Will, 1986), others believed that the special education classification and placement system needed to be researched and improved, but not discarded (see, e.g., Kauffman, Gerber, & Semmel, 1988, as well as other articles in this issue of the *Journal of Learning Disabilities;* Oakland & Cunningham, 1990). Proponents of major restructuring (see, e.g., Gartner & Lipsky, 1987; Reynolds et al., 1987; Will, 1986) criticized the effectiveness and the ethics of special education in the same terms that were used in the 1960s with regard to segregated special classes as being "racially biased, instructionally ineffective, and socially and psychologically damaging" (Skrtic, 1991, p. 149). These reformers rejected the four assumptions that they believed were basic to special education as typically implemented:

(a) disabilities are pathological conditions that students have, (b) differential diagnosis is objective and useful, (c) special education is a rationally conceived and coordinated system of services that benefits diagnosed students, and (d) progress results from rational technological improvements in diagnostic and instructional practices. (Skrtic, 1991, p. 152)

Although defenders of the current special education system agreed that some of these assumptions needed to be rejected, they also were concerned that, in spite of the lack of evidence supporting special education, "the current system and its associated practices should be retained for political purposes, given the nonadaptability of the general education system and the fact that special education practices can be improved" (Skrtic, 1991, p. 157).

The central issue in the debate, then, became whether and how mainstream general education could be strengthened sufficiently to provide support for the growth and development of every student. In particular, the focus was on what alternative structures and supports would be necessary in order for students to be successful within the mainstream so that the need for special education and other similar structures (e.g., Chapter 1 programs) could be avoided.

Supporting General Education as an Alternative to Separate Services

If, in fact, general education can be an appropriate, less stigmatizing setting for students at risk for failure, the question to be addressed is how to create a more adaptive orientation in the mainstream of American education. According to Nevin and Thousand (1987), research findings support several responses to this question. First, both special and general educators need to change their beliefs about integration of students with learning and/or behavior problems: "special educators . . . must believe that general education systems *can* appropriately serve students with handicaps. . . . general educators must believe they can positively affect the education of students with handicaps . . . and that they will receive necessary administrative and educational support for integrating students with handicaps" (Nevin & Thousand, 1987, p. 275). Two critical assumptions are embedded here.

First, how learning problems are understood is important; they may be defined as internal deficits within children or as a mismatch between student abilities and the school's attempts to meet student needs. Each of these assumptions reflects different attitudes and beliefs. As long as individual student disability is perceived as the dominant cause of school failure, public education will be able to avoid undertaking the kind of reforms needed for all students to succeed (Skrtic, 1991).

The second underlying issue is that of administrative support for educating all students. A well-founded concern of parents, advocates for the disabled, and ethical professionals is that inclusive models of educating disadvantaged, disabled, and at-risk students will become programs of "dumping," that is, placing students into classrooms without providing adequate support services. In order to allay these fears, administrators and policy makers must demonstrate a commitment to funding appropriate, restructured services. Also required are guarantees to maintain special education and pupil personnel services (albeit in restructured form), adequate student–teacher ratios, and evaluation of outcomes. In some districts this has meant waivers for continuing to fund special education personnel as the number of labeled students has decreased. Ultimately, change will be impossible unless there is basic trust that resources will not be withdrawn as the number of labeled handicapped students decreases and that administrators will not place students with special needs into classroom settings without adequate support to the classroom teacher.

Changing beliefs and attitudes and building administrator support is not enough. Skrtic (1991) suggests that there are underlying organizational regularities and cultural practices that contribute to the failure of schools to address diverse student needs; that is, schools are not able to adapt to student needs at the classroom level because of the way schools are organized. One critical regularity involves how teachers consider their role. It has been suggested that educational reform has failed because it "has either ignored teachers or oversimplified what teaching is about" (Fullan & Hargreaves, 1991, preface). Teachers are encouraged not to personalize or adapt their instructional programs, but rather to master and improve their ability to deliver these programs. They are evaluated in terms of how well they present their curricula, rather than on how much students learn. There is empirical evidence that "teachers rarely view their instructional practices as a potential source of the problem in special education referrals, and that the special education referral and classification process is oriented to place the blame for failure on the student rather than on the standard programs in use" (Skrtic, 1991, p. 203). Special education serves to protect teachers and schools from acknowledging the limitations of these standard programs and teaching practices, thus removing a potential source of innovation as well:

> In organizational terms, student disability is neither a human pathology nor an objective distinction; it is an organizational pathology, a matter of not fitting the standard programs of the prevailing paradigm of a professional culture, the legitimacy of which is artificially reaffirmed by the objectification of school failure as a human pathology through the institutional practice of special education. (Skrtic, 1991, p. 169)

Skrtic proposes the importance of reconceptualizing the organizational structure of schools from that of a professional bureaucracy, premised on perfecting standard skills and programs by teachers, to an *adhocracy*, configured as a problem-solving organization. He suggests the analogy of the National Aeronautics and Space Administration (NASA) during the 1960s. Because there was no standard program available to put an American on the moon, professionals worked on an ad hoc basis. No specialty or profession had all the answers in its standard repertoire, so collaboration and mutual adjustment were the bases for the division of labor within the NASA Apollo program. Likewise, as schools cope with the uncertainty that is inherent in the problems they are being asked to address — namely, student diversity, equity, and excellence — they must institute an *adhocracy* based on problem solving.

The Problem-Solving Culture as a Necessary Condition for Reform

The creation of an effective problem-solving culture in the schools is the fundamental construct underlying the collaborative, interdisciplinary consultation process described in this book. It is also one of the major operating assumptions of the school reform and restructuring movement of the 1990s. For example, Fullan and Hargreaves (1991) define a major problem in education as "not enough opportunity and not enough encouragement for teachers to work together, learn from each other, and improve their expertise as a community" (p. 1), and they introduce the concept of "interactive professionalism," which redefines "the role of teachers and the conditions in which they work" (p. 63). Embodied within this concept are the following dimensions:

- collaborative work cultures.
- norms of continuous improvement where new ideas are sought inside and outside one's setting.
- reflection in, on and about practice in which individual and personal development is honoured, along with collective development and assessment. (p. 63)

Although there are many specific strategies and techniques available, the critical factor is the need for "new ways of thinking and acting" to "permeate the daily life of schools" (Fullan & Hargreaves, 1991, p. 63). Rosenholtz (1989) describes the uncertainty inherent in the profession of teaching, given its nonroutine nature and activities, and stresses the need to develop problem-solving and renewal capabilities. Among the varying reform initiatives presented in the literature, some of which are in conflict with one another (Rowan, 1990), one common theme has emerged: To create innovative and productive changes in the ways schools operate, the roles of all the stakeholders — parents, teachers, administrators, special educators, pupil personnel staff, and students — must be restructured to increase collaboration and problem solving among school personnel and to change the school culture fundamentally around the norms of teaching. Kerr (1983) has suggested that schools need to be redesigned as workplaces:

> If Saab and Volvo could make what would appear to be inherently tedious work, the assemblage of automobiles, engaging at all and especially engaging over time, then surely we should be able to restructure teaching in a way that would build in new challenges.... Indeed, teaching would appear to be a case of an inherently interesting activity that schools have, in effect, reduced to a numbing repetition. (p. 143)

Current restructuring efforts, whether they be nationally initiated achievement tests or locally initiated drug prevention programs, often focus on the primary goal of impacting students. Student outcome goals are often expressed in terms of wanting students to achieve and to be contributors to society. Although such goals are appealing, we believe they represent goals that are either too narrow (increased student achievement) or too broad (student contribution to society). Perhaps a more functional aspiration for schools is to prepare students to be learners and problem solvers within the world they will ultimately face. However, if schools are to reach this goal, they must address how classroom and school culture can be adapted to contribute to the desired outcome. If school reform is to succeed, the conditions of teaching and learning must occupy a central place (Elmore & Associates, 1990).

In order for schools to produce learners and thinkers, school culture must provide problem-solving and learning opportunities for staff as well (Fullan, 1993; Sarason, 1990). "For whom do the schools exit?" Sarason (1990) asks, suggesting that no restructuring can occur until consideration is given to professional relationships and functioning within the schools. He is concerned about "the complete inability of educational reformers to examine the possibility that to create and sustain for children the conditions for productive growth without those conditions existing for educators is virtually impossible" (p. 147). In fact, the educational community has voiced the need to produce an environment of professional collaboration, reflection, and problem solving to address the problems of diversity, equity, and excellence (e.g., Elmore & Associates, 1990; Fullan, 1993; Grumet, 1989; Sarason, 1990). Moreover, we assume that not only will teaching professionals benefit from increased collegial interchange, but that all school staff need such opportunities. It is essential for interaction among school personnel to be interdisciplinary in nature because the nature of the problems

8   *The Context for Change*

in a given school, like those facing the Apollo group, do not have standard answers.

There is increased emphasis on the idea of the school as a learning organization (Fullan, 1993), a place in which teachers as well as students learn (Rosenholtz, 1989; Sarason, 1990). Creating a collaborative environment where all individuals within a school can become learners and thinkers represents a unified end result. To increase student achievement toward the goal of producing learners and thinkers, we must in some way increase teacher learning and thinking. In this context, to resolve problems regarding a student's difficulty in learning simple math processes implies that teachers be able to learn and think about math processes in different ways. The bottom line is that looking for deficits within a student benefits neither the teacher nor the student in reaching the ultimate goal. To create learners and thinkers means that teachers need the support and resources to move themselves and their students toward this target.

A problem-solving culture has yet another advantage. It has been demonstrated that research on effective teaching practices cannot be transformed directly into classroom practice; "even the best research-based practices must be transformed by teachers" (Anders & Bos, 1992, p. 475). This transformation requires a school culture that encourages reflection and provides support. Gaskins, Cunicelli, and Satlow (1992) concluded in their project that teacher instructional change occurred when teachers were encouraged to be active partners in the process and when collaborative methods provided teachers with the opportunity for learning, supportive feedback, and reflection. Kline, Deshler, and Schumaker (1992) studied barriers to the implementation by special education teachers of students with learning disabilities of "strategy instruction." Kline et al. found an array of potential factors limiting the use of research-based instructional strategies including "setting factors (e.g., lack of administrative support and high start-up costs), teacher factors (e.g., a poor mind-set and failure to use critical teaching skills), programmatic factors (e.g., lack of overall plans that specify how strategy instruction will be incorporated into ongoing instruction, and competing role expectations for resource room teachers), and instructional factors (e.g., high rates of interruptions during strategy instruction, bogging down during the instructional process, and not insuring that students demonstrate mastery and generalization of the strategy)" (p. 397). However, they also found a number of techniques to improve implementation, including "affording teachers an opportunity to meet regularly as support teams for the purpose of interacting with other teachers to share ideas and to solve problems" (p. 397).

The Importance of Collaborative School Cultures

Neither problem solving nor collaboration are new concepts to schools. Although most professionals in the schools have been trained "to function individually as expert problem solvers" (Friend & Cook, 1992, p. 12), schools are constantly bombarded with the demand that they become collaborative. There are many definitions of collaboration in schools as well as prescriptions for how to achieve collaborative school cultures (e.g., Elmore & Associates, 1990; Grumet, 1989; Little, 1990). Friend and Cook (1992) suggests that there is general agreement that "collaboration includes working together in a supportive and mutually beneficial relationship." In addition they offer their own definition of collaboration, which focuses on the interpersonal relationship itself—that is, *"a style for direct interaction between at least two coequal parties voluntarily engaged in shared decision making as they work toward a common goal"* (p. 5).

Little (1990) stresses the importance of a hard look at the concept of collaboration, "at the circumstances that foster or inhibit it, and at the . . . consequences that follow from it" (p. 510). Critical elements of this analysis include the degree to which the tasks of teaching are structured to "require and reward interdependence among teachers" (Little, 1990, p. 511), as well as the "beliefs, ideas, and intentions" (p. 511) that are supported by the collaborative exchanges. Interestingly, these same collaborative exchanges raise the possibility that, under some circumstances, teacher collaboration may serve to confirm commitment to present practice. This potential brings into question whether "teachers' time together advance(s) the understanding and imagination they bring to their work, or . . . teachers merely confirm one another in present practice" (Little, 1990). As Little (1990) notes, group problem solving is not, in and of itself, a positive structure unless care is taken to avoid problems such as *groupthink.*

Further, as with most organizational variables, there are costs associated with professional collaboration in schools (Fullan & Hargreaves, 1991). Structuring collaboration among teachers reveals both the strengths and the weaknesses of individual teachers and school norms. Additional costs of collaboration include the increased time involved in orchestrating opportunities for collegial interactions and the difficulties in gaining personal investment and commitment to the resolution of problems (Fullan & Hargreaves, 1991; Hord, 1986). The traditional lack of external rewards for teaching together, the pressure for immediate responses to problems, and the inherent complexity of interpersonal interactions also often work against the development of collaborative environments (Bredo, 1977).

When collaboration is in the context of giving help, there may be "psychological and social costs: the costs to one's own sense of competence, the status one has with important others, the obligations one incurs by accepting resources" (Little, 1990, p. 516). These costs result in several dilemmas that have been associated with giving help, for example, "the attributions of competence or incompetence that either person makes about the other, the tensions surrounding nominal status differences introduced by . . . title, and the demands for reciprocity" (Little, 1990, p. 517). The critical question becomes, then, how to develop patterns of interaction that will support innovation or commitment to more effective instructional policies for all students rather than an unconditional and nonreflective enthusiasm for collaboration.

An example in the recent past of an unsuccessful attempt to increase collaboration was the move toward open classrooms in the 1960s. To cope with the isolation of teachers, open classrooms were built to encourage professional collaboration, team teaching, and other cooperative methods of teaching. The idea that physical changes in school building structure alone would produce collaboration clearly was mindless. We would never consider, in the hopes of increasing collaboration among physicians, tearing down the walls of examination rooms. The thought of "examining wards" would be overwhelming for most physicians as well as patients. And yet physicians frequently collaborate, especially within institutional settings. In fact, a frequent phenomenon in schools built with open classroom space is that teachers have recreated their individual teaching space; they have rebuilt walls. Clearly, introducing the collaborative problem-solving mode of functioning in schools has not been an easy sell.

Developing Collaborative Problem-Solving Teams

One of the recent major school reform initiatives designed to increase teacher collaboration involves the concept of the collaborative problem-solving team. Team models that have as one of their goals an increase in professional collaboration include grade level teams (Friend & Cook, 1992), multidisciplinary teams (MDTs) for special education decision making (Yoshida, 1980), teacher assistance teams (e.g., Chalfant, Pysh, & Moultrie, 1979), as well as teams involved in site-based management and school reform programs (e.g., Maeroff, 1993). One result is that many schools now have a proliferation of teams working to complete discrete mandated functions.

Teams of various types have a long history in organizations, spanning the fields of business, industry, and mental health as well as education (Maeroff, 1993). Within schools, teams have been seen as one way to provide services to students having learning and behavior problems. Routine use of MDTs in the schools became the standard with P.L. 94-142, but their benefit has been uncertain. Maher and Pfeiffer (1983) presented the differing viewpoints about the use of MDTs:

> Some individuals . . . have asserted that MDTs are valuable because team members bring differing and important perspectives to bear on the education of handicapped and potentially handicapped children. Other individuals, in contrast, have argued that the MDT is an inefficient vehicle for managing pupil cases and that the MDT interferes with specialists' providing direct service to pupils, their parents, and families. (p. 123)

Other problems identified include "increased role ambiguity, and confusion concerning responsibility for decisions" (Abelson & Woodman, 1983, p. 125). Often none or few of these team members have received any training in additional skills for teaching and managing the learning process or in the team process itself. Further, there is often restricted, or nonexistent, financial support for such teams; thus teachers are required to "make time," work extra hours, or reduce their instructional time to participate on these teams.

As concerns about the special education referral and placement process have grown, teams have been utilized in prereferral or teacher support team initiatives (e.g., Chalfant & Pysh, 1984, 1989; Fuchs & Fuchs, 1988; Hayek, 1987; Ott, 1990; Rosenfield, 1992). Fudell and Dougherty (1989), in their survey of state education departments, documented that 13% of the 57 state and protectorate education departments that responded had mandated some form of teacher support team, and 66% indicated the existence of consultative team models that were either functioning or in pilot form. There are many team formats, stated functions and compositions, as delineated in Table 1.1. The concept of a school-based team has emerged as a normative and accepted structure within the school building. One variation on this structure, IC-Teams, is the focus of this book.

BELIEFS AND ASSUMPTIONS OF IC-TEAMS

This book provides a description of a particular collaborative consultation model—IC-Teams—and a set of guidelines for a change facilitator to introduce, implement, and institutionalize this team structure

TABLE 1.1. Variations of Problem-Solving Teams Found in Schools

Team name	Team composition	Leadership	Team focus	Team function	Formal training package indicated	Primary organization of service delivery	Principle investigator/reference
Assistance Teams	Multidisciplinary	Principal	At-risk students	Expedite referral process for the assessment and placement of students	Yes	Whole team	Barrs (1980, cited in Stokes, 1982)
Building Teams	Multidisciplinary building-based staff	Principal	Student/teachers	Helping teachers help targeted students; inservice of staff	None indicated	Whole team	W. Mickler (cited in Stokes, 1982)
Instructional Support Teams	Multidisciplinary building-based staff	Varies	Building issues/teachers	Support; inservice	None indicated	Whole team/teacher/consultant	Horvath & Baker (1982)
Staff Support Teams	Multidisciplinary	Shared by team members	Staff	Problem-solving forum; expedited referral and evaluation process; inservice	None indicated	Whole team	Stokes & Axelrod (1982)
Teacher Assistance Teams	Primarily teachers	Teacher member	Teachers	Problem-solving unit	Yes	Whole team	Chalfant & Pysh (1989); Chalfant, Pysh, & Moultrie (1979)
Local School Teams	Multidisciplinary	Principal	Student/teachers	Individual student planning; consultation with school personnel	None indicated	Whole team	Cole, Siegel, & Yau (1990)
Teacher Support Teams	Multidisciplinary; no regular classroom teachers	School psychologist/special educator	School organization	Collaborative problem solving	Yes	Whole team	Ott (1990)
IC-Teams	Multidisciplinary	Designated systems manager	Teacher/student/organization	Collaborative problem solving; instructional improvement	Yes	Case manager/consultant; whole team	Rosenfield (1992)

in a school setting. Although instructional consultation (Rosenfield, 1987), as a service delivery option, was originally designed for individual consultants, its integration into a more comprehensive school-based team model evolved over a number of projects with which we were involved. Table 1.2 provides descriptions of the sites in which earlier versions of IC-Teams were implemented.

As implementation of these projects occurred, it became clear that there was an underlying rationale that needed to be explicated to participants early in the process in order for them to make sense of the change. Without an understanding of these fundamental assumptions, IC-Teams became a series of activities rather than a connected pattern with meaning for the participants. For example, assessment activities introduced to support teachers in structuring classroom instruction became part of traditional psychoeducational assessments, a purpose for which these assessment techniques sometimes had insufficient validity (Shinn, Rosenfield, & Knutson, 1989).

Within a multidimensional conception of school change, one of the critical dimensions is the necessary "alteration of *beliefs*" (Fullan, 1991, p. 36). As Sarason reminds us, we are all at the mercy of our world view, that is "our unverbalized assumptions about the way the world is and should be" (Sarason, 1983, p. 83). Our beliefs and assumptions about how the world works inform our behavior but we usually do not

TABLE 1.2. School-Based Consultation Team Projects

Project	Initial year	District	Schools	Location	Major funding source
Early Intervention Project (CT)	1985	8	12	Urban	State
Child Study Team Prereferral Project (NY)	1985	1	5	Suburban/ rural	District
Project Link (PA)	1988	19	26	Suburban/ rural	State
Instructional Consultation/ School Support Team Project (PA)	1989	1	1	Urban	District
IC-Teams (MD)	1991	1	16	Suburban	District

consciously consider them. Because beliefs help us to define our behavior and organize our knowledge, they "are instrumental in defining tasks and selecting the cognitive tools with which to interpret, plan,
and make decisions regarding such tasks" (Pajares, 1992, p. 325). Increasingly it has become apparent "that the very questions we ask—
either personally or in scientific and applied psychology—emerge from
a particular world view that is responsible for validating them as well
as creating them" (Plas, 1992, p. 46). As educators and pupil services
personnel begin the process of interdisciplinary functioning, it is critical that they begin with an appreciation of the assumptions that un-
derlie IC-Teams and of how these assumptions compare to previously
held beliefs.

A Historical Perspective

What is the origin of our most basic beliefs about how schools should
operate, how children learn, and how we should address learning and
behavior problems of students? In the 1800s in America, schools began to take on some of their defining parameters. Writing from the
perspective of an educational historian, Finkelstein (1989) notes that
in the 19th century, the public schools in America were created in large
part by reformers who set out "to expand and civilize schools and the
children who would attend them" (p. 17). The classroom environment
was "designed to stamp out differences among students, to secure con-
formity to rules and regulation, to substitute the rule of law for the
rule of personal persuasion" (Finkelstein, 1989, p. 15). As teachers phys-
ically and psychologically moved away from the communal experience
of the one-room school house, the pedagogical process of teaching reading and writing became a private, asocial experience. As the bureaucrati-
zation of schools grew, students came to be increasingly treated as
standardized entities. This need to homogenize rather than accept diversity in students has remained a part of our school culture. Students
who are not standard have continued to be seen as a challenge to the
school culture and many "nonstandard" students have been labeled as
defective.

The dominant paradigms of special education and school psychology have reinforced this deficit-driven belief system about the etiology
of problems. Sarason (1981) has described American psychology as
"quintessentially a study of the individual organism unrelated to the
history, structure, and unverbalized world views of the social order"
(p. ix). He contends that a basic axiom for psychologists is that "if you
really understand the psychological structure of the individual, you have
the means either for changing or for controlling or helping him"

(p. 58). This individual, acontextual perspective has been a central theme in American child psychology as well, which is permeated by a belief in the individual, self-contained child:

> The child—like the Pilgrim, the cowboy, and the detective on television—is invariably seen as a free-standing isolable being who moves through development as a self-contained and complete individual. Other similarly self-contained people—parents and teachers—may influence the development of children, to be sure, but the proper unit of . . . analysis and the proper unit of . . . study is the child alone. . . . We have never taken fully seriously the notion that development is, in large measure, a social construction, the child a modulated and modulating component in a shifting network of influences. (Kessen, 1979, p. 819)

This emphasis on the individual as the basic unit for study has permeated the way problems in school are defined and interventions developed. Thus, when a student is experiencing academic or behavioral problems, the emphasis is on collecting data about the referred student. Usually few intensive and/or specific questions are asked about the instructional and management design that the teacher or parents have used or the child's progress under the specific adaptations developed. Such questions, when asked, are often perceived as blaming the teacher (or parent), and there is often great relief when a presumption of biological deficit is found (such as a learning disability or an attention deficit hyperactivity disorder), which can then elicit sympathy for the student and blame for no one.

Moreover, for legal and policy reasons, much attention over the past 20 years has been devoted to labeling individual students who demonstrate problems in learning and/or behavior and to determining the place where such students will receive assistance. Considerable special education and pupil personnel service resources are currently devoted to this sorting and placement process. However, as has been stated earlier in this chapter, there is growing belief that this system needs change because of problems in the credibility of the diagnostic process itself (see, e.g., Ysseldyke et al., 1983) as well as lack of documented efficacy for the current system (e.g., Reynolds et al., 1987; Rosenfield & Reynolds, 1990; Skrtic, 1991; Slavin et al,1990).

IC-Team Assumptions: Learning Communities and Educational Change

Given this brief historical background, the design of IC-Teams is based on the acceptance of three critical assumptions:

Assumption 1: All students are learners. The most basic belief is that the focus should be on facilitating learning for all students, not on documenting learning failures. When a student is not making acceptable progress, the match between the student, the task, and the instructional setting is examined. To maximize the learning of each student, attention is focused on the classroom environment and the delivery of instruction rather than predominantly on the deficits of individual students. Bloom (1976) provided a model of school learning that focuses on assessing alterable variables and modifying the conditions of learning rather than on identifying the deficits of learners.

Assumption 2: Focus on instructional match, not place. Placement in special education or remedial reading or retention is not an intervention. It is not where intervention occurs, but the match between the entry-level skills of the student and the instructional and management strategies used that is the key factor and should be the focus of problem solving.

A commitment to learner outcome based on alterable characteristics represents, for some school staff and parents, a major shift in basic beliefs about their tasks, in part because of the history described above. Just as it is common for teachers to evaluate themselves on the quality and the delivery of their lessons, school psychologists sometimes evaluate themselves on how comprehensively their psychoeducational evaluations define learner deficits. For students with handicapping conditions, the focus is often on the label the student will wear and the place in which the student will learn. However, with IC-Teams, there is a shift from examining largely nonalterable input variables, such as intelligence, to evaluating how to improve outcome in learner-centered terms, beginning with the general classroom setting. It is not where intervention is done, but rather the strategies used—instructional and management—that need to be the focus of problem solving. The goal is to work collaboratively to explore the entry level characteristics of the child so that instruction is pegged at the child's instructional level, utilizing research-based effective instructional and management interventions, and then to monitor progress to determine the child's rate of learning, improvement in behavior, or both.

Assumption 3: Build a problem-solving learning community in the school. A school culture based on shared technical expertise and norms of collaborative problem solving is the context in which students' academic and behavioral development can be addressed most effectively. When the school itself becomes a learning community for faculty and staff, it can more easily succeed in providing a strong learning community for students, particularly for those at the margins. A collaborative school culture helps provide the context for improved learner outcomes. Unlike the "egg carton" metaphor for the school (in which teachers all work in separate compartments called classrooms, and students are sent to other compartments when they are labeled as defective), there is a shared responsibility for student learning and behavior outcomes based on continuous professional discussion. In our experience, teachers have responded to the collaborative problem-solving culture positively, internalizing the notion that teachers are professionals—like doctors and lawyers—who consult and collaborate with one another on work-related problems.

In conceptualizing reformed structures, more support and collaboration between teachers and other professionals in schools have been recommended. It is not just the student who has existed in isolation. Teachers also have worked alone, with little collaboration with one another or with other professionals in education. Although there is a considerable literature supporting the pervasive nature of isolation and individualism in the teaching profession (see, e.g., Huberman, 1983; Lortie, 1975; Rosenholtz, 1989), research has demonstrated benefits from teacher collaboration in terms of student achievement, teacher morale, support for innovation, and support for new teachers (Little, 1990).

However, as indicated earlier (Little, 1990), closer attention needs to be paid to the type of teacher collaboration and collegial involvement that supports positive classroom and teacher outcomes. According to McLaughlin and Yee (1988), schools that work well often have highly collegial, problem-solving orientations. They provide many opportunities for teachers to interact and to provide feedback, support, and ideas to one another in nonevaluative contexts. Teachers discuss instruction and classroom practice and are infused with norms of ongoing professional development and interaction. Scant attention, however, has been directed at collegial models that encourage such interaction among all the various professionals who work in schools.

The development of a shared technical culture, to use Lortie's (1975) term, and norms of problem-solving interactions that are based on respect and equality among all school professionals interacting around learning and behavior concerns are important goals for IC-Teams. Achieving these goals, however, requires a change in school culture and the creation of new norms of interaction.

Change Process Assumptions

"What would it take to make the educational system a learning organization—expert at dealing with change as a normal part of its work, not just in relation to the latest policy, but as a way of life?" (Fullan, 1993, p. 4). In the literature (e.g., Hall & Hord, 1987; Fullan, 1993), change is described not as an event but rather as an ongoing process, which encompasses alterations in structures, beliefs, and behaviors. Likewise, IC-Teams require a variety of structural and normative changes, involving a process that assumes change will be neither immediately visible nor magically imposed. Fullan (1991) suggests that the time frame for "even moderately complex changes take from 3 to 5 years, while major restructuring efforts can take 5 to 10 years" (p. 49).

An increasing body of research on the process of change in schools has focused on

> both the *what* and the *how* of change. . . . It is possible to be crystal clear about what one wants and be totally inept at achieving it. Or to be skilled at managing change but empty-headed about what changes are most needed. To make matters more difficult, we often do not know what we want, or do not know the actual consequences of a particular direction, until we try to get there. . . . The problem . . . is one of how those involved in change can come to understand what it is that should change and how it can be best accomplished, while realizing that the what and how constantly interact and reshape each other. (Fullan, 1991, p. 5)

Out of the many failed innovations in the name of school reform in the early 1960s and 1970s came the recognition that several key factors improved the probability that planned change would be implemented and institutionalized. Change efforts may be directed at the following:

1. Dissemination of technical, research-based innovations to change practice;
2. Professional development for teachers and staff to change people;
3. Development of organizational capacity in problem solving to change organizational functioning; and/or
4. Systemic reform that incorporates the first three but goes beyond the school to include the district, state, and the community (Sashkin & Egermeier, 1993).

The fundamental assumption of this book is that the more attention given to each of these factors, the more likely that implementation will occur and change eventually will be institutionalized.

The "What" of IC-Teams

Early in our work, the importance of clarity concerning the IC-Team approach became apparent. Without it, schools and districts were unable to make informed decisions concerning adoption of IC-Teams as a service delivery system. Furthermore, they could not determine if program implementation had been successful. As a result, IC-Teams concepts were translated into an *innovation bundle,* that is, a set of structures and practices to be implemented as a package. Without a description of the essential elements of the model, a well-developed training package, and a method to evaluate implementation, schools may adopt the rhetoric of collaborative consultation without the substance. Many innovations in schools fail because their critical components are never implemented with integrity (Fudell, 1992). Further, no model of service delivery can be replicated unless it is clearly articulated. For all of these reasons, the details of IC-Teams are presented in Chapters 2 and 3.

The "How" of IC-Teams

For effective implementation of school-based consultation in the form of IC-Teams to occur, the process of transition itself needs to be integrated with the innovative package. In this way, real schools can make the changes necessary to offer services, utilizing concepts derived from the knowledge dissemination and utilization literature. It is not enough to have an innovation. There must also be a process by which change is introduced and supported. It is assumed here that underlying successful change is a multistage process of initiation, implementation, and institutionalization, each with its own business to be accomplished. Transcending the stages of change is the need for planned professional development, including supervised practice. Finally, we have come to view the necessity of well-trained facilitators as critical to effective change. We address these factors in depth in Chapters 4 through 8.

SUMMARY

This chapter presented the context for IC-Teams. There is much talk about educational reform in both the general and special education communities, based on dissatisfaction with current outcomes. The IC-Team approach has drawn upon several major themes in this context: for example, collaborative interaction among school personnel, focus on the learning environment for the student, and an understanding of the change process. If the reader is happy with current practice and outcomes and feels no pressure to consider change, there is no need to read further. However, if change toward a collaborative, problem-solving team model is appealing, the next section describes a specific innovation, IC-Teams, that has been developed based on the major themes delineated above. The third section of this book provides a guide for becoming skilled at facilitating the adoption and implementation of this specific innovation in a school or district.

2

The Collaborative
Consultation Process

The concept of instructional consultation (Rosenfield, 1987) was originally developed for the individual practitioner in the school to provide a framework for working with teachers' concerns about classroom learning and management problems. IC Tcams are a product of efforts to implement the concepts of instructional consultation at the school level that originated from school-wide projects (see Table 1.2) designed to change the process of referral for students about whom teachers had instructional and/or behavioral concerns. These projects were located in urban, rural, and suburban settings across four states, involved populations of diverse socioeconomic status and ethnic background, and sprang from different motivations for initiating the change. In each project, one or both of us participated, providing consultation and/or working on site as a change facilitator.

Although the projects differed in many respects, they all shared a commitment to two outcomes. The first involved a conceptual and behavioral shift in determining the etiology of learning difficulties and in perceiving what constitutes effective interventions. Rather than viewing a teacher or parent concern about a student as the result of a defect within the student (a medical model paradigm) that requires extensive psychoeducational diagnosis, school-based professionals in these projects came to perceive that such problems reflected an inadequate match between a particular student and the setting. Intervention was not seen as a place to send a student with a plan, but as a series of carefully structured activities developed from classroom-based assessment. The focus in these programs was on restructuring settings to facilitate the students' academic, social, and/or behavioral development. The second outcome centered on restructuring the school to develop a more collaborative, problem-solving culture in which an interdisciplinary team structured the service delivery framework (Rosenfield, 1992). These two features have been combined into IC-Teams, a model developed through continuous exploration and evaluation in school settings.

In order for an innovative model to be replicable, its critical components must be articulated and evaluated, and there must be a process for implementating these components. IC-Teams is a complex innovation package, organized around three features (see Figure 2.1): a problem-solving, instructional consultation process (Rosenfield, 1987); a delivery system structured around an interdisciplinary team; and an evaluation design to ensure that the innovation package has been implemented with integrity (Rosenfield, 1992). We address the delivery system and evaluation components in Chapter 3. The consultation process is presented in this chapter.

The IC-Team delivers instructional consultation (Rosenfield, 1987), a stage-based, collaborative, problem-solving process among professionals. When fully implementing IC-Teams, building staff routinely utilize the consultation process to address classroom academic and behavior issues and problems, as well as to plan proactively for maximum student achievement and development. After a teacher requests assistance, the system manager, or in some schools the team, assigns a case manager to work with that teacher. (Note that the terms "consultant" and "case manager" will be used interchangeably in this book, as will the terms "consultee" and "teacher.") The case manager and the teacher then engage in the consultation process.

The instructional consultation process serves as a scaffold for a variety of assessment and intervention methods that professionals can call upon in working through issues and concerns. Because the scaffold itself is relatively content free, there is room for individual schools with differing curricular orientations to adopt the process. However, it is essential that the assessment and intervention practices and strategies are ones supported by research. For example, it does not matter whether the problem area is reading, math, or classroom behavior; whether direct instruction or whole language is used in teaching reading; or whether behavioral or other types of classroom management techniques are used, so long as practice reflects state-of-the art instructional, motivational, and management strategies.

Successful consultation entails two key elements: (1) There must be an authentic working relationship between the partners in the process, and (2) the business of each stage of the consultation process must be effectively completed (Block, 1981). This chapter describes the type of relationship required for engaging in collaborative problem

Process Variables	Delivery System Variables
Collaborative consultation process for problem solving:	Structures by which the collaborative consultation process is delivered and maintained within a school:
• Establishing a consultation relationship between case manager and teacher which is collaborative and based on the use of effective communication.	• Team functioning: Representative team membership that meets regularly
• Stages of problem solving: Entry and contracting Problem identification and analysis Intervention planning Intervention implementation Resolution/termination	• Clearly articulated referral process: Referring teachers become part of the problem-solving process Active administration support and participation Use of case management
	• Documentation of cases and student progress

Evaluation Design

• Evaluation of training
• Evaluation of implementation
• Evaluation of outcomes

FIGURE 2.1. Three critical components of IC-Teams.

solving. It reviews the problem-solving process in terms of the tasks required at each stage. Although this chapter describes the consultation process, extensive supervised practice is required to achieve mastery of the process itself. The training process is presented in Chapter 6.

THE CONSULTATION RELATIONSHIP

Central to the problem-solving consultation process is the establishment of a collaborative relationship between the case manager (consultant) and the teacher (consultee). Although both parties are, in truth, responsible for the success of the problem-solving process, one of the case manager's tasks is to negotiate and monitor the quality of the consulting relationship. The case manager needs to be aware that the consultation process operates on multiple levels and that he or she must attend to the relationship as well as to the problem-solving tasks of each stage.

It is also fundamental that a collaborative school culture encourages professionals to work together without high personal cost; a task of the IC-Team is to work toward building this culture for the school.

There is consensus that, at each stage, consultation involves verbal interactions that are facilitated by clear communication strategies and the development of a working relationship based on authentic and collaborative interactions. However, the collegial, consultative relationship is also mutually influenced by each participant. Thomas Jefferson was reported to have attributed Benjamin Franklin's success as a diplomat to the fact that he never heard Franklin directly contradict someone else. In consultation, it is essential to appreciate the consultee's point of view and to enable movement in a different direction when a consultee is stuck.

The Collaborative Relationship

The collaborative consultation relationship is best described as a "working" relationship (Fisher & Brown, 1988). It is a nonhierarchical relationship between professionals; the case manager exerts an influence without direct power to enforce his or her position. Fisher and Brown (1988) recommend that we disentangle the process (how we handle a situation) from the substance or content being discussed. They remind us that we are most likely to have immediate substantive concerns on our minds: "However important the *way* we deal with each other may be, it often looks less urgent than our immediate goal" (Fisher & Brown, 1988, p. 17). The teacher is clearly intent on finding a solution to a perceived problem, not on constructing a relationship with the case manager. Unless the relationship is well structured, however, the partnership will be at a disadvantage, particularly when there is conflict or disagreement. As with most professional activities, setting the guidelines in advance minimizes difficulties later. Block (1981) stresses the importance of negotiating the relationship early, suggesting that the likelihood of a consultee implementing interventions is directly related to the extent of collaboration built into the process.

Working relationships cannot be bought by concessions; neither do they hinge on total agreement. What, then, are the rules for building a working relationship? According to Fisher and Brown (1988), the golden rule for building a working relationship is to do only those things that are both good for the relationship and good for each partner, whether or not the other person reciprocates. To apply this principle, the case manager should accept the consultee as worthy of consideration and care, trying to understand the consultee's frame of reference and to address matters that affect him or her. Irrespective of the consultee's behavior, the case manager should be reliable and be open to learning from the consultee. In addition to trying to persuade the consultee, the consultant should be open to persuasion. These guidelines are congruent with much of the interpersonal literature in consultation, which advises case managers to be empathic, authentic, and good listeners (see, e.g., Friend & Cook, 1992; Rosenfield, 1987).

It is the quality of authenticity that is perhaps most difficult to convey to new case managers. Block (1981) describes authenticity as behavior that puts "into words what you as a case manager experience as you work" (p. 31). Trust develops as the teacher becomes increasingly aware of the genuine nature of the interactions. Clear expression of the case manager's own needs and wants in the situation is important as well, and is part of being authentic. For example, it is sometimes difficult for new consultants to be clear about what is convenient for them when making arrangements to meet, and we have witnessed several of them feeling martyred and exasperated by inconvenient meetings they had agreed to attend. When the case manager has a hidden agenda with respect to a given teacher or student, the case manager's capacity to be authentic is compromised. This aspect of becoming an effective consultant needs discussion and coaching, as it is often difficult for new case managers to balance their own perspective on the case with norms of good manners, desires to avoid any hint of disagreement or selfishness, and wishes to avoid confronting a colleague.

Communication Strategies

The basic listening and communication skills of the helping process are known to facilitate clear communication in consultation. Perhaps one of the distinguishing aspects of collaborative consultation is extreme care in the use of questions. In working with teachers, the case manager needs information, but the question–answer format places the case manager in an expert stance. Dillon (1990) suggests a number of potential problems with obtaining information in this way: questions are suspected of producing blocking, reducing input, cutting off conversations, and inhibiting responses. Alternative strategies should be selected whenever possible, and these include requesting clarification, paraphrasing, perception checking, and examining actual student work samples. Because learning to use these and other consultation communication skills effectively is recommended, activities designed to teach good consultation communication strategies should be part of training (for further information, see, e.g., Friend & Cook, 1992; Parsons & Meyers, 1984; Rosenfield, 1987).

THE PROCESS OF INSTRUCTIONAL CONSULTATION

Over the past 25 years, the consultation field has been influenced by a number of disciplines, with school consultation researchers and practitioners taking a leadership role (Zins et al., 1993). Within school consultation, many models exist (for a review of the literature, see Idol & West, 1987; West & Idol, 1987; Zins et al., 1993). Instructional consultation (Rosenfield, 1987) is the major consultation framework used by IC-Teams. It is similar to other consultation models in its emphasis on the problem-solving process, the consultation relationship, and working with a consultee, usually a teacher who is concerned about the progress of a child or class. However, it is more focussed on the classroom instructional environment.

Instructional consultation takes a transactional perspective, emphasizing three interacting components of an instructional system. The learner is obviously one part of the system, with the focus on determining the student's entry level skills (or readiness to undertake the instructional task) and rate of progress. Curriculum goals, or the objectives as they are operationalized into classroom tasks that the learner is expected to master, make up the second component of the instructional system. The third major system component consists of the instructional and/or management strategies that enable, or potentially enable, the learning process.

There is considerable consensus that it is helpful to view consultation as a problem-solving model with specific stages, although authors differ in their characterization of the stages (West & Idol, 1987). Within instructional consultation, the stages are (1) entry and contracting, (2) problem identification and analysis, (3) intervention planning, (4) intervention implementation, and (5) resolution/termination. There is a strong emphasis on collecting data and relying on data for decision making throughout the process. Each stage has specific tasks that must be accomplished before moving on to the next stage. However, cycling through one or more of the stages again is sometimes necessary. A brief description of each stage follows. A more in-depth description of the tasks for each stage can be found in *Instructional Consultation* (Rosenfield, 1987).

Entry and Contracting

Entry is usually accomplished at the school and system level, and involves the decision to use consultation as a process for problem solving in a building and/or district. Chapter 5 focuses on IC-Team initiation and discusses the entry process at length. Contracting is a similar process at the individual level, in which the rules of the consultation relationship are discussed by the consultant and the consultee. Contracting provides an opportunity to set some ground rules for how the teacher and case manager will work together. It concludes with an explicit agreement between the teacher and the case manager to engage together (or the decision not to do so) in the consultation process.

Table 2.1 delineates the specific content that must be discussed at this stage. It is important for the classroom teacher as consultee, to know that the process will not begin with a hunt for solutions. Rather the teacher and case manager will be working collaboratively to frame the problem in classroom-based terms and to plan and develop an intervention strategy.

Contracting, which can take from 5 to 20 minutes, depending on

TABLE 2.1. Contracting

Case manager *negotiates* contract

    Introduces self as case manager

    Reviews process
        Reviews system
        Clarifies team function
        Checks teacher awareness of process

    Reviews problem-solving stages
        Goal setting
        Problem identification and analysis
        Intervention planning
        Intervention implementation
        Resolution/termination

    Clarifies problem ownership
        Problem owned by case manager and teacher
        Team involvement in problem

    Discusses time involvement
        Need for time
        Amount of time

    Explains data collection
        Baseline data
        Kinds of baseline data
        Who will collect data
        Continuing data collection

    Explains confidentiality, student's and teacher's
        Not used for teacher evaluation
        School policy on student confidentiality is followed

    Gains consultee agreement to be part of process

how familiar the consultee is with the process, is a discussion, not a speech by the case manager. Moreover, this discussion must occur even if there has been a presentation at a faculty meeting about the consultation process because it is never possible to know how individuals interpret the content of a presentation. The contract session must provide a genuine opportunity for dialog about joint responsibilities and for the teacher to refuse to participate. An agreement stipulates the time that will be required and a commitment to participate in the problem-solving relationship. At any time, the agreement can be renegotiated. Usually, it is the case manager who becomes aware of problems in the relationship and raises the issue of renegotiating a contract that is not pleasing to one or both parties.

Prior to any contract session or faculty presentation, the team must have clarified, first among themselves and then with the staff in the building, the limits of confidentiality between teachers and case managers. There are always risks to consultation, both intrapersonal and job-related, for teachers who assume the role of consultee, and the teachers need to be aware of how information from the consultation process will be used and by whom. Given that the principal is usually a member of the team (and is sometimes assigned as a case manager), this issue becomes particularly salient.

Another critical issue is how the problem-solving process interacts with the mandates of the special education laws and regulations. In most well-functioning IC-Team schools, direct referral for special education is rare without first going through the problem-solving process. This is not an attempt to subvert the law, but rather a concentrated effort to provide appropriate services to students without an intervening labeling process that diverts resources. However, the procedures must be known and understood by the relevant stakeholders in the school system and community, including parents, and a system of accountability for monitoring student progress must be in place.

There are a number of common pitfalls in the contracting process, the most frequent of which is simply a failure to discuss all of the issues delineated above. A second contracting problem occurs when the case manager presents the contract information as a lecture, rather than a dialog, about the process and concludes with a pro forma request for questions. Silence or simple acquiescence is not the same as commitment to engaging in the consultation process. Finally, there is an unfortunate tendency to skip the contracting process, often due to the press to move into the problem identification stage without delay. A teacher may be pressing to begin discussing the "real problem," that is, the student, and if the case manager is at all hesitant about "wasting time contracting," it is likely that this stage will be short-circuited.

Problem Identification and Analysis

Perhaps the most critical stage of the problem-solving process is that of problem identification and analysis. Although the original written or oral description of a "problem" by a teacher or parent is often the starting point for a full evaluation of a student by a multidisciplinary team, IC-Team case managers do not assume that the initial concern is even an adequate representation of the problem, much less a reason to assume an evaluation of the child is needed. Instead, the referral is the beginning of a process, conceptualized from a language systems perspective, of problem setting (Schon, 1983; White, Summerlin, Loos, & Epstein, 1991)—"professional practice has at least as much to do with finding the problem as with solving the problem found" (Schon, 1983, p. 18). In practice, the situations in which problem setting occurs are characterized by "uncertainty, disorder, and indeterminacy" and by "unique events" (p. 16) that make a "cookbook" (i.e., standardized) approach to diagnosis untenable.

The goal in problem identification is to develop a problem statement that is meaningful to all the participants and is respectful of their understandings and perspectives, yet is framed so that there is room for new ideas and new meanings that provide "a context for change to develop" (White et al., 1991, p. 350). For example, the teacher who initially believes a child has an attention deficit disorder must not feel that her beliefs about causality are demeaned or ignored as the problem is reframed from an internal deficit in the student to a delineation of the specific behaviors that concern the teacher in the classroom. This restructuring of the problem to specific behaviors empowers teachers to feel more optimistic about resolving problems (Tombari & Bergan, 1978).

Problem setting involves the construction of the "reality" of a problem through conversation by the individuals involved. Indeed, "consultation can be seen as the 'management of conversation' with persons who are connected by their active communication about someone or something that is being described as problematic" (White et al., 1991, p. 349). Together, the case manager and teacher "create a reality, or meaning system" (p. 350), each contributing ideas, values, and prejudices.

In sum, this stage is important in two respects. First, the problem itself does not exist in any meaningful way separate from how we talk and think about it. A behavioral psychologist and a psychodynamic psychologist, both observing a first grader sucking her thumb during reading class, are likely to perceive very different problems. A related aspect of the problem identification process is the avoidance of labeling, particularly early in the consultation conversation. Labeling behavior or academic functioning as problematic

> makes a value judgment about the meaning of that behavior, but does little to describe that behavior. . . . The act of labeling tells more about the assumptions and attitudes of the labeler with regard to normative and pathological functioning than it tells about the particular problem. (White et al., 1991, p. 350)

Secondly, the way we choose to talk about the problem can have specific consequences, not only for how we might intervene, but also for the possibility of resolving the problem in the least restrictive environment. Diagnostic labels, such as learning disability, call forth in the minds of teachers, the need for interventions beyond their expertise, and can short circuit their problem-solving efforts.

The important work of problem setting is the goal of the problem identification stage. Care is taken to avoid premature closure or diagnosis as well as those procedures that result in labeling a child. The conversation, in which all perspectives are respected, if not explicitly accepted, attempts to define a problem in such a way that the participants can resolve the situation by moving the student toward more positive growth and development.

The initial step in this stage is for the case manager and the teacher to meet to discuss the problematic situation. The problem is always defined in terms of a perceived discrepancy between the actual achievement and/or behavior of the student and that which the teacher feels is appropriate. The language used must specify the behaviors that define the discrepancy for the classroom teacher. The purpose of each session and activity devoted to problem identification is to move the consultant–consultee dyad closer to a mutual understanding of the perceived discrepancy between the student's current functioning and the level of functioning that the teacher expects the student to maintain, either in classroom social or academic behavior. Table 2.2 describes the specific areas to be explored, depending on whether the area of concern is academic or behavioral. There are three techniques that facilitate the problem identification process: interview, observation, and assessment.

Interview

The interview process itself contributes to problem identification. The case manager is responsible for directing the conversation toward clarifying the discrepancy between the student's current and desired

TABLE 2.2. Problem Identification and Analysis Content

Major Purpose: To identify teacher concerns in observable and measurable terms. To explore, define, and analyze referral concerns.

1. Review referral and teacher's perception of the concern.
2. Prioritize and then target specific problems for intervention.
   - Ensure student is working at instructional level.
3. Clarify concern and impact within classroom environment.
   - Review available information.
   - Describe events that occur before and after that affect the problem.
   - Explore previous and current instructional and management strategies.
   - Explore conditions under which student does achieve.
4. Describe problem in observable/measurable terms.
5. Select data collection method and establish baseline.
6. Specify "gap" between current and expected performance.
7. Establish short-term goal (4–6 weeks).

performance in behavioral terms. Doing this collaboratively allows the teacher to retain ongoing responsibility for the student's progress. The specific information that helps to clarify the discrepancy includes (1) the student's social behaviors and/or academic skills, including entry level skills in these areas; (2) the nature of the tasks being required of the student; and (3) the instructional and/or management strategies used, both effective and ineffective. Further, data collection is necessary in order to help frame the discrepancy, to pinpoint the entry level, and to document progress made under different interventions.

Because the teacher and case manager do not always have essential information, additional assessment activities may be required. In particular, two strategies have been found to be helpful in clarifying the discrepancy between desired and actual classroom behavior: (1) classroom-based assessment of academic skills (see, e.g., Gickling & Rosenfield, 1995; Rosenfield, 1987; Rosenfield & Kuralt, 1990); and (2) behavioral observation of the task, the student's behavior, and the instructional/management strategies (Rosenfield, 1987; Ysseldyke & Christenson, 1993).

Classroom-Based Academic Assessment

Student assessment is a multibillion dollar activity of the American educational establishment, but relatively little is known about one of its most essential aspects, the "sleeping giant—the truly huge and complex world of classroom assessment" (Stiggins & Conklin, 1992, p. 2). Existing research suggests, according to Stiggins and Conklin (1992), that there are quality control problems and that, in fact, teachers themselves are concerned about how well they assess student learning. Several concerns of Stiggins and Conklin (1992) are related to the problem identification stage. The first problem is that "teachers tended to rely on mental recordkeeping to manage some kinds of performance information" and that they "remain unaware of the dangers of bias inherent in such recordkeeping methods" (p. 142). Additionally, information about affective performance, such as student motivation, is "based on various kinds of measures. . . . However, quality control in this arena of assessment often receives little or no attention" (p. 142). A further problem emerges in the relationship between assessment and instruction. Again, according to the research of Stiggins and Conklin (1992),

> in most of these classrooms, teachers view instruction and assessment as separate activities. Integration of the two is done haphazardly and rarely to full advantage. . . . Most teachers either do not take the time or do not know how to make good use of assessment in presenting instruction, in evaluating it, and in making it more effective and meaningful. (p. 148)

Poor measurement in the classroom context is likely to lead to inadequate instructional decision making: "At the very least, poor decisions mean inefficient instruction, and at worst they can lead to failure to learn and an attendant loss of student motivation to participate in the learning process" (p. 196).

Case managers, therefore, must have some understanding of how to assist teachers in generating appropriate and sound information for assessing the discrepancy that the teacher perceives. One of the critical techniques for this task has been curriculum-based assessment (CBA), which is defined as "a system for determining the instructional needs of a student based upon the student's ongoing performance within existing course content in order to deliver instruction as effectively and efficiently as possible" (Gickling, Shane, & Croskery, 1989, pp. 344–345). There is often a mismatch between the entry skills of students about whom teachers are concerned and the demands of the classroom tasks the students encounter. Correction of these mismatches leads to a better, less frustrating instructional environment for a student. Both curriculum and instructional modifications may be needed to create an appropriate instructional match for such a student, but the beginning point is gathering data about the student's entry level of skills and knowledge.

There are 5 key questions that CBA addresses (Gickling & Rosenfield, 1995):

1. What is the outcome that the teacher expects for the student, that is, what does the student need to do to be successful within the curriculum?
2. What discrepancies, if any, are there between the expectations and the student's performance?
3. If a discrepancy exists, what knowledge and skills need to be developed for the student to be successful?
4. As instruction progresses, is there continuous monitoring of the match between the student's entry level and the curriculum?
5. Is progress assessed regularly and used for instructional decision making?

CBA is a criterion-referenced form of assessment, which begins with the curriculum objectives of the classroom and school as these objectives are operationalized in classroom tasks. Assessment is a process of evaluating the discrepancy or match between the student's actual functioning and the expectations of the teacher. Specific techniques for implementing CBA have been developed (see, e.g., Gickling & Rosenfield, 1995; Gickling et al., 1989; Hargis, 1987; Rosenfield, 1987; Rosenfield & Kuralt, 1990). One outcome of IC-Teams introducing CBA in schools is that classroom teachers have used these assessment activities more regularly and effectively; developed charting and graphing techniques; and changed attitudes toward the importance of regular assessment procedures for guiding instruction.

Observation Techniques

Classroom observation is not new to consultation or to the more traditional psychoeducational evaluation process. However, it is too often approached as a mandated activity rather than as a specifically tailored data gathering stategy to answer a referral question. Observation is not recommended until the case manager and teacher have a purpose to guide the observation process. Moreover, meaningful observation can rely on either formal or informal systems, but in our experience it is too often casual and anecdotal, rather than systematic. Because of the complexity of classroom life, it is critical to develop observational techniques that minimize bias and provide useful information for decisionmaking. The following are the three key questions to ask: (1) What do I want to know? (2) How does my observational system answer my question? and (3) Am I being objective in reporting what I see? (Boehm & Weinberg, 1977). Information about developing useful observation techniques is available in most applied behavior analysis texts. A useful system for observation of classroom instructional activities has been developed by Ysseldyke and Christenson (1993).

Successful Completion of Problem Identification

Conclusion of the business of the problem identification stage occurs when the teacher–case manager dyad has consensus on the following:

- A behaviorally defined statement of the problem in terms of a discrepancy between expected and actual student performance;
- A goal directed towards diminishing or eliminating the discrepancy;
- Baseline data on the goal behavior; and
- An understanding of the ecology (the antecedent and consequent conditions) surrounding the behavior in the setting in which the behavior occurs.

As teachers become increasingly able to provide these types of information at the consultation sessions, the interview process becomes more efficient. Case managers often assist classroom teachers in building skills to obtain the needed data or may collect the data personally when that is necessary, although they usually do not take on major responsibility for assessment of the student.

Intervention Planning

Only after the problematic situation has been identified, i.e., in behavioral terms and as a discrepancy between the desired and current behavior, to the satisfaction of the teacher and case manager, is it time to consider interventions. In many cases, teachers are able to develop good intervention plans for themselves when the problem has been identified in specific observable terms. Remediating a math disability is not always perceived by teachers as being within their technical range of knowledge. Knowing that the child does not have the relevant multiplication skills for the math lessons in the classroom, on the other hand, may prompt a teacher to generate, or be a partner in generating, a plan to fill in the gap. In other cases, the teacher and case manager find it necessary to strategize together about an intervention plan that is feasible, research- and data-based, and acceptable to all concerned. In some difficult cases, the consultation dyad may require the assistance of the team itself in generating an acceptable intervention plan, either because of the expertise of members of the team in addressing a particular problem or because of the need for more resources that can only be provided at the school or district level.

The intervention planning stage is complete when an intervention plan has been worked out in detail and is considered realistic and reasonable by those who must actually conduct the implementation. The data documenting the current discrepancy are considered the benchmark for the plan. The plan itself must include answers to the following questions:

- What will be done; that is, is there a detailed description of the specific strategy to be implemented?
- When will it be done? How often? With what materials?
- Who will do it?
- How will effectiveness of the plan be monitored; that is, are there data collection methods to evaluate progress during implementation?
- When will progress be monitored; that is, what are the checkpoint times to monitor progress?

When each of the details in response to these questions has been worked out and all concerned parties agree on their responsibilities during the implementation stage, intervention planning is considered complete. Although this degree of preliminary organization does not guarantee that the intervention itself will be implemented, it provides a framework for troubleshooting problems that occur during implementation, and it builds commitment to the intervention.

An important issue in intervention planning is the quality of the intervention design. Intervention recommendations are considered from an idiographic perspective, given the unique situation of the particular teacher, classroom and school ecology, and student involved. Since the consultation process is considered a scaffold for a variety of different assessment techniques, interventions, and curriculum content, the process is not wedded to a particular theoretical orientation regarding interventions. Some teachers view behavioral interventions as acceptable and some do not; there are schools committed to direct instruction and those committed to whole language instruction in their reading programs. However, instructional strategies that do not have a base in either theory or research are inappropriate. The team has an ongoing responsibility to the continuing professional development of the school faculty on effective, research-based instructional and classroom management strategies, as well as for the general upgrading of the quality of instruction in the school.

Team members often request "cookbooks," or lists of acceptable intervention strategies, as they struggle to develop appropriate intervention designs. Maintaining a problem-solving perspective for each situation while building a repertoire of intervention strategies is an important team goal. As new types of situations are encountered, teams recognize the need for continuing professional development. For example, in a school district with a research-based writing program, the teams across schools came to a similar recognition that they needed more strategies for assessing and intervening with students who were not making adequate progress in writing skills. They developed an inservice program in this curricular area, bringing in consultants from a local university to provide information and coaching.

Intervention Implementation

Planning and conducting interventions are two different stages. It is not until an intervention is implemented that its feasibility and effectiveness are really tested. The case manager continues to maintain the collaborative relationship with the teacher, and any others, conducting the intervention. If problems in the practicality of the intervention occur, these become the focus of problem solving. If the data show that the intervention is not effective, then a modification in the intervention may be necessary. It is likely that at least one modification in the intervention will be needed to maximize effectiveness.

Resolution/Termination

It is important to bring the problem-solving process to a formal closure, whether or not the problem has been effectively resolved. First, accountability for the student's progress requires that the consultation process not be allowed to fade away when the process is not working well, and that a different approach to the situation be considered. The team may need to become involved at this point. The teacher should be allowed to terminate the contract, with the option to renegotiate. This presents an ethical dilemma for the team when a student is not making progress but the teacher is unwilling to consult. This possibility needs to be discussed in advance by the team and options clarified with the entire faculty.

Alternatively, when the consultation clearly has been successful, it is appropriate to end the process. Often, the dyad is reinforced to continue meeting regularly by the progress that the student is making, and neither party wants to terminate a relationship that has proven mutually beneficial. However, given the scarcity of human resources in most schools, time is a precious resource. Success should be celebrated, the teacher should have a procedure to re-access the case manager if problems develop, and the case manager should be free to move on to a new consultation relationship.

The written record of the consultation process is not a traditional formal report. Whatever system the team utilizes for its record keeping, there should also be a method to provide documentation to the teacher. It may be a summary, in memo form, to the teacher that includes the original concern, assessment data, interventions conducted, and results. Another option is a series of charts/graphs, described in Chapter 3, that specify the problem addressed, the intervention conducted, and the results. The teacher should be a partner in constructing and completing these records. At the end of an academic year, there may be a series of instructional recommendations prepared for the receiving teacher of a particular student. However, these procedures do not eliminate the need for a centralized record of the consultation process for accountability purposes, in the event that future problems develop. In addition, such records may be accumulated by the team to determine their ongoing effectiveness. Good record-keeping policy also requires that outdated records be eliminated.

SUMMARY

Within the IC-Team model, the instructional consultation process is a critical functioning element. When the case managers are not sufficiently skilled in this process, the entire IC-Team is compromised. Effective consultation requires an understanding of the nature of both the working relationship and the stages of the problem-solving process. Further, there must be a commitment to using research-based intervention strategies in teaching and learning, rather than relying on preferences that may feel good to the professional but are not based on empirical results. Finally, there is a need for documentation and accountability regarding the progress of the student. When each of these components are in place, the implementation stage has been reached for this aspect of IC-Teams. In later chapters, the training and evaluation procedures for instructional consultation will be presented.

3

The Instructional Consultation Team Delivery System

The collaborative consultation process discussed in the previous chapter cannot occur in a vacuum. The context for the process is the delivery system, which must be clearly established and defined. The IC-Team delivery system is a centralized and systematic process by which teachers with classroom-based concerns can access collaborative support. The system is characterized by accountability to referring teachers and students and by a commitment to decisions based on objective data gathered through a problem-solving process. In designing the delivery system of IC-Teams, considerable weight has been given to the underlying assumption that teachers and school staff, as professionals, are entitled to consult and collaborate, and that well-designed collaborative structures in schools facilitate student academic and social development. This assumption is actualized in both the professional atmosphere encouraged in the consultation process and by the actual components of the delivery system. Figure 3.1 presents details of the core indicators that must be structured for the delivery system to be in place. These include an appropriately comprised team which has established functions, a process by which school staff can access the team as a resource, and procedures for documenting case and student progress.

COLLABORATIVE TEAMING

In each building, an IC-Team is created to serve as a centralized problem-solving unit, to model interactive professionalism (Fullan &

Team Functioning

Has representative team composition.
Meets regularly for team business and team maintenance.
Assesses team needs and plans for ongoing training.
Receives and tracks requests for assistance from classroom teachers.
Monitors effectiveness of individual case consultation process.
Facilitates organizational interventions based on requests received.
Documents proceedings and outcomes.
Assists in evaluating the effectiveness of individual case consultations and team effectiveness in the building.

Request for Assistance

Request for Assistance Form includes:
Teacher's name
Teacher's available times to meet
Student's name and DOB
Brief statement of concern
Parental contact
System manager
Receives all requests for assistance.
Tracks all cases using Tracking Form.

System Tracking Form includes:
Referring teacher name
Student name and DOB
Grade level
Case manager assigned
Date of referral
Date of first contact
Status of case
Case manager
Collaborates with teacher.
Is responsible for coordinating case.
Reports to team.
Is responsible for efficient contacts and documentation of case meetings using Case Documentation Form and collaboratively using student progress monitoring.

Case Documentation

Case Documentation Form includes:
Date(s) of contacts
Brief summary of consultation
Plans, date, and time for next meeting

Student Documentation Form includes:
Name of student
Statement of problem in observable terms
Statement of objectives for solving problem
Description of intervention
Data collected during baseline and intervention phases

FIGURE 3.1. IC-Team delivery system content.

Hargreaves, 1991), and to operate as a consultant panel for each other and for teachers in a building. While the multidisciplinary teams spawned by P.L. 94-142 have typically interpreted their function as determining if a referred student has a handicapping condition, determining the nature and etiology of the student's problem, and developing an individualized educational plan — all within the legal boundaries of due process for the student and the parent, the IC-Team views the referral problem as a work-related concern of the teacher, brought to the team for professional consultation.

The IC-Team can be best described as a collaborative team based upon the defining elements as cited by Thousand and Villa (1992). According to Thousand and Villa, teams are most effective when there is:

1. Face-to-face interaction among team members on a frequent basis.
2. A mutual "we are all in this together" feeling of positive interdependence.
3. A focus on the development of small group interpersonal skills in trust building, communication, leadership, creative problem solving, decision making, and conflict management.
4. Regular assessment and discussion of the team's functioning and the setting of goals for improving relationships and more effectively accomplishing tasks.
5. Methods for holding one another accountable for agreed-upon responsibilities and commitments. (p. 76)

Team Composition

Members are recruited to represent major school building stakeholders, including, but not limited to, general and special education teachers; pupil personnel staff; such specialists as librarians, reading teachers, or physical education teachers; and the building administrator. For example, the team at an inner-city school serving approximately 650 students in grades K–5 consists of the principal, a special educator, three general classroom teachers, reading and math specialists, and the school nurse. Table 3.1 displays team membership in a recent implementation of IC-Teams, and provides examples of differing team compositions that still are considered representative.

Administrator participation. It is critical that the building administrator, or someone designated by the administrator and perceived as legitimately able to speak for the administrator, be on the team. As teams begin to operate, norms of the school culture begin to be called

TABLE 3.1. Examples of IC-Team Memberships in 9 Project Schools

School	Team size	Team composition (number of members by role)						
		Psyc	Guid	Adm	Read	SpEd	Teacher	Other
A	11	1	1	2	1	2	2	2
B	13	1	1	2	1	1	3	4
C	11	1	1	2	1	1	3	2
D	11	1	1	2	1	2	3	1
E	11	1	1	2	0	1	4	2
F	14	1	1	2	2	3	3	2
G	11	1	1	2	1	3	3	0
H	9	1	1	2	1	1	2	1
I	14	1	1	2	1	1	5	3

into question. A statement commonly heard on new teams is, "We aren't allowed to do it that way." Without the principal there, progress is immediately halted. Even with the principal there, the perception of an ever-present "them" determining rules may be overpowering to team members. We were present at a team meeting where two staff members insisted that the principal forbade them from doing something, even though she was there and kept insisting that they had her permission.

Size. Although there is little research to document the appropriate size of IC-Teams, teams seem to function collaboratively when they consist of 8 to 14 permanent members. It is difficult to establish a representative team with fewer members, and a team of more than 14 members results in a cumbersome team process.

Rotation. It is important to rotate teacher members so that each faculty member in the building who wishes to do so has the opportunity to be a member of the team. However, rotation of teacher members off the team should occur only after the teacher has received sufficient training and support and has served as a case manager.

Credibility. It is highly recommended that when the team is initiated in the building, well-respected teachers who volunteer are selected.

Balance. More general education teachers than special education teachers should be on the team. Pupil services need to be represented, even if the pupil services staff members are not based at the school full time.

Team Functioning

Work groups are created primarily to address specific tasks; in this respect, IC-Teams are no different from other work groups. The tasks are to receive referrals and supportively collaborate with teachers who express concerns regarding classroom or student issues. Well-functioning teams also begin to examine school regularities and curricular issues that impede the growth and development of all children, particularly those who need more individualized educational and social interventions. The functions of the IC-Team are outlined in Figure 3.1 and are described in more detail below.

The team meets regularly for team business and team maintenance. Competing demands on team members' time are a primary concern. Regular meetings are essential and are structured carefully into the school schedule. The team meets weekly at regularly scheduled times, and, once teams understand the importance of regularly scheduled meetings, they being to insist on protecting this time.

The team assesses team needs and plans for ongoing training. One function, rarely considered in schools, arises from the norm of continuous improvement (Fullan & Hargreaves, 1991), that is, ongoing team member training. Prior to IC-Team implementation, team members are trained in the skills necessary to be effective instructional consultants and team members. To ensure effective functioning, the group process is discussed and monitored. At the beginning of each subsequent year, the team conducts a needs assessment and structures training based on needs identified within the team and the school. In addition, there are established processes by which new members are inducted into the team, including a procedure for providing training and support and for redistributing leadership periodically.

The team receives requests for assistance from teachers and monitors the effectiveness of each case consultation. A major goal of the team is to ensure that all concerns about students' learning and behavior are addressed. Teacher concerns about individual students are initiated through the referral process. Team business includes receiving and tracking all requests for assistance from classroom teachers, meeting regularly to update and review cases, documenting and recording case progress, coordinating resources to support other teachers and team members, evaluating case outcomes and intervention effectiveness. Referring teachers are included in team deliberations whenever necessary. Other activities are performed that support successful consultation between team members and referring teachers.

The team facilitates organizational interventions based on referrals received. More widespread concerns about learning and management in the school may require organizational interventions on the part of the team. Planning and conducting inservice programs, introducing new or modified instructional materials at particular grade levels, or generating organizational modifications in the school may be activities of IC-Teams.

The team documents proceedings and outcomes. One justifiable concern of parents and teachers, and a due process issue as well, is that consultation is often treated as an informal procedure without adequate documentation of the process and outcome. Documentation protects both the student and the school staff by ensuring that progress is monitored. A number of specific case procedures and forms, illustrated later in this chapter, facilitate this documentation.

The team assists in evaluating the effectiveness of individual case consultations and team effectiveness in the building. It is also the responsibility of the team to monitor the effectiveness and efficiency of its procedures and processes. Skill level of team members, outcomes of student concerns addressed by individual consultants, and the integrity of IC-Team implementation all need to be considered. An evaluation design is utilized that assesses the implementation of all the phases of IC-Teams, of training, and of student outcomes.

Request for Assistance

A major function of the team is to provide consultation resources so that teachers have the opportunity for professional collaboration on learning and management concerns within their classrooms. In order for this to be accomplished, staff members need a clear and efficient process for contacting the team and a structured set of procedures by which the consultation process is conducted and monitored. The entire faculty is informed, in a well-planned and carefully executed presentation about who, where, and what is involved in accessing the IC-Team, with the system manager becoming the direct link between faculty and team. Efficient access to the team reduces duplication of existing referral patterns in a school and ensures that no teacher request falls between the cracks. The major components of this process include a Request for Assistance Form to access the team, a system manager to track all requests using a structured set of procedures, and a case manager to collaborate with the teacher and to monitor the consultation process and outcome. The use of these components together operationalizes IC-Teams' emphasis on accountability in this system.

Request for Assistance Form

The use of the term "request for assistance" has evolved as a major distinction between IC-Teams and traditional team models in schools. The
use of Request for Assistance Forms emphasizes that it is the teaching
professional who is requesting assistance in helping students, rather
than the student being referred to determine if there is an innate deficit
or pathology.

The timeliness of response to teachers' concerns is another important issue addressed in the process of accessing assistance. Experience
shows that referral of students, particularly since the inception of P.L.
94-142, has become a complicated process that, in many cases, impedes
teacher requests for professional collaboration. Lengthy referral
processes have been designed so that teachers receive assistance only
if they have performed the required number of classroom interventions, contacted the required number of support personnel, and
documented their efforts throughout. Teachers sometimes indicate that
they believe the goal of the referral is to show how much effort they
can expend in isolation prior to admitting defeat and/or incompetence.
Once teachers do find their way through the maze of referral requirements, there is strong evidence that students are almost guaranteed the
traditional psychoeducational assessment (Ysseldyke, 1983), while
teachers are offered little, if any, support within the classroom. Therefore, if the student is not found to have a disability, services may not
be forthcoming to address the teacher concerns that prompted the referral in the first place.

The request for assistance process of IC-Teams is therefore based
upon the following premises:

- Teachers are professionals who are entitled to consult and collaborate.
- Students and teachers are best served if assistance is received early, when problems are relatively small and can still be resolved
  within the classroom setting.
- A collaborative framework, developed around problem identification and continued through the evaluation of specified strategies, supports problem solving.

The form is intentionally brief and inviting in order to encourage
teachers to request assistance often and early (see Figure 3.2). It contains only the information necessary to determine the type of concern
and the times teachers are available to meet with an IC-Team member:
the teacher's name; times the teacher is available to meet; the student's

DATE _____

I need help with _____

_____

_____

_____

_____

_____

You may contact me on the following days and times:

_____

_____

_____

_____

_____

Name _____

Student name _____ DOB _____

Room number _____ Grade _____

Date of parental contact _____

FIGURE 3.2. Example of Request for Assistance Form for the M. Hall Stanton School in the school district of Philadelphia.

name and date of birth (DOB), if applicable (sometimes teachers access the team for more general curriculum/management assistance); a brief statement of the teacher's concern; and information about previous parental contacts.

There is an inherent understanding and profound trust that teachers, as with any profession, do not request assistance unless they have exhausted their personal resources or have come to the conclusion that additional input is necessary. A request does not reflect inadequacy or failure on the part of the teacher; nor is it a quest for finding a student deficit. Instead, it is a problem-solving strategy that is part of the teacher's professional functioning. The Request for Assistance Form is also congruent with the goal of institutionalizing a process that encourages teacher collaboration prior to student failure.

One aspect of the form that each school must consider within its own culture is whether to specify previous parental contacts or, instead, to require parental permission. Although IC-Teams are structured to provide consultation to teachers, and a request does not indicate that a student is suspected of having a handicapping condition, school systems differ in their relationships with parents. Some school systems are comfortable in using this procedure without parental permission, whereas others are concerned about doing so. We encourage full discussion of this issue within the school. In all cases, parents and relevant community stakeholders need to be informed fully about the purpose of IC-Teams and the process itself. More will be said about this issue in Chapter 5.

System Manager

Team members rely upon the system manager to organize and document team functioning. Receiving requests for assistance, scheduling team meetings, and maintaining team records are some of the functions of the system manager. Any one of the team members may volunteer to perform this role, and this individual usually does fewer case consultations in exchange for undertaking these responsibilities. In one school,for example, a teacher who felt unable to undertake the consultation process, but who wanted to remain a functional member of the team, volunteered to be the system manager.

One role of the system manager is to track all requests for assistance onto the System Tracking Form (described below) and to document carefully the progress of each request.

System Tracking Form

Each IC-team utilizes a tracking system to document the progress of teacher requests for assistance. Figure 3.1 provides a list of the essential components required in a tracking form while Figure 3.3 offers one example of a tracking system. As designed, the tracking system documents that the following vital aspects of IC-Team functioning occur:

- Teacher requests are addressed in a timely fashion (typically within 1 week of receipt of referral).
- All students involved in case consultation through the team are accounted for and receive documented service.
- A case manager is assigned and contact with the teacher is implemented.

- Case progress is recorded and documented.
- All requests for assistance are centralized in order to provide an organizational perspective on the concerns expressed within a particular building.

The System Tracking Form is thus designed to provide the basic information necessary to ensure accountability and uninterrupted service to teachers who access the team.

The system tracking process also provides a broader picture, through the patterns of recurrent problems, of grade and/or school needs. For example, one IC-Team that received a substantial number of requests for assistance involving first-grade students was thereby alerted to the need to redistribute resources and provide additional support. Several school-wide strategies occurred, including reducing the student–teacher ratio to better match instruction for these students, assigning extra resource services to the first grade, and providing classroom consultation to first-grade teachers. Any school—indeed any organization—is limited by the resources available. The system tracking process of IC-Teams allows schools to utilize resources more strategically and to document whether allocations provide the expected outcomes.

Case Manager

While schools have relied on the team concept in addressing classroom teacher concerns, such processes are often inefficient and, in some cases, impediments to effective problem solving (Maher & Pfeiffer, 1983). For example, most existing teaming models require that a referring teacher meet with the entire team to identify problems and develop strategies (Chalfant & Pysh, 1989; Cole, Siegel, & Yau, 1990; Stokes, 1982). The need for repeated meetings to address one concern, combined with the difficulty of creating time for 5 to 9 school personnel to meet, creates a heavy resource demand. In addition, when problems are not solved within one or two team meetings, an insidious perception quickly emerges that the student must have a very serious problem if nine professionals working together cannot solve it. Further, throughout this process the teacher is often totally responsible for maintaining a classroom, creating time to meet with the team, and implementing strategies without support.

Problem solving in IC-Teams is an ongoing and often recursive process that does not typically fit neatly into one meeting, regardless of the number of people present. The IC-Teams model has extended the teaming concept by incorporating a case management process

STATUS REPORT

Child's name (1st name & last initial)	DOB / Grade level	Teacher Homeroom	Referral date	Case manager	Date of 1st contact	(Use status code here)				Comments

FIGURE 3.3. Example of System Tracking Form.

(Figure 3.4). As suggested by others (e.g., Bardon, 1983; Pryzwansky & Rzepski, 1983), requests for assistance may be assigned to individual team members on the basis of "a match between initial referral information . . . and the talents, interests, and professional skills of the various team members" (Bardon, 1983, p. 188). The assigned team member becomes the case manager and has major responsibility for communicating with and assisting the teacher.

Once assigned, the case manager is responsible for collaborating with the teacher and for documenting case progress (see Figure 3.1). The case manager employs the systematic problem-solving and effective communication skills, acquired during training and refined through on-site facilitation, in collaborating and consulting with the teacher.

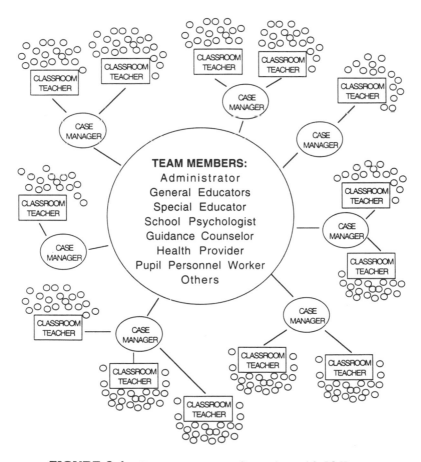

FIGURE 3.4. Case manager configuration with IC-Team.

Progress of the case is documented on a Case Documentation Form (see Figure 3.5) and updates are regularly provided to the team as a whole by the case manager. In this regard, the case manager represents a link between the teacher and the IC-Team. The case manager maintains regular contact with the teacher and, when individual students are involved, ensures that documentation is maintained to account for student progress (i.e., completion of Student Documentation Form, see Figure 3.6). Case managers use the team for consultation and support when progress is slow or when a full staffing of a case is deemed necessary by the team. At such times, the teacher is invited to attend the team meeting.

Given the differences in the composition of IC-Teams across schools, assignment of requests for assistance to case managers varies depending on the school and the team. In some schools, cases are assigned by grade level to particular team members. In other schools, the nature of the concern dictates which case manager is assigned. For example, if the request involves academic concerns in reading, the reading specialist or special educator is assigned as case manager. Occasionally, interpersonal relationships among staff have been considered. Another influence that can affect case assignment is the best match between the times that a teacher and case manager are available to meet.

The expertise, comfort, and time availability of team members often culminate in forming unique and inventive mechanisms for the assignment of cases. However, although classroom teachers on the team find the process interesting and stimulating, experience suggests that they can reasonably serve as case manager on only one or two cases at a time.

Case Documentation Form

Figure 3.1 lists the components of a Case Documentation Form while Figure 3.5 provides an example of a Case Documentation Form that has been developed across several implementations of the IC-Team process. Figure 3.7 provides an example of a completed Case Documentation Form. Because case managers are updating the entire team as to progress of each case, the Case Documentation Form provides a consistent record of meeting dates, consultation activities, and proposed follow-up activities.

Student Documentation Form

Whenever a student or group of students is the focus of the collaborative consultation process, documentation is maintained on a Student

Date	Summary of consultation	Follow-up activities & next meeting

FIGURE 3.5. Example of Case Documentation Form.

Documentation Form (Figure 3.6). As indicated in Figure 3.1, the Student Documentation Form includes (1) the name and DOB of the student, (2) a clear behavioral description of the problem, (3) the goals and objectives established in addressing the identified problem, and (4) any intervention proposed and implemented. In addition, data are maintained, beginning with baseline data, to determine whether a particular intervention is effective. The example of a Student Documentation Form depicted in Figure 3.6 requires all of the above components and utilizes a graph format for the presentation of data. The design of this particular recording form is based upon the growing body of

Student name _____ Grade _____ Teacher _____ Date(s) _____

School _____ Case manager _____ from ___ to ___

Operational definition of
behavior/academic concern: _____

Statement of current functioning: _____
(based upon above graph) _____

Statement of desired performance: _____
(specify time period) _____

Describe intervention(s): _____
_____

FIGURE 3.6. Example of Student Documentation Form.

research that suggests that the use of direct and frequent measurement enhances student progress (Fuchs & Fuchs, 1986). In addition, the Student Documentation Form graphically summarizes data, thereby providing a visual representation of student progress.

Our experience with case monitoring is that there is often resis-

Case manager: *Winnie Q.*   Teacher: *Karen M.*   Student: *John D.*

Date	Summary of consultation	Follow-up activities & next meeting
2/25	Cancelled due to snow.	Rescheduled for 3/1
3/1	Karen related concerns and identified 2 major areas of concern. Reviewed current behavior program in use.	Schedule for 3/4 for further problem ID. Karen will bring and think about changes to current behavior sheet.
3/4	Reviewed current behavior program in use. Continued problem ID and decided to target on-task behaviors before lunch. Set time for observation and CBA in area of reading.	Meet again 3/11. Observation on 3/5, 3/6, 3/7 for baseline. Conduct CBA on 3/10.
3/11	Cancelled. Reschedule for 3/12.	
3/12	Reviewed observation data with Karen. Also reviewed anecdotal information of Karen's. Observation indicated on-task on avg. 65%. Reading level is currently frustrational according to CBA.	Meet again on 3/19 to discuss options for reading placements. Bring material.
3/19	Reviewed appropriate reading materials and finalized behavior program. Set goals for on-task behavior.	Karen will implement new behavior sheet beginning 3/20. Meet again 3/26.
3/26	Determined that behavior program in place, had to adjust reading materials once again based upon quick CBA.	Observe over next 2 weeks and then meet again in 2 weeks to monitor.
4/14	Met to review observation data. Will continue to monitor behavior sheet and observe.	Meet again in 3 weeks.

FIGURE 3.7. Example of completed Case Documentation Form.

tance to completing forms early in the implementation process, in part because team members may have limited skills in monitoring individual student progress. Problems with completing forms, brought about behavioral definitions, and collecting baseline data (Green-Resnick & Rosenfield, 1989) have brought about changes in the form and more extensive training procedures. However, team perseverance in acquiring skills and establishing norms of data collection result in higher teacher satisfaction and ease in measurement of effectiveness.

EVALUATION DESIGN

Evaluation is often presented in a final chapter, almost as an afterthought, for many programs. However, evaluation is deeply embedded in IC-Teams (Rosenfield, 1992). The three components to the evaluation design are presented in Table 3.2: evaluation of implementation, evaluation of training, and evaluation of outcome. Each is integral to IC-Teams and occurs at a different point in the change process.

Evaluation of Implementation

There are two essential reasons for evaluating implementation. First, it is critical to know that the innovation has been implemented with integrity (Gresham, Gansle, Noell, Cohen, & Rosenblum, 1993). No matter how useful and well-designed an innovation package might be, unless it is implemented with integrity, its effectiveness cannot be meaningfully evaluated. Level of implementation, defined as "the degree to which the various elements of an innovation have been operationalized as intended" (Fudell, 1992, p. 10), must be measured prior to outcome evaluation to document that the intervention is actually a relevant factor in the outcome being measured (Cook & Poole, 1982). A second use for level of implementation measures is to provide valuable data for formative evaluation. Results can be used to identify specific dimensions of the innovation that have not been well implemented, as well as to pinpoint where additional training is needed.

Defining Critical Dimensions

The first step in evaluating the level of implementation is to identify the key components and critical dimensions of the innovation. Critical dimensions are the essential characteristics and activities of the program, and are "specified in statements that describe the model and are

TABLE 3.2. Evaluation Components of IC-Teams

Evaluation of implementation

> Defining critical dimensions
> Developing IC-Team LOI
> Administering IC-Team LOI
> > Formative
> > Summative
> Collecting data on site variations in implementation

Evaluation of training

> Defining goals of training
> Developing formats for evaluating training
> > Retrospective pretesting
> > Formative process for feedback
> > Summative evaluations
> Administering training evaluations

Evaluation of outcome

> Clarifying outcome goals
> > Goals related to model
> > Goals related to individual sites/projects
> Selecting options:
> > Attitude change
> > Referral and placement patterns
> > Student achievement
> > Teacher–student interactions
> > Cost/benefit analysis
> Relating critical dimensions to outcomes

measured by the observance of particular behaviors and materials" (Fudell, 1992, p. 11). Although there is considerable room for individual schools to adapt dimensions to their culture, the critical elements of each dimension *must* be adopted for IC-Teams to be considered implemented.

The critical dimensions for IC-Teams were originally identified by Fudell (1992), in research on Project Link teams. A group of project facilitators and one of the program designers (Rosenfield) validated the list of critical dimensions. The critical dimensions of IC-Teams (presented in Appendix A), modified from both Fudell (1992) and Rosenfield (1992), expand and specify the collaborative process and the delivery system. As IC-Teams evolve, changes are specified within the level of implementation dimensions and appropriate new measurement procedures designed and validated.

Developing the IC-Team LOI

To determine the actual level of implementation of IC-Teams (or any innovation), data need to be collected about the critical dimensions. The IC-Team LOI Scale is presented in Appendix A. An earlier version of this instrument was field tested by Fudell (1992), and refined through additional evaluations of IC-Teams (Fudell, Gravois, & Rosenfield, 1994).

Administering the IC-Team LOI

The IC-Team LOI Scale is administered for formative and summative purposes, as described above. It is recommended that, during the first year of implementation, the measure be administered two times. At midyear, results provide information about the progress of the team and assist the facilitator and team in designing ongoing training. As the year concludes, a second administration of the scale provides summative information about the year and formative information to set the course for training in the second year of implementation. Change facilitators may wish to conduct an initial administration very early in the implementation stage to establish a baseline and to verify training needs of team members. Regardless, the IC-Team LOI should be administered regularly until criterion level is established, and thereafter, periodically to ensure continued integrity of the program.

Scoring the IC-Team LOI

It is recommended that the performance indicators of the critical dimensions be assessed according to whether or not they are actually present, with criterion levels of performance established for each indicator (Rubin, Stuck, & Revicki, 1982). The overall degree of implementation is obtained by calculating a percentage of the number of dimensions in place. Criterion levels are set for high, average, and low levels of implementation. For IC-Teams, the level of implementation has been set at 80% of the dimensions in place. Extreme caution should be used in evaluating student outcomes as indicators of the effectiveness of IC-Teams until the IC-Team LOI is at the required criterion level. For formative purposes, the percentage is not considered an issue of success or failure, but a benchmark of the team's current performance and an indicator of where further training and emphasis are needed. Comparisons across sites, and within and across districts, also provide information relevant for later replications of IC-Teams.

Evaluation of Training

Essential to the implementation of IC-Teams are both consultation process skills and skills in the content areas of classroom-based assessment (including CBA and observation), graphing and charting, and intervention strategies. These specific skills are delineated in Chapter 2. Team members reach criterion level in these skills in order to implement IC-Teams with integrity. As one might expect, individual team members are at different skill levels prior to implementation, and the goals of training are related to the level of skills of the participants.

Evaluation, both formative and summative, of skill level may be accomplished in many ways, each method with its own issues and concerns for the change facilitator. Although pretesting is a useful strategy for planning training, it at times creates resistance among new team members who are uncomfortable demonstrating lack of expertise in front of one another. Further, it is often difficult for individuals to assess what they do not know before they have had training in those areas. For example, many school psychologists and special educators have had some experience with consultation and perhaps some didactic work in their training program related to the topic. However, there is evidence that many school professionals serving on multidisciplinary teams do not have sufficient understanding of consultation to know the limitations of their skill level (Hughes, 1994). Retrospective pretesting (Campbell & Stanley, 1963; Rippey, Geller, & King, 1978), which asks participants to judge their pre-training level after receiving sufficient training for self-assessment, can be helpful in providing information to help team members evaluate their growth.

The major purpose of the training evaluation is to provide formative feedback to the individual and the training coordinator about the level of skill of each team member. Summative assessment provides information that is useful in making judgments about IC-Team effectiveness. If the participants as a group have not acquired the skills, there is little likelihood that IC-Teams can be implemented with integrity. Training evaluations may be administered at different stages of the process, but generally are used most often during the early stages of implementation. This subject will be discussed in more detail in the chapter on training.

Evaluation of Outcome

Although there are some outcome measures that have been consistently used during implementation of IC-Teams, it is also important that the goals of the schools, district, and, possibly, funding agencies of a particular implementation site be elicited early in the initiation process. Common variables included in evaluation are attitude change of staff and community, referral and placement patterns, student achievement and behavior, teacher–student interactions, and cost/benefit analyses. Research on the IC-Team process itself might also include relating specific critical dimensions of IC-Teams to outcomes.

SUMMARY

In this chapter, two key components of IC-Teams have been described: (1) the delivery system including the team, request for assistance procedures, case management and documentation; and (2) the evaluation components designed to determine if IC-Teams have been implemented with integrity, if individual team members and the team as a whole have reached criterion level in training, and if desired outcomes have been obtained. Together with the process of collaborative consultation presented in Chapter 2, these three components define IC-Teams.

4

The Change Facilitator

As increasingly complex changes are being introduced to schools and as the goals of change are becoming more comprehensive, the skills required of school staff have become more complex as well, requiring greater support (Fullan, 1991). Research on the role of facilitators has determined that they contribute "in the short run, . . . to the development of support, technical help, and clarity about the innovations being implemented. In the longer run, to greater mastery, confidence, and ownership" (Fullan, 1991, p. 217).

There has been much disappointment over the past 30 years in education as reform efforts have failed to make significant change in schools. However, as Doyle stated in 1978, regarding implementation of federally supported innovations, "Many of the problems that decreased the likelihood that planned change would occur could have been predicted. . . . But the knowledge educators have about barriers to change and about facilitators of change is usually ignored by both local and federal actors" (p. 99). In addition, because change is basically a human process, Backer (1994) reminds us that

> those responsible for guiding educational innovation and change must pay attention to human factors — such as the need for teachers and others to feel rewarded and involved in the change process, the need to work through fears and anxieties about change, the need to have information about innovations presented in readily understandable language, and the need for reliable evidence that innovations are effective and don't have terrible side effects. (p. 2)

Moreover, once a particular innovation has been accepted, individuals must have ongoing opportunities to learn new skills and receive support for changing their behavior.

Given the history of efforts to change schools and attend to the students at the margins, we believe that, in order to implement IC-Teams effectively, it is necessary to understand the process of change and the role of the change facilitator. In this chapter, we describe the attitudes, knowledge, and skills that on-site school facilitators of IC-Teams will find useful in their work. Our emphasis will be on the development of on-site school facilitators, although many of the issues are relevant to district level facilitators as well. First, an understanding of change from a personal philosophical perspective will be presented. Then the specific skills needed to participate as a change facilitator, and their application to IC-Teams, will be described. Finally, the concerns of change facilitators who have been involved in introducing IC-Teams will be presented, along with some recommendations for coping with these issues.

THE PROCESS OF CHANGE

The introduction of school-based teams into educational settings represents change as much as the introduction of any other complex innovation. A substantial literature exists about the conceptual basis of change from both an organizational and individual level. Several major theoreticians and researchers (e.g., Fullan, 1991; Hall & Hord, 1987) have viewed educational change from a stage-based perspective. These stages of change provide guidance in assisting schools to adopt innovations, and they serve as guideposts to judge the progress of change. But for the change facilitator, an understanding of the organizational dynamic is not enough. What is also required is a guiding philosophy of change, a philosophy that allows the change facilitator to go to work each morning with a deep understanding of the processes occurring on a daily basis and to remain sane. The philosophy that we adopt as change facilitators determines the way in which we operate to offer supportive help while respecting the dignity of others.

Adopting a Personal Philosophy of Change

Guiding the process of change is an awesome responsibility, and it requires an understanding of one's own philosophy about change as well as a set of specific competencies. Change itself is neither good nor bad, but it introduces a transition process that needs to be understood (Schlossberg, 1989). Whenever a person's life is altered in meaningful ways — and a school-based innovation can be considered such a transition to those affected — the individual involved needs to develop ways

to cope with the transition process itself. Further, the change will affect individuals differently. A school psychologist who values the assessment process and loves testing children will feel less enthusiastic
about the introduction of IC-Teams than a psychologist who views testing as a time-consuming barrier to providing effective classroom-based
assistance. Even so, the second psychologist will be equally subject to
challenges of the transition process as she struggles to learn new skills
and develop a comfortable style as a consultant, if these have not previously been part of her repertoire.

The school change process has been compared to attempting to
repair a flat tire on a moving vehicle. However, that is not the whole
story. Change can also be energizing. Many teachers, school psychologists, and others have reinvented themselves and their practices by participating in the IC-Team process, citing a decrease in feelings of
burnout, more investment in their work, decisions to put off retirement,
and the like. The point here is that it is not the transition itself that
is the major problem, but "understanding how — and how much — these
changes alter our lives, and what we can do about coping with them"
(Schlossberg, 1989, pp. 29–30).

Our values and beliefs are a deeply ingrained part of each of us.
Professionals are usually acutely aware of their professional frame of
reference or theoretical/philosophical orientation — school psychologists, for example, may describe themselves as psychodynamic, behavioral, or eclectic in orientation. But the reality is that at some level
the professional frame of reference is attached to more personal beliefs and values. These impact both the way we define our world and
the way we choose to interact with it. As change facilitators implementing alternative delivery systems, it is important to reflect upon our own
values and beliefs that determine our personal capacity to implement
particular innovations.

The type of change described in this book will be easier or more
difficult to sustain depending on the individual's belief system. Chapter 1 articulates the basic beliefs and values underlying IC-Teams. This
might be a good time to return to that chapter and consider these beliefs from the perspective of participating as a change facilitator for
IC-Teams. Obviously, we are more apt to embrace a change viewed as
being for the better (or at least neutral) than one perceived as being
negative. To a large extent, it is the evaluation of change that will make
it either easier or more difficult to sustain. For school psychologists
and special educators who believe that psychoeducational assessment,
and the labeling and placement process, do not contribute to the well-
being of children, the consultation process described here has been
viewed as a positive change.

Basic Beliefs about Change

We also have beliefs about change itself. As we have implemented IC-Teams with the assistance of multiple facilitators, it has become apparent that it is important to reflect upon our own beliefs regarding change as well as beliefs about how individuals and systems respond to change. Establishing a better self-understanding allows a greater capacity to work freely within the educational setting, offering assistance as needed and, most essentially, not blaming others for their failure to change. While such beliefs are related to the adoption of innovative practices and systems, they are also relevant to the consultation and collaboration processes, in which consultees who are being asked to consider change may have their own substantial reasons for not doing so.

There are several basic assumptions that we have adopted regarding change. Whereas some have been espoused by researchers in the area of educational change (e.g., Fullan, 1991; Hall & Hord, 1987), others originate in areas such as family and systems therapy (Satir, 1988; Satir & Baldwin, 1983). The following assumptions have become axiomatic:

• Change is inevitable. There is no preventing change from occurring. However, the direction and outcome of change can be influenced.

• Change is a process, not an event (Hall & Hord, 1987). A school staff does not make a decision to become more consultative one day, and the next day, have in place every aspect of IC-Teams, or any other innovative practice for that matter.

• Change is an additive process, a process of ever-increasing options in how people behave (Satir & Baldwin, 1983). People change when they get, are given, learn, or discover something new that is deemed to be more personally valuable than what they currently have. It is when new and different ways of behaving are valuable and useful that old and ineffective ways of behaving can be stopped — not discarded. The person can always resume previous behaviors and thus has the choice to change.

• Many of the events that occur during the change process can be anticipated (Hall & Hord, 1987). The change facilitator should be aware that there are personal and organizational reactions that are predictable, and some negative reactions can be prevented by appropriate interventions

• The change facilitator's job is, just as the name implies, to facilitate change rather than *make* change. It is important to understand that people can be given only the opportunity to change. The change facilitator is one person who can create safe and rewarding opportunities that may enable change to occur.

• Change in one part of a system necessarily results in change in another part of the system. A pebble thrown in a pond creates ripples that impact the homeostasis of the entire water surface. Likewise change in one part or person of a system impacts the functioning of the other parts and ultimately the entire system.

• As facilitator, you can only start where you and others are currently functioning. As Satir (1983, 1988) stresses, people are often doing the best they can with the knowledge and skills they possess, and when they can do better, they will. People are to be respected for where they start the change process. They cannot know more than what they know or be expected to see the desired change the way it is planned; the change facilitator must create awareness, educate, model, and provide feedback in order to help people move.

As one works as a facilitator, these axioms provide an understanding that is useful in coping with the roller coaster ride that the change process creates.

Theory of Change

There are numerous theories of change from which a facilitator may choose. Figure 4.1 presents a theoretical view of change that has guided our work and is grounded in the literature on family and systems theory (e.g., Satir, 1983, 1988).

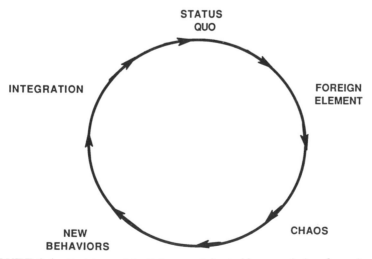

FIGURE 4.1. Satir's model of change. Adapted by permission from Avanta: The Virginia Satir Network, 310 Third Avenue NE, Issaquah, WA 98027. Copyright 1989 by Avanta: The Virginia Satir Network. All rights reserved.

Status Quo

Status quo represents that phase of change that appears to have achieved homeostasis. Before a change facilitator enters, the system is at equilibrium, irrespective of the problems that exist. A school operates within the context it has created. Influences from both inside and outside affect the culture that has developed. Within any school there is an accepted culture with norms and rules, both implicit and explicit, supported in some way by every individual within the building. Being able to learn, understand, and respect the importance of the status quo, or the existing culture, is a critical competence for any change facilitator. It is vital because the status quo, whether dysfunctional or not, represents the reality of that school. It is the starting point for everyone involved, including the change facilitator.

Status quo also applies to each individual who contributes to the school system. Each person fulfills a specific role and function and has developed ways of functioning that promote personal survival. Whether an individual's behavior has been developed in reaction to bureaucratic policies or through proactive measures, each individual has developed mechanisms for surviving within the school environment. For the change facilitator entering the building, such behaviors may appear to indicate incompetence, burnout, or just plain eccentricity. Whatever the behavior, it is important that the change facilitator know and respect the utility of that individual's current state of functioning. Where there are no indications of harm to self or others, the change facilitator is only in the position *possibly* to help that individual develop more appropriate and effective ways of functioning.

Introduction of Foreign Elements

Anything that upsets the status quo is considered a foreign element. Foreign elements may be unexpected, such as a sharp increase in high school dropouts, or may be requested, as when schools ask for the opportunity to participate in a project introducing a particular innovation. The change facilitator, too, is a foreign element. This is true even when that person has been a school or district staff member assigned to different activities. It is true whether the facilitator was asked directly to be involved by those with a vested interest (e.g., the principal, teachers, etc.) or whether directed from the outside (e.g., central office) to create change. Of course, the innovation or change being advocated is also a foreign element.

Chaos

The result of the introduction of a foreign element is chaos—on both a system and an individual level. Chaos is marked by a myriad of behaviors and feelings, many of which are directed at reestablishing the status quo, rather than supporting the system toward change. School systems, for example, often develop bureaucratic layers to cope with foreign elements rather than actually deal with root causes. Schlechty (1990) refers to the creation of positions to monitor perceived incompetence (i.e., curriculum specialists are hired to monitor school-based personnel after the reading achievement of first graders decreases) rather than deal with the possibility that the curriculum is inadequate or that teachers are not fully trained in the curriculum. Some consider special education a second system to protect the general education system from undergoing the necessary changes of becoming more adaptive to individual differences in students (Reynolds et al., 1987; Skrtic, 1991). In some cases the behavioral reactions of systems to foreign elements have produced innovative outcomes; however, the goal of reactions is often to protect the status quo.

Individuals also experience chaos with the introduction of a foreign element. There are numerous reactions to chaos, many of which reflect inappropriate and ineffective ways of coping. When under stress and experiencing chaos, such as with the introduction of IC-Teams, individuals tend to demonstrate identifiable patterns of responding. Satir (1988) notes that ineffective and seemingly dysfunctional behaviors are in reality survival stances and can be observed in participants' verbal and nonverbal communications. For example, when in stressful situations, according to Satir (1988), individuals tend to function in one of four dysfunctional communication patterns: blaming, placating, computing, or distracting.

People who have adopted a blaming stance tend to assume that "no matter what happens, it's always the other person's fault" (Schwab, Baldwin, Gerber, Gomoir, & Satir, 1989, p. 82). Because they don't take responsibility for their own behavior or acknowledge others' feelings or thoughts, they are not able to recognize their own need for change. Placators typically agree to any and everything that is introduced, even when possessing no energy, intention, or ability to participate in change. Because their only purpose is to please others, there is no investment in self-reflection and learning new behaviors. Some individuals faced with change and stress assume a computing stance, completely ignoring their feelings and focusing on the logic of the situation. For example, in IC-Team implementation, these individuals may remain stuck asking for clarification of directions rather than acting upon them. They typically attune to small details that make minimal impact on change and often want others to listen to them as experts. These behaviors prevent them from acting within the chaotic situation, which may cause uncomfortable feelings. Finally, the distractor stance is noticeable in individuals who, when faced with stress, cannot attend to the task or subject at hand, tend to be constantly in motion, cracking jokes, and carrying on irrelevant conversations. They ignore their own and others' feelings related to change.

Although these survival stances are not the most functional responses to stressful and chaotic situations, they do serve a purpose for the individual (Satir & Baldwin, 1983), that is, to help maintain an individual's sense of self-worth. Further, these ways of communicating are not considered "rigid and unchangeable" (Satir & Baldwin, 1983, p. 201), but instead are learned, exist, and are fostered in situations where others are also engaging in ineffective ways of operating and communicating. Often individuals who participated in poorly implemented innovations will comment about how they got burned or were unsupported "the last time." One school psychologist commented that she was not sure whether IC-Teams was a miniskirt or a tweed suit—that is, a fad not worth her commitment, or a solid change for the better, one to which she needed to pay attention.

Such comments and examples reflect how upset and vulnerable the participants may feel about the change process, requiring safeguards. From the change facilitator's perspective, it is often difficult to distinguish between criticism for a particular event and blame for creating the chaos the individual experiences. Likewise, it is equally important to recognize that all individuals experience concerns as change is introduced. In fact, such concerns related to IC-Teams are identified and discussed later in this chapter. However, it is the ability to cope with such concerns that has been described here. Hence, the change facilitator must keep both the concerns and coping behaviors of participants in mind when attempting to intervene or support. To do so requires much self-reflection on the part of the change facilitator, in addition to collegial supervision to determine whether the individual reactions of change participants are appropriate responses to particular issues or are a product of the uncertainty of change. When individuals assume one of the survival stances described above, it is often easy for the change facilitator to fall into the trap of responding similarly, rather than listening and helping the individual clarify the difficulty of undergoing change.

Practicing New Behaviors

The experience of chaos also provides an opportunity to introduce new behaviors, some of which may be those integral to the innovation and supported by the change facilitator. Other new behaviors may help participants learn to cope with stress and to communicate their feelings about change more appropriately. The value of the particular behavior for the individual who is experiencing change determines which behaviors will be learned. If the change facilitator presents new knowledge, techniques, and strategies that are seen as valuable, team members will be more likely to utilize them and ultimately integrate these new behaviors into regular practice. The change facilitator must present and model new ways of communicating and interacting so that team members have alternatives to the ineffective patterns that were described above.

Integrating New Behaviors

As systems and individuals are supported with appropriately timed and presented knowledge, skills, and strategies, the new behaviors increasingly become a part of the way of doing business. The change facilitator recognizes that "learning is enhanced and maximized when the person feels supported and thus willing and able to take risks. This does not mean that learning will always be pleasant and that the learner will not know times of discouragement and despair" (Satir & Baldwin, 1983, p. 182). The change facilitator's skill at creating safe and comfortable learning environments ensures that as this process continues, a new status quo is developed and awaits another foreign element.

Concerns of IC-Team Members during Implementation

A more realistic view of implementation is fostered if there is an understanding of the normal issues and concerns that participants experience when adopting an innovation. The concept of personal and organizational readiness for change increasingly has been emphasized in the change literature. Hall and Hord (1987), for example, have articulated a Concerns Based Adoption Model (CBAM) to the study of change. Their research confirmed the presence of a "set of developmental stages and levels teachers and others moved through as they became increasingly sophisticated and skilled in using new programs and procedures" (p. 7). The stages of concern basically fall into three categories: self, task, and impact. Specific types of concerns are defined and presented in Table 4.1, adapted from Hall and Hord (1987).

These same concerns have been documented for the IC-Team process; two research studies have assessed the concerns of IC-Team members at different stages of implementation (Gravois, Rosenfield, & Greenberg, 1991; Rosenfield & Feuerberg, 1987). Note that the team members' concerns, not those of the general faculty, were investigated and are presented here, although research documenting the latter's concerns would be valuable as well.

Gravois et al. (1991) investigated concerns expressed by team members of 11 school-based Project Link teams during their fifth month of implementation. Structured interviews with the teams were conducted and audiotaped. When analyzed, 694 concerns were generated across the 11 teams and categorized according to the type of concern expressed. The 10 subcategories of concern mentioned most frequently across the 11 schools are presented in Table 4.2.

The concern mentioned most often was the difficulty team members experienced in integrating different models of service delivery simultaneously. It is not uncommon for IC-Teams to be introduced where there are multiple teams operating (e.g., multidisciplinary eligibility teams for special education services, screening and prereferral teams, teacher assistance teams). Many of these teams, although all are providing services to at-risk children, are based on different underlying philosophical assumptions. Team members begin struggling early with questions about how IC-Teams fit into existing school culture and how to implement one team while maintaining others.

TABLE 4.1. Hall and Hord's (1987) Stages of Concerns

0— *Awareness:* Little concern about or involvement in the innovation is indicated.

1— *Informational:* There is a general awareness of the innovation and increased interest in details. However, participants are unworried about self with regard to innovation.

2— *Personal:* Uncertain of demands of innovation; concerns regarding how innovation will affect self.

3— *Management:* Attention is focused on process and task of using innovation and most efficient use of time, resources, etc.

4— *Consequence:* Focus is on impact innovation will have on students.

5— *Collaboration:* Concern about coordinating and collaborating with others regarding innovation.

6— *Refocusing:* Exploration of additional benefits for students, including modifying or replacing innovation.

Note. Data from Hall and Hord (1987).

Another major concern of team members was how other faculty within the building would receive IC-Teams. Team members were concerned about how to introduce a new way of providing services to students — one that team members were still learning — to the entire faculty. There were related concerns about how to develop and clarify a systematic process for the team to receive referrals and document student progress. Again, at 5 months of implementation, many team members were still unclear about how the delivery system functioned. Other issues, although less important at 5 months of implementation, were concerns about time for consultation and feelings of lack of support from district level administrators.

Rosenfield and Feuerberg's (1987) study provides insight into the types of concerns that are expressed later in the implementation stage. During the second year of implementation of early intervention teams, the most frequently expressed concerns involved practical implementation issues, including time (or lack thereof), excessive workload, excessive caseload, and excessive paperwork relating to documentation. Problems involving general education faculty (i.e., staff resistance to change, culture of school not supportive, and staff–administrator conflicts) represented 18% of the responses. In addition, a scant 6% of team members indicated feeling lack of personal competence in providing case management services, and only 6% indicated that they had difficulty conceptualizing the innovation.

As the literature on introducing innovations would predict, these results suggest that the initial concerns of the team members centered on getting the team established within the school and continuing to gain additional knowledge about the details of IC-Teams and the collaborative problem-solving process. As implementation progresses, concerns appear to relate to management of time between professional duties and teams duties. These latter concerns are congruent with the more general CBAM formulated by Hall and Hord (1987), as concerns move from awareness and information levels to management and consequence-related concerns (see Table 4.1).

In these studies, and in our experience, time concerns are present from the very beginning and continue throughout the implementation process. At a fundamental level, time is the most precious resource available to teachers and students. Teachers, team members, and principals will quickly indicate that the lack of sufficient time poses the greatest stress on the collaborative consultative process.

There is no single answer to resolving the issue of time. In schools that have achieved successful implementation, referring teachers and team members come to accept that the time invested in training for and implementing IC-Teams benefits student learning. A well-trained

**TABLE 4.2. Ten Most Frequently Mentioned Concerns
by Team Members at 5 Months of Implementation
(Subcategories across Teams)**

Subcategory	Percentage of total concerns expressed
Old/new model configuration (P)[a]	13
Faculty perception of team or innovation as negative (F)	10
Concerns introducing innovation to staff (P)	9
Delivery/referral system unclear (P)	7
Team functioning unclear (P)	6
Faculty's willingness to participate uncertain (F)	6
Specific innovation components unclear (P)	6
Time (P)	4
Excessive load (P)	3
Inadequate skills (I)	3
Inadequate support from district administrators (A)	3

Note. (P) practical management concerns; (F) faculty/staff concerns; (I) individual concerns; (A) administrative concerns.
[a]Broad area.

and prepared team is more likely to succeed in creating changes in student performance over the long term than a team that sacrifices adequate training in order to begin implementation. Unprepared teams often find themselves spending more time using trial and error learning during case consultations, leading to frustration for everyone involved and negative perceptions on the part of referring teachers concerning the benefit of the process.

Many schools have experimented with scheduling in order to create more time, while other schools have doubled classes for library, media, music, or physical education. What works for one school may or may not work for another. It is here that creativity and the adaptation process merge, often with extraordinary results. One principal, with the aid of classroom assistants, taught the entire fourth and fifth grades herself in order to free individuals for training. It was a sight to behold: one individual, in front of nearly 300 students in the school auditorium, using videotapes, think–pair–share, and whole-class responses to actively engage students. Although this particular strategy is not likely to be replicated, other suggestions—each tested by a team—for creating more time are included in Table 4.3.

The change facilitator must be aware that individuals react to foreign elements differently and that, for some individuals, the idea of change is more threatening than the actual change itself. It is also important to accept that it is normal and natural to have personal concerns (stage 2 concerns in CBAM), both for the facilitator and for the participants in the process. Facilitator concerns are addressed later in this chapter.

THE CHANGE FACILITATOR

The change facilitator is the individual (or individuals) at the local level who is responsible for "introducing and responding to new ideas and, more important, in following through with new programs to support implementation and continuation" (Fullan, 1991, p. 216) over time. There is a three-step developmental progression for IC-Team facilitators: experienced case manager/team member, on-site school facilitator, and system level facilitator. First, all facilitators should have an understanding of the process based on experience as a team member. New facilitators, where possible, should work first as case managers to gain mastery of the instructional consultation process through practice with feedback and to work within the team delivery system structure. The second step is that of on-site school facilitator, whose role in a school is to help initiate the process, develop a team and delivery system, provide training, and coach individual team members on the instructional consultation process. The third step is that of the system change facilitator, who assists a district in making the decision to adopt IC-Teams, helps select the first schools and facilitators, trains and supports the facilitators, and copes with system organizational concerns. Our focus in this section, and for most of the book, will be on the work of the on-site school-based facilitator.

TABLE 4.3. Creative Ways to Find Time for Consultation

1. Hire a permanent substitute for 1 day each week.
2. Have the principal, assistant principal, or other administrator take a teacher's class.
3. Group children for related arts classes—librarian can take extra children.
4. Meet before school, after school, or at lunch time.
5. Use related services personnel to cover classes.
6. Set up the bell schedules or master schedules so that people are free for common planning times.
7. Have other teachers cover a class—that is, use time when movies or videos are being shown, or other large group activity is appropriate.
8. Have breakfast meetings where food is provided by PTA or principal, or is rotated among staff.
9. Use existing planning times for case consultations.
10. Provide compensation time for team members and teachers who consult by allowing them to leave building early, come in late, or be released from other duties.

Cox (as cited in Fullan, 1991), reviewed a large sample of innovations and suggests that effective facilitators engaged in several clusters of activities as follows:

- located and helped select the new practice;
- knew the content of the new practice, its purpose, and the benefits that were to result from its use;
- helped arrange and conduct training in the new practice, working with external assistance;
- arranged funding and other support from the district or other sources;
- obtained endorsements for the new practice from the superintendent, school board, principal, and teachers;
- worked with teachers using the practice in the classroom, working out "bugs" and overcoming obstacles;
- assisted in evaluation; and
- helped plan how to continue and institutionalize the new practice. (pp. 217–218)

In summarizing the results of the available research, Fullan (1991) concluded with the following insights concerning the role of the local facilitator, another term for on-site facilitator as we are using it here:

> First, if local facilitators work just on a one-to-one basis, they will have limited impact because they will reach only a minuscule percentage of teachers. Second, if they are in a district that does not have a coordinated plan for managing change, it will be extremely difficult for them to set up activities involving the continuous assistance and follow-up so necessary to support change in practice. . . . Third, local facilitators have to access and balance expertise in both the content of change and the process of change. Fourth, . . . local facilitators must take into account each school and classroom context with which they wish to work. Finally, local facilitators must develop ongoing complementary working relationships with other change leaders—principals, vice-principals, department heads, resource and other lead teachers, central office administrators, and other district consultants. (Fullan, 1991, pp. 220–221)

Given this set of activities for effectively conducting the change facilitator role, Saxl, Lieberman, and Miles (1987) empirically generated 18 key skills for successful implementation, which are presented in Table 4.4. These generic facilitator skills were applied to IC-Teams by Rosenfield and Gravois (1992), who investigated the types of skills employed by the on-site IC-Team facilitator in an inner-city school. During the second year of implementation, the facilitator's audiotaped logs were collected and analyzed. Figure 4.2 represents the hypothesized configuration of key facilitator skills for IC-Teams, with numbers corresponding to the skills found in Table 4.4.

TABLE 4.4. 18 Key Facilitator Skills

Skills and description	*Examples*
1. *Interpersonal ease* Relating to and directing others.	Very open person; nice manner; has always been able to deal with staff; knows when to stroke, when to hold back, when to assert; knows "which buttons to push"; gives individuals time to vent feelings, lets them know her interest in them; can talk to anyone.
2. *Group functioning* Understanding group dynamics, able to facilitate team work.	Has ability to get a group moving; started with nothing and then made us come together as a united body; good group facilitator; lets the discussion flow.
3. *Training/doing workshops* Directing instruction, teaching adults in systematic way.	Gave workshops on how to develop plans; taught us consensus method with five-finger game; prepares a great deal and enjoys it; has the right chemistry and can impart knowledge at the peer level.
4. *Educational general (master teacher)* Wide educational experience, able to impart skills to others.	Excellent teaching skills; taught all the grades, grade leader work, resource teacher; has done staff development with teachers; was always assisting, supporting, being resource person to teachers; a real master teacher; much teacher training work.
5. *Educational content* Knowledge of school subject matter.	Demonstrating expertise in a subject area; showed parents the value of play and trips in kindergarten; knows a great deal about teaching; what she doesn't know she finds out.
6. *Administrative/ organizational* Defining and structuring work, activities, time.	Highly organized, has everything prepared in advance; could take an idea and turn it into a program; good at prioritizing, scheduling; knows how to set things up.
7. *Initiative taking* Starting or pushing activities, moving directly toward action.	Assertive, clear sense of what he wanted to do; ability to poke and prod where needed to get things done; had to assert myself so he didn't step on me.
8. *Trust/rapport building* Developing a sense of safety, openness, reduced threat on part of clients; good relationship building.	In 2 weeks he had gained confidence of staff; had to become one of the gang, eat lunch with them; a skilled seducer (knows how to get people to ask for help); "I have not repeated what they said so trust was built"; did not threaten staff; was so open and understanding that I stopped feeling uneasy.
9. *Support* Providing nurturant relationship, positive affective relationship.	Able to accept harsh things teachers say, "It's OK, everyone has these feelings"; a certain compassion for others; always patient, never critical, very enthusiastic.
10. *Confrontation* Direct expression of negative information, without generating negative affect.	Can challenge in a positive way; will lay it on the line about what works and what won't; is talkative and factual; can point out things and get away with being blunt; able to tell people they were wrong, and they accept it.

(continued)

TABLE 4.4. continued

Skills and description	Examples
11. *Conflict mediation* Resolving or improving situations where multiple incompatible interests are in play.	Effected a compromise between upper and lower grade teachers on use of a checklist; spoke to the chair about his autocratic behavior and things have been considerably better; able to mediate and get the principal to soften her attitude; can handle people who are terribly angry, unreasonable; keeps cool.
12. *Collaboration* Creating relationships where influence is mutually shared.	Deals on same level we do, puts in his ideas; leads and directs us, but as peers; doesn't judge us or put us down; has ideas of her own, but flexible enough to maintain the teachers' way of doing things too.
13. *Confidence building* Strengthening client's sense of efficacy, belief in self.	She makes all feel confident and competent; doesn't patronize; "You can do it"; has a way of drawing out teachers' ideas; injects a great deal, but you feel powerful; makes people feel great about themselves; like a shot of adrenaline boosting your mind, ego, talents, and professional expertise.
14. *Diagnosing individuals* Forming a valid picture of the needs/ problems of an individual teacher or administrator as a basis for action.	Realizes that when a teacher says she has the worst class, that means "I need help"; has an ability to focus in on problems; picks up the real message; sensitive, looks at teacher priorities first; knows when an offhand joke is a signal for help.
15. *Diagnosing organizations* Forming a valid picture of the needs/ problems of the school organization as a basis for action.	Analyzes situation, recognizes problems, jumps ahead of where you are to where you want to go; anticipates problems schools face when they enter the program; helped us know where we should be going; helped team look at the data in the assessment package.
16. *Managing/controlling* Orchestrating the improvement process; coordinating activities, time, and people; direct influence on others.	Prepared materials and coordinated our contact with administration and district; is a task master and keeps the process going; makes people do things rather than doing them himself.
17. *Resource bringing* Locating and providing information, materials, practices, equipment useful to clients.	He uses his network to get us supplies; brings ideas that she has seen work elsewhere; had the newest research, methods, articles, and ideas and waters them down for our needs.
18. *Demonstration* Modeling new behavior in classrooms or meetings.	Willing to go into classrooms and take risks; modeling; showed the chair by his own behavior how to be more open.

Note. From Saxl, Lieberman, and Miles (1987). Copyright 1987 by the *Journal of Staff Development.* Reprinted by permission.

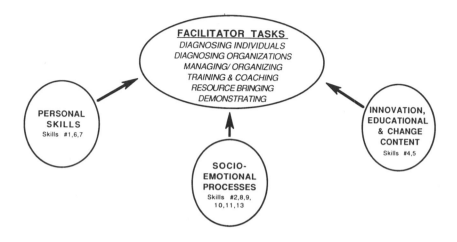

FIGURE 4.2. Hypothesized configuration of key facilitator skills within IC-Teams.

There are basically six tasks that the facilitator is required to do (numbers in parentheses refer to Table 4.4) diagnoses individuals (14), diagnose organizations (15), manage and control the change process (16), conduct training and coaching (3), bring resources to the process (17), and model and demonstrate the process (18). In order to do these tasks, the facilitator must have mastery of the content of the innovation (5) and a general grasp of educational issues and content that relate to the innovation package (4) (and, we might add, a commitment to the assumptions underlying the innovation model). But these skills are not enough. There are socioemotional skills that are required in order to be effective in supporting change. The change facilitator must have a good understanding of group functioning and have skills in facilitating the team (2), thus building collaborative relationships between the facilitator and participants as well as among the school personnel. This requires being able to build the trust of the participants (8), but also the ability to confront (10), when that is needed, and to resolve conflicts (11). The capacity to provide appropriate support (9), which also builds the confidence (13) of the participants, is required. Personal skills include interpersonal ease in relating to others (1), initiative taking (7), and the capacity to organize the work, time, and activities (6). Figure 4.3, using comments from audiotaped logs of a change facilitator, depicts how change facilitators apply the specific skills

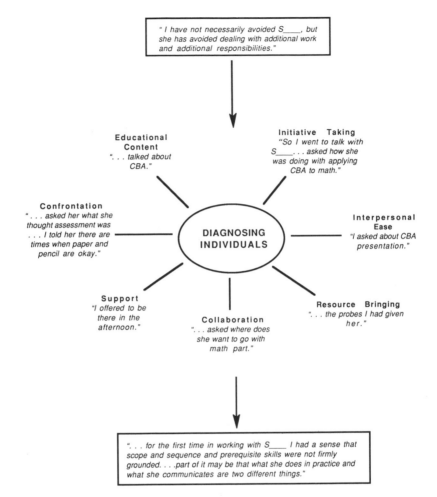

FIGURE 4.3. Example of individual diagnosis utilizing key facilitator skills.

described by Saxl et al. (1987; see Table 4.4) to diagnose a team member's skills and knowledge.

Selection and Training of IC-Team Facilitators

IC-Teams can be introduced most effectively into a school building or district when individuals have been selected and trained to support the change process. Before selecting a facilitator for any innovation, the two following critical factors must be considered: (1) the belief system of the innovation must be compatible with the candidate's belief system; and (2) the individual must have skill, knowledge, and experience regarding the elements of the innovation, as well as demonstrated competence in the key facilitator skills. It is impossible to help another to change if the content of the change is not valued and has not been mastered by the facilitator.

In the case of IC-Teams, the fundamental level of competency required is that of collaborative consultation. Consultation training is increasingly included in the curricula of school psychology and special education programs, and there is an increase in the number of individuals who have basic skills in the stages and interpersonal skills of consultation described in Chapter 2. At the inservice level, there are opportunities for training and coaching, sometimes with the assistance of outside university consultants, sometimes drawing on internal system resources (see Reschley, 1993; Rosenfield & Gravois, 1993). Peer-supported professional development activities, written and media-based materials, workshops, and the use of audio- and videotaping with structured feedback can all be incorporated into the process of developing basic consultation skills. It is critical that school systems and individuals genuinely committed to implementing this, or any other consultation model, make a firm commitment to training in the basic skills. Too often, the local trainer of the model is not effective because he or she never reaches mastery on the skills needed for the innovation itself. We have, in some districts, worked with facilitators who were learning the instructional consultation process while they were facilitating the development of the team. Whereas earlier we compared the change process to changing a tire on a moving vehicle, trying to teach others before reaching mastery is like simultaneously learning "how to drive while changing not only the tire but the whole mechanism," an analogy used by Meier (1992) in a similar case regarding teachers (p. 609). It is a situation with obvious drawbacks, resulting in frustration for team members and the change facilitator, and it usually results in delays in reaching acceptable levels of implementation.

There are several models for training of school change facilitators (see, e.g., Reschley, 1993). The training program for new IC-Team facilitators was formulated when we were faced with implementing IC-Teams in a large number of schools with only one or two trained facilitators. The process of training facilitators, which evolved as the project expanded, includes the following:

• Individuals are provided with a thorough overview of the consultation process and theory combined with practice in applied situations utilizing feedback and coaching. This has typically been accomplished by having the interested individuals either enroll in inservice training conducted by the local university or sit as members of an existing team and receive training as case managers under the direction of a trained IC-Team change facilitator.

• Individuals are selected for the on-site school change facilitator role based on their demonstrated competence in consultation and case manager skills and on their demonstration of key change facilitator skills (see Table 4.4). The individual assuming the role of on-site school facilitator has internalized the content of instructional consultation, especially that of collaborative problem solving, and can apply the problem-solving structure to concerns, issues, and problems at the individual, team, and school level. Few individuals typically demonstrate these two sets of critical skills, and most remain in the important role of team member/case manager.

• Individuals selected as new change facilitators at the building level are typically trained with their new IC-Team by an experienced system facilitator. The system facilitator supports new on-site school facilitators through group support on a biweekly basis and through individual coaching. This ensures continued acquisition of necessary facilitator skills and assists in implementing IC-Teams and the problem-solving process at the school building level.

• The system facilitator is an individual who has gained experience as an on-site school facilitator, typically in two or more implementations of IC-Teams in schools. Beyond the necessary skills described above, system facilitators demonstrate understanding of organizational and systems functioning, awareness of the change process as it relates to both the individual and the system and, most importantly, the collaborative problem-solving capabilities to maneuver through the bureaucratic obstacles with which they are faced. Our limited experience in developing individuals for this role has shown that the unique qualities of newly designated system facilitators are maximized and enhanced by a close mentoring relationship with a more experienced system facilitator.

Given the high stress of the change process, we recommend that facilitators link with each other for support, regardless of level of facilitation.

Concerns of Change Facilitators

As Hall and Hord (1987) suggest, concerns theory is applicable to those at all levels of participation in change, including change facilitators, who are experiencing and facilitating change simultaneously. Hall and Hord also recognize that the content of the concerns expressed across levels will vary. Thus, it is important for facilitators to remain aware of their own personal and task concerns, but not be so preoccupied with them as to limit their ability to be minding the store, so to speak. In order to maintain one's own comfort and confidence in facilitating the process, IC-Team projects in districts have regularly provided opportunities for facilitators to share problems, so that support and assistance would be available to address concerns. Common concerns and some solutions to address these concerns have been generated by IC-Team facilitators and these general concerns are presented below. Specific concerns related to initiating, training, implementing, and institutionalizing IC-Teams are presented in the next four chapters, along with a variety of strategies that experienced facilitators have used to resolve or minimize these concerns.

The general concerns we have encountered most often involve administrative support, time, and feelings of stress. These concerns are discussed below with several ideas for coping which have proven useful for experienced facilitators.

Administrative Support

Facilitating an innovation, particularly one that involves complex school restructuring of norms and regularities, is a risky business for the facilitator. Often the on-site school facilitator is a school district employee who has volunteered to undertake this role. Therefore, one of the bottom-line concerns for the school-based facilitator is obtaining the support of administrators both at the district level and in the school itself.

The key strategy for obtaining administrative support is to successfully complete the tasks in the initiation stage, which are described in detail in the next chapter. It is at this stage that district and school-based administrators make a commitment to support IC-Team implementation on the basis of an extended contracting process. But, despite good intentions, as the change process unfolds during implementation, support may wane and/or the facilitator may perceive the need for additional support so as to move forward through a particularly difficult issue.

One useful strategy is to maintain good communication with administrators at all levels throughout the years of implementation. It is recommended that facilitators be as authentic as possible about their needs and "wants" regarding the support of case managers in their work with teachers. As Block (1981) suggests:

> One of the most critical skills in flawless consultation is to put directly into words what you, the consultant, want from the client to make a project

successful. . . . Essential wants are the things you must have as a minimum.
. . . If you do not get an essential want from a client, then you would do
better not to proceed. . . . If we give in on an essential . . . we will be sor-
ry. Giving in on an essential means the project will be on shaky grounds,
and we risk failure. (p. 62–63)

It is important that these "wants" be expressed clearly during initiation
and, equally, that the facilitator have a functional working relationship
with their building administrators so that these commitments remain
in force during the implementation phase when there is most apt to
be slippage. For example, it is common for meeting time to be infringed
upon during the school year, as the press of other business becomes
more urgent. Allowing meetings to be canceled or poorly attended is
not tolerable when this happens regularly. The need for the school-
based administrator to attend team meetings is also nonnegotiable. Yet,
the busy principal may begin to find compelling reasons to miss meetings. The facilitator needs to be clear about why it is essential for the
principal to attend meetings, and needs to be skilled in presenting the
case to the administrator. It is crucial to have an authentic relationship with the principal so that these issues, and other issues that are
bound to arise, can be put "on the table. " We have found that more
facilitators are able to be collaborative and collegial than are able to
negotiate their wants and needs (ones essential to implementation) effectively with administrators. Being able to do the latter is a necessary
condition for successful implementation.

Time

There is no problem more often mentioned in our work with teams
and facilitators than time — or the lack of it! Make no mistake, however;
the issue of time is not unique to developing innovations in schools.
The crush of assessments for the busy school psychologist, the end of
year madness for the teacher — all these reflect the "Great American
Time Crunch, which is fueled by the perception that there's never
enough time to get everything done and no matter how fast you move,
someone — or something — is bound to get there faster" (Baldwin, 1994,
p. 52). Sometimes, in fact, our perspective becomes distorted: "distinc-
tions get blurred between *what* has to be done, *how much* has to be done,
how fast it has to be done, and *what is worth sacrificing* to get it done"
(Ristau & Ryan, 1994, p. 56). The problem is exacerbated by our inability to judge how long a project is likely to take, usually erring on the
optimistic side: "A project expected to take a half day takes two full
days. A meeting scheduled for two hours needs three. I mean, really:

If my colleagues and I were as bad at estimating space as we are at estimating time, we'd be crashing into the furniture and dropping coffee cups off our desks" (Kelly, 1994, p. 63). Kelly suggests that our belief that we can somehow learn to control time, to make the hours conform to our demands "might be touching if it weren't so absurd" (p. 63). The problem of time cannot be resolved by continuing to try to do more and more in the same amount of time (e.g., we have worked with some teams that wanted to continue to treat all referrals for consultation as candidates for psychoeducational evaluation), and we certainly are not suggesting that facilitators throw in the towel when time, as it inevitably will, causes grief. Although there are no easy solutions, recommendations about time use are found throughout this book.

Facilitator Stress

A concern of IC-Team facilitators which has repeatedly arisen and deserves special consideration, centers on the feelings of anxiety and stress experienced by facilitators as they engage in and engage others in the change process. There are many reasons why facilitators feel stressed in the change role. Comprehensive innovations, such as IC-Teams, necessarily create upheaval, as the old order evolves into the new. Even though facilitators report positive and even euphoric affect at times, stress is a reality and part of the change process. Although not exhaustive, the following suggestions represent effective ways of addressing the stresses experienced in facilitating IC-Teams.

Arrange for professional support. The facilitator needs to know where professional support can be found. In district or large project implementations, groups for facilitators — to provide training, problem solving, and personal support — are a common feature. In smaller projects, facilitators may reach out for support to university personnel, to their colleagues and supervisors, and/or to other facilitators in similar settings or geographic proximity. The advent of electronic mail makes a network of school-support-team change facilitators a practical possibility.

Develop a personal support system. We encourage facilitators to find personal ways to deal with the stress of the process. Each individual needs stress reduction techniques such as exercise, supportive family members, or other personally meaningful strategies.

Accept that time will be an issue. Do not be surprised that time seems insufficient. Time was insufficient before IC-Teams were introduced and will be insufficient after IC-Team implementation. But it is important to be aware that more time is needed during the early phases, as skills are still incipient for many of the participants; the staff becomes

more efficient as they master the consultation process. It is particularly difficult for professionals, accustomed to perceiving themselves as
skillful, to muddle through the messy process of consultation in the
early stages, and there is a danger that professional staff will want to
"save time" and be more efficient by returning to traditional ways of
doing things. This may also be true of facilitators.

Set priorities. There will always be choices to be made. Failure to
set priorities and anticipation that everything will get done, are likely
to lead to frustration. Work with the team to set priorities for meetings, training, and cases. For facilitators, tracking their own schedules
to see how time is actually spent and then establishing priorities for
use of time is a helpful strategy as well as good modeling for team
members.

Schedule and plan. One of the surest indicators that implementation is moving forward and likely to be successful is when teams, administrators, and facilitators begin discussing how to schedule for
success. Reworking the school's schedule for specials within the building to free teachers for consultation and team meetings, and planning
team meetings by reviewing master calendars are signs that the issue
of time is being addressed proactively.

SUMMARY

The on-site school change facilitator is a pivotal player in the development of IC-Teams. An understanding of the change process, both in
general and in personal terms, is basic for undertaking this role. Commonly encountered responses and concerns of participants engaged
in change have been reviewed to provide the change facilitator with
an increased awareness of the multifaceted impact of implementing
IC-Teams. Further, the tasks of the change facilitator in relation to these
concerns and responses have been delineated, along with the personal
and professional characteristics that are necessary. Finally, generic concerns of change facilitators across multiple projects have been presented, along with strategies that have been found useful by those in this
role.

Although the task may seem overwhelming and the stress considerable, for those individuals whose beliefs are compatible with the model,
who have achieved mastery of the IC-Team process, who have prepared
for the tasks of the development stages, and who have developed a support system, the rewards have been compelling. We now move on to
describe the process that change facilitators must manage.

5

Initiating the Process

Initiation is defined as "the process leading up to and including the decision to proceed with implementation" (Fullan, 1991, p. 50). It involves mobilizing a system's energies, proposing new ideas, and choosing to begin a change (Miles & Ekholm, 1991). Emphasis in initiation is given to what Fullan (1991) terms the "three R's": Relevance, Readiness, and Resources. *Relevance* includes actions that help clarify and assess system needs in relation to the innovation being proposed. Even when a particular innovation appears to fit the needs of the organization, the change facilitator must also analyze the organization's *readiness* for change—that is, the current status and capacity for change of the individuals within the organization and of the organization itself—to determine whether the intended outcomes are worth the costs of implementation. Backer (1994) defines readiness as a "willingness—a 'state of mind' that is the precursor of actual behaviors needed to adopt an innovation (or to resist it). People have to *believe* that change will make a difference, and that adopting a particular innovation will help, before they are likely to commit to change" (p. 2). Finally, Fullan (1991) indicates that the *resources* of the organization and individuals must be assessed to ensure the ability to carry out the implementation.

CONSIDERATIONS IN IC-TEAM INITIATION

Table 5.1 lists what we believe are the critical activities to address during initiation of the IC-Team innovation. Embedded within this guidelist are the three R's cited by Fullan. Whether initiating a change at the system level or in one school, these elements remain important.

TABLE 5.1. Considerations in Initiation—A Guidelist

Innovation quality
System needs: Dealing with competing realities
Awareness and support of stakeholders
  District-wide
    Superintendent
    Teachers
    Union
    Director/supervisor of special education
    Director of categorical programs
    Director of pupil personnel
    Principal(s)
    Curriculum coordinator
    Other
Administrator who will be responsible for project
Selection of participating school(s)
  School-wide awareness and support
Selection of participating team members
  Team size in proportion to faculty size (8 to 14 members)
  School-based administrator, preferably principal who attends all meetings.
  Regular education teacher(s)—number in proportion to faculty
  Special education teacher(s)
Additional team members
  Psychologist
  School nurse
  Guidance personnel
  Reading specialist
  District administrator (especially if first team in district)
  Other(s)
Voluntary, informed, written commitment of administration and team members to:
  Attend inservice meetings
  Attend team meetings
  Implement the collaborative process
Informed, written consent from district level
  Informed, written consent of principal
Awareness and support of other critical stakeholders
  Parents of school students
  Community
    Advocacy groups
    Social service agencies
    Juvenile justice
    Other
  Continue new faculty awareness
Development and presentation of training plan
  Sequence and schedule of training
Accessing resources
Evaluation planning
  Development of comprehensive evaluation that is both formative and summative
    Evaluation of training
    Level of implementation
    Selected outcomes

A Prologue to Initiation

Prior to attempting IC-Team implementation, change facilitators should thoroughly familiarize themselves with IC-Teams' knowledge base and processes. Chapters 2 and 3 have delineated the essential elements of IC-Teams to assist the change facilitator in identifying areas that may need further training and skill development. As a self-assessment, the facilitator should evaluate which aspects of the model are well understood and which ones require additional training. Only after gaining understanding of, comfort with, and skill in the framework can the facilitator accurately communicate the demands, challenges, and rewards of implementing IC-Teams to those undertaking change. A thorough understanding of IC-Teams by the facilitator is prerequisite for beginning the initiation phase.

As discussed in Chapter 4, an additional concern is personal acceptance by the change facilitator of the basic assumptions of IC-Teams. The stress of the change process is considerable in and of itself. If the facilitator is not convinced that the IC-Team innovation is an improvement over the status quo, support for change will not be delivered with integrity. Although ideological commitment is not required, and questions by change facilitators about the model need to be addressed, the change process is jeopardized without an acceptance of the underlying ecological and collaborative assumptions of IC-Teams.

Innovation Quality

The quality of an innovation is largely determined by its research base and effectiveness in reaching intended outcomes. Often innovation quality is initially based on researched results of previous implementations. In the case of IC-Teams, development was, in large measure, a process of integrating previously researched components, including those related to collaborative consultation, prereferral interventions, classroom-based assessment, and intervention strategies (Rosenfield, 1992). This does not, however, relieve the developer of an innovation, and those who clinically replicate it, from the need to continue to evaluate the framework. As research has emerged on various aspects of IC-Teams, the data have been shared during initiation with the schools and systems considering its adoption.

An essential piece of innovation quality to be considered is the nature of the technical assistance available during implementation. In the case of IC-Teams, technical assistance has been defined to include a local facilitator who is available to provide weekly, on-site training and coaching for innovation participants. Such assistance is considered a crucial element for long-term success (Miles & Ekholm, 1991).

While it is understood that IC-Team projects, like any innovation, must be adapted to particular contexts, it is clear that adaptation has its limits. There is an important distinction between adoption and adaptation in the initiation and implementation of an innovation. IC-Teams, as defined and described in Chapter 2, require certain conceptual and practical elements. Taken as a whole, these elements *are* IC-Teams. There is an expectation, then, that the components outlined as critical dimensions (Figure 2.1) will be present in all fully implemented IC-Teams, including, for example, an interdisciplinary team that utilizes a systematic and centralized process to deliver collaborative support to classroom teachers.

However, it is also anticipated that each school and district will adapt the model to its particular culture and community. In fact, such adaptation is documented as necessary to ensure ultimate implementation (McLaughlin, 1990). One adaptation that occurs naturally is the division of tasks typically attributed to the system manager. It is often practical to have other individuals assume some of the responsibilities, such as setting the agenda or maintaining the minutes. Some IC-Teams have chosen two individuals to assume these responsibilities whereas other teams have rotated some of these responsibilities. While the primary function of the system manager is to collect all referrals to the team and to maintain accurate documentation of case progress, other duties may be negotiated among the teams. However, adaptations must be done with careful thought and with the understanding of the full team. The change facilitator must monitor the extent of modification or adaptation in the innovation to ensure that the conceptual underpinnings remain intact. In order to maintain the integrity of the innovation, the facilitator has the important task of helping to differentiate what cannot be modified and where adaptation is possible.

System Needs

No matter how exceptional an innovation, unless the adopting system perceives that innovation as meeting its needs, successful implementation will not occur. Two aspects in organizations are key for change facilitators: the goals of the organization and the means to reach those goals. Innovations should be considered as a means to reach goals, and hence, must fit the overall goals of the system. While Miles and Ekholm (1991) warn that elaborate needs assessments and endless committees and task forces are often more harmful than helpful in mobilizing action, there must be some profound sense that the innovation proposed will fulfill a substantial need of the system and ultimately lead to the achievement of set goals.

An alternative to elaborate needs assessments is to confer with concerned parties in the system, including those stakeholders identified in the guidelist. In the case of one implementation of IC-Teams in a large, suburban school district, such dialog began when the school psychologist, newly assigned, began informally speaking with the building administrator, the special education resource teacher, the reading specialist, and classroom teachers about the difficulties they faced. Such discussion—occurring in the halls, before and after meetings, and in the lounge—provided invaluable information about the needs at the building level. When the "stories" were shared with school psychologists based at different schools, it became clear that the concerns expressed were widespread across the district, and this, in turn, validated the needs expressed. Again and again the same words regarding the lack of alternative support for teachers and students came from different people, in different professional roles, and in different schools.

Issues at the teacher or classroom level included a decreased sense of teacher professionalism, limited access to support for both students and teachers, and limited availability of technical assistance. At the building level the principal was seeking ways to assist the teachers to collaborate more in order to serve children better and support one another. Although the school had instituted grade level teams several years before, the principal did not see teachers engaging in active problem solving to resolve classroom concerns.

At the district level, there was a commitment to inclusion and to more equitably serving the diverse population of the district. One central office administrator expressed the concern that a disproportionate number of minority students were evaluated and placed in special education, that too many students were referred for special education evaluation in general, and that there were inadequate mainstreaming options for students identified and receiving special education services. The district was located in a state that had begun to move toward a policy of inclusion of special education students in general education classrooms. It became the school psychologist's job to communicate how IC-Teams would meet the diverse needs of all stakeholders.

As has been noted in earlier chapters, the major goals embedded within IC-Teams include providing teachers with increased skills in collaborating and consulting for problem solving. Such collaborative skills are often missing in the professional training and practice of teachers, although they are a prized aspect of many other professions including nursing, medicine, and law. The skills provided through the IC-Team training have the potential to further teachers' ability to support one another and to enable resource personnel to maximize support for teachers and students. If the IC-Team is successfully implemented, a

key desire of the principal, that of collegiality among teachers, is accomplished. Because collaboration maximizes support for teachers and
students, it benefits all students, especially those who are considered
to be at risk or in need of additional support. Hence, the district level
issues of overreferral and disproportionate placement in special education are addressed if alternative services are created to support
teachers and students.

In this example, the IC-Team innovation was perceived to fulfill
and fit system needs that existed from the classroom to the central office.
The more an innovation taps common or similar needs among key
stakeholders, the greater the chance for change. It is when the change
fits one sector without fitting another that we are apt to see partial implementation or inappropriate use.

It is empowering, however, to know that readiness is a factor that
can be enhanced, rather than being a fixed characteristic of either individuals or systems. Interventions that enhance readiness lead to an
increased probability of successful change. Backer (1994), for example,
suggests several methods for enhancing readiness including persuasive
communication that addresses issues of discrepancy and efficacy, and
active participation that encourages key people to get involved in activities related to the innovation process.

Awareness and Support of Stakeholders

Key people who influence an innovation's success must be consulted
during the process of initiation. Such people range from classroom level
teachers who wield informal power to district level superintendents
and associate superintendents with legitimate power to support or
squelch any innovation. A major goal in the early stages of introducing school-based support teams is to educate those whose approval
would sustain an innovation. An all too common scenario in educational innovations has been top-down implementation of an innovation by district level personnel several places removed from the
classroom (Fullan, 1993). Yet once an innovation is adopted, district
administrators may unknowingly (and sometimes knowingly) undermine the innovation after countless hours of committed effort on the
part of school-based personnel. This undermining can take many forms,
including removing necessary financial and personnel supports, increasing incompatible demands, or directly stopping the innovation.

To combat the possibility of central office undermining, facilitators initiating school-based support teams undertake a process of *frontloading*. Frontloading encompasses all of the meetings and informing
activities in which the change facilitator engages to ensure that key peo-

ple truly understand what the change is prior to making a decision to adopt it. A certain amount of public relations is built into creating awareness of and support for the innovation. The change facilitator must continually cite the assessed system needs as related to the innovation. Understanding the culture of the school and system allows the change facilitator to provide a realistic perspective of what IC-Team implementation can do for a system while gaining support for the innovation.

It is always good to bear in mind what one principal stated about her own district: "In this system, it's better to underpromise and overdeliver rather than overpromise and underdeliver." In that district, almost 6 months were dedicated to introducing, describing, clarifying, and reintroducing the proposed innovation to anyone and everyone who would be impacted by the implementation. The change facilitators began meeting with an associate superintendent and his executive advisory council in mid-August. When initial responses of this group were enthusiastic about commencing the project then and there, the facilitator presented the project to lower level district personnel for feedback. The following months were filled with meetings with the various bureaucratic levels of the school organization: first with executive supervisors, then supervisors, then individual directors, then pairs of directors and/or supervisors until all the key players had been informed and commitment to the model developed.

Because of the interdisciplinary nature of IC-Teams, the change facilitator met with curriculum, pupil support, instructional, and special education personnel. These meetings not only provided an opportunity to gain support for the project, but also served as an ongoing assessment of the district's needs and available resources. The change facilitator heard from district personnel about whether the innovation affected them, how it impacted their responsibilities, and the degree of support they felt for the innovation. The meetings also provided the opportunity to answer questions, many of which were asked again and again. For example, special education and pupil support personnel often ask questions regarding fit between such early intervention programming and the federal, state, and local directives for supporting children who exhibit learning difficulties. Principals often ask practical and management-oriented questions centering on the time required, impact in other and similar schools, and how to build responsiveness in faculty.

The importance of such meetings cannot be overstated. It is interesting to note that it was in one of the many introductory meetings that one supervisor mentioned the possibility of providing financial resources that later materialized as support for outside training costs.

Hence, while these meetings may be tedious at times and often appear redundant, the support and understanding established ensure greater success during implementation and ultimately impact the likelihood of institutionalization.

The identification of a district level administrator to serve as liaison, or "point person," for the innovation should be an outcome of the awareness process. During the activities described, an interested and informed administrator often is identified. This individual then provides the necessary district office support to make the project happen and to maintain commitment during the inevitable problems that arise during implementation.

How frontloading works within any particular school depends largely on whether the change facilitator is internal (an employee with defined responsibilities, whom district and school staff trust to be committed over the long run) or external (an outsider introducing change), and the magnitude of change proposed (i.e., whether it is system-wide or in only one school). There are inherent advantages when a change facilitator is internal to a system. There may already be a foundation of trust and rapport between school personnel and an internal change facilitator upon which to build the change. Discussing needs and communicating ways to meet those needs is a rarity in education, and some administrators are pleased to have this support and initiative. On the other hand, there are advantages to a facilitator being from outside the system, given that school personnel often respect experts and may listen more carefully to them than to internal change facilitators. Although there is little evidence to suggest that external facilitators alone are correlated to successful implementation, research has documented the powerful effect of external and internal facilitators working collaboratively (Fullan, 1991). The critical issue is to develop good working relationships between the external and internal facilitators so as to maximize the potential contribution of each.

While much of this book is directed at systems change, individual practitioners in schools can also use these concepts to change and introduce IC-Team concepts into their own schools. Carner's (1982) case study demonstrates how a school psychologist can initiate changes in school psychological service at the individual level. Whether school professionals are attempting a change in their individual roles or working toward major structural changes, there are many similar activities that must occur during the initiation stage. Carner (1982) introduced a change in service delivery from traditional to consultative school psychological services, and those experiences provide a valuable lesson for all change agents: There is, in reality, the potential for a great deal of latitude in creating new roles or structures in schools, and it is up to the individual professional proposing the change to inform and demonstrate what is possible.

Selection of Participating Schools

Whether selecting 1, 10, or 100 schools to participate in implementing IC-Teams, one must follow the same process, based upon the same criteria. First, there must be sufficient resources available for implementation, both within the school and from external sources. The greater the external resources, the less are needed from the school itself. Conversely, if there are limited external resources, then schools must increase their commitment for support of the innovation. It is essential for participating schools to commit some resources; doing so helps build commitment to the innovation over the long run. Second, principals and staff must indicate explicit commitment. Commitment includes realistic understanding of the innovation by the building administrator and faculty, ideas on how to create necessary time for meeting and training, faculty interest and support, and willingness to take part in evaluation activities.

One research-based factor for successful change is a sense of ownership of the innovation by administrators and teachers (Miles & Ekholm, 1991). An informed, voluntary decision to adopt the innovation facilitates ownership. Moreover, there is consensus in the school change literature that the principal has a primary impact on the success of an innovation at the building level (Hall & Hord, 1987; McLaughlin, 1990). Thus, the selection of schools for participating in IC-Teams necessarily begins with dialog sessions between school principals and change facilitators. School principals are provided with an overview of IC-Teams and the change process, including the underlying philosophical beliefs. These are communicated in relation to the assessed needs and accepted goals of the system and school. Any effort to create schoolwide awareness begins with the consent of the principal.

In one school district, an initial presentation was made to all elementary school principals during their regularly scheduled monthly meetings. This presentation was facilitated by the supervisor of elementary instruction, a district administrator who had been involved in earlier district meetings and who supported the innovation by creating time during a heavily booked meeting. Of 29 principals in attendance, 6 expressed interest in participating in a pilot implementation. A second process of dialog was initiated with these principals and the faculty of their schools. Interested principals often requested that a presentation be made to their faculty members. Many valid questions concerning the innovation and its implementation in the school were raised by faculty members. These questions and concerns are not considered resistance, but rather legitimate personal and professional issues that need to be discussed in the early stages of adoption (Hall & Hord, 1987).

Sometimes we have worked with schools that have made a commitment with limited or apparently absent financial support. In the case of a recent IC-Team implementation, the creation of school-based teams was proposed with no financial support from external sources. During selection of participating schools, attention focused on the schools' ability to deal with limited resources and their willingness to experiment to create the time necessary for training and meetings. Principals and teachers presented ideas for creating more time by utilizing working lunches, sacrificing nonessential meetings, and utilizing parent volunteers to augment existing resources. Some school districts are working to negotiate professional development credits for team members who go through the training as a way to compensate them for time. This idea was generated by team members. During years of implementation of IC-Teams, we have encountered many creative solutions for inadequate financial resources. These are presented in Chapter 7.

Selection of Participating Team Members

Once participating schools are identified, school administrators are assisted by the facilitator in determining the IC-Team composition. It is the change facilitator's task to assure the interdisciplinary nature of the team and to clarify the necessity for general and special educators as well as administrators to be active participants. The number of general educators included on the team should be proportional to the number of faculty and should be greater than the number of special educators on the team. Remaining team members may be selected from support personnel, including the school psychologist, guidance counselor, nurse, and reading specialist, with the number of team members totaling between 8 and 14.

Team composition is more complex than simply selecting members based on their professional roles. As with the selection of participating schools, team members are invited to participate based on certain criteria, including their interest in and understanding of the model, their formal and informal power positions within the school, and their capacity and commitment to implement the collaborative process. Within the parameters indicated above, consideration is given to those faculty and resource people, including key formal (e.g., principal, union building representative) and informal leaders (e.g., the teacher whom everyone respects and considers competent) who not only demonstrate competence, but who also would increase the likelihood of success for the innovation process. Creating a team of well-intentioned and capable people who have no political clout within the building often slows the rate of change within the school. A thorough understanding of the school and its culture will greatly assist in determining the most appropriate team membership.

Throughout the selection process, change facilitators should maintain awareness of additional teams existing within the school. Schools are bombarded by a proliferation of school-based teams. Systems and schools often choose to train existing teams in an effort to "collapse" the number and redundancy of teams. The task of the change facilitator is to uphold the core IC-Team concept, including representative membership from the general and special education classrooms, while assisting schools and districts in meeting the very valid need of combining and consolidating teams whenever possible. In an IC-Team implementation in a large, inner-city school, the existing School Support Team and School Improvement Team, both mandated teams, were combined and expanded to meet the criteria of the IC-Team model. In a suburban implementation, state mandated Pupil Support and Section 504 Teams, as well as federally mandated eligibility teams for special education are being combined. It is important to point out that the integrity of IC-Team concepts can be maintained while meeting the mandates of these teams. Because many of these other mandated teams have not offered any structures or training, schools have utilized the IC-Team and its comprehensive training to add integrity to these other teams.

Written Commitment of Districts and Schools

During the process of initiating IC-Teams, facilitators can expect to obtain informal commitment to the innovation. However, the level of commitment and number of schools interested often will decrease as more formal commitments are required. Formal commitment to the IC-Team model is obtained largely through the use of written contracts. Such commitment addresses the various sectors of the school system involved (e.g., district office administrators, building administrators, and team members) and attempts to create additional support for the innovation. For example, some implementations of IC-Teams developed individual contracts for district, school, and team members, whereas other implementations developed a combined contract (see Appendix B) between the school, district, and project facilitators. Creating a single, combined contract provided everyone with the assurance that there was widespread support and understanding of the project. The contract typically addresses commitments for attendance to inservices and team meetings, and an overall willingness to support and implement the collaborative process.

Awareness of Other Critical Stakeholders

Once schools and districts have made a decision to participate in IC-Team implementation, there are additional activities required to inform other key stakeholders including parents, community members, and outside agencies. The change facilitator and selected team members should make presentations to Parent Teacher Associations (PTAs) and to school board meetings to provide information about the upcoming innovation. Although to begin such dialogs during the initiation stage may sound premature, it is always better to develop understanding among and support from these key people early on rather than deal with misrepresentations of the innovation that are likely to occur later. In addition, the change facilitator can assess parental and community needs and resources through these introductory meetings. Parents who become concerned that their children will not receive important and mandated services can seriously undercut the implementation process. When they are fully informed, however, parents may become partners in supporting the program and have, in our experience, been willing to attend Board of Education meetings to lobby for IC-Teams.

Development and Presentation of Training Plan

Inservice education, to be truly empowering, must in no way smack of being an add-on (Maeroff, 1988). During the initiation phase, the change facilitator develops an awareness of the level of commitment and resources required for training by presenting a well formulated, systematic plan of training to participants and key stakeholders. Table 5.2 provides a sample training plan which estimates the total time required for direct training to be approximately 30 hours across 5 months. This estimate does not include time for the change facilitator to prepare and follow up training. When more than one school is involved in implementing IC-Teams, awareness activities and didactic training can be done in large, combined team trainings. However, on-site change facilitators are critical for ensuring the effective application of skills on the part of participants. The amount of time spent directly in training activities does not represent the total training experience. The training process is recursive in nature, and much additional training occurs over time throughout the implementation stage. The training plan

TABLE 5.2. Sequence of IC-Team Training (January through June)

Date	Topic of training	Time needed
1/13	Team needs assessment	1 hr
1/24	KICK OFF. Problem-solving process	1 day
1/27	On-site guided practice in problem-solving process Ongoing	2 ½ hr
2/3	Effective communication skills	2 hr
2/10	Effective communication (cont'd)	2 hr
2/24	CBA	1 day
3/2	CBA (cont'd)	2 ½ hr
3/9	On-site guided practice/coaching (test case solicited)	1 hr
3/16	Introducing model to faculty	2 ½ hr
3/23	Graphing and charting	1 hr
3/30	On-site guided practice/coaching	1 hr
4/6	On-site guided practice/coaching	1 hr
4/13	SPRING BREAK	
4/21	Testing School-wide student achievement testing	
5/4	On-site guided practice/coaching (team indicated training)	1 hr
5/11	On-site guided practice/coaching	1 hr
5/18	Evaluation procedures	As scheduled
5/25	On-site guided practice/coaching (action plans developed)	1 hr
6/1	Evaluation procedures	As scheduled
6/8	Action plans (cont'd)	

should reflect all aspects of the IC-Team training and implementation process. For example, the change facilitator should meet regularly with individual team members, and the training plan should indicate such support as an ongoing occurrence. Further, the training plan should reflect the degree of intensity required to obtain a particular skill. It is during the planning and scheduling of training that the amount of time and commitment on the part of participants, schools, and districts becomes obvious.

Accessing Resources

Evans (1990) noted the critical importance of training and support in building effective consultation skills. Communicating the financial, including personnel costs, of training and implementing IC-Teams demonstrates respect for the right of individuals, schools, and districts to make informed decisions. Financial cost should be accurately portrayed; substantial funding is required during the training and implementation phases. The personnel costs require the presence of an on-site facilitator, not only for training, but to support the team members as well.

The change facilitator begins assessing resources during initiation in order to determine what resources exist, what additional resources can be obtained, and how those resources can be utilized to support the IC-Team process. However, training and implementation costs are, as Evans (1990) termed it, "time-limited" and should be balanced against the long-term cost of continuing with the present system of servicing at-risk and mildly handicapped students. After years of implementing IC-Teams on shoe-string budgets, experience dictates that adequate resources can be found. In most districts, the pilot or experimental, implementation of the model has been carried out on a limited budget. However, when districts want to go beyond one or two buildings, there is a need to allocate more substantial funding. Comprehensive training and implementation involves major changes in the attitudes and behaviors of many personnel (Evans, 1990). An optimum amount of resources exists for any innovation. Having too few resources results in despair and frustration; however, having too many resources results in waste and a dispersion of responsibility. When resources are limited, the most likely victim of cuts is the evaluation of training and implementation effectiveness.

What are the resources needed when implementing IC-Teams? First, and essential, is support for a competent change facilitator. Experience has shown that, for best results, the change facilitator should be available 1 day per week per school during the year in which a school begins the implementation process. This time is dedicated solely to the duties of creating and implementing the change.

In addition, there is the issue of supporting the team members and schools who elect to participate. Funds are needed to pay training costs including stipends, consultant fees, and released time for teachers. Money is typically allocated to hire substitutes for classroom teachers on the teams so they may attend several training sessions. Funds are also needed to support the on-site training that occurs during the beginning of implementation—for example, for substitute time for team members as they practice skills or meet with the change facilitator for feedback and coaching. These costs may range from zero, if strategic scheduling allows free time for consultation, to the cost of providing substitutes so that team members have released time to practice skills. Figure 5.1 presents a worksheet for estimating training costs.

The time and resources required for the team to meet to conduct its work and to engage in problem solving should be supported with the school's existing resources. Paying team members and teachers to

# of Schools _____
Change facilitator salary for 1 day per school _____
Consultant fees _____

Training costs _____
    30 hours workshop pay per team member:
        $_____ per hour × 30 = $_____ × (N) Team members

    Substitute costs:
        $_____ per day × 2 days per year × (N) Teachers on team

Materials/supplies/printing/refreshments _____

FIGURE 5.1. Worksheet for estimating training costs.

conduct team and case manager business is discouraged. From the start, it is important for the school to struggle to find a way to sanction such collegial interaction without relying upon external sources. The opportunity to consult, using a systematic problem-solving process, can be intrinsically rewarding for school staff. The danger of paying teachers to consult is that when these funds are cut (and eventually innovation funds always are), the resulting resentment will be detrimental to the process. For these reasons, it is important that the school confront early on the need to embed the process into the budget and norms of the organization.

Accessing resources includes developing creative uses of existing resources, as well as obtaining new financial resources. Space for meeting is a resource to be negotiated within each school. Released time for team members may occur through the hiring of substitutes, but it may also occur by strategic scheduling within the building to allow common planning times, double classes, or efficient use of classroom assistants. (Table 4.3 in Chapter 4 contains additional suggestions for effective and efficient use of school resources to support professional collaboration.)

Evaluation Planning

Evaluation of the teams remains an evolutionary (and sometimes revolutionary) process, much like IC-Team development itself, with certain essential evaluation components routinely addressed. Three broad areas of program evaluation are articulated by Rosenfield (1992): evaluation of training, evaluation of the integrity of team implementation, and evaluation of specified outcomes. During the initiation stage, the change facilitator emphasizes the need to design an evaluation plan that encompasses these three areas and helps to develop a clearly articulated evaluation design acceptable to all stakeholders. Ensuring resources, both financial and staff, for conducting the evaluation is also an initiation phase activity. Opportunities to involve students (including, e.g., school psychology interns or student teachers) or university faculty for this activity should be explored, if possible.

Evaluation, especially that of individual professional skills, is not the norm in most educational settings. Rosenfield (1992) found that "while satisfaction measures of training are easy to obtain, there seems to be considerable reluctance among professionals to be assessed on content aspects of training" (p. 33). Hence, it is critical that all details of evaluation be discussed throughout the initiation process, especially when selecting schools and teams, and that all participants are aware of the parameters of evaluation prior to making a decision to participate. Although these steps do not guarantee success in obtaining compliance with evaluation activities, they go a long way toward preventing the hostility that may arise if evaluation is "sprung on" participants after implementation begins.

The evaluation of training requires assessing both the quality of training provided (i.e., formal evaluations of participant satisfaction with workshop presentations) and the impact of that training on the participants' ability to apply skills in actual practice. Written exercises are an efficient means to assess participants' initial understanding and conceptual control over communication skills, stages of problem solving, and charting and graphing. Role-play, audiotaping, and observation during actual practice allow for coaching to occur and for the simultaneous evaluation of participant application of skills. We continue to seek reliable and valid procedures for assessing training that can be conducted within applied settings. Creativity on the change facilitator's part is a valuable asset when designing training evaluations.

The importance of assessing the integrity with which the model is implemented has been discussed in Chapter 3. The complexity of IC-Teams is reflected in the comprehensive nature of the IC-Team LOI Scale, which is currently used to measure the IC-Team implementation. The IC-Team LOI Scale (Appendix A) consists of a combination of interviews, record reviews, and observations, all of which are time consuming. The change facilitator needs to include time and personnel required to complete the scale into the implementation plan.

In addition, during initiation the change facilitator works closely with key stakeholders to identify which outcome variable(s) are of interest and how to assess the changes that result from implementation. Schools and school systems that have decided to initiate IC-Teams do so to meet specific needs. Outcomes included within the evaluation design should logically relate to these needs.

The change facilitator does not necessarily assume responsibility for conducting the evaluation, but instead retains responsibility for ensuring that a three-part evaluation plan is considered during the initiation stage. Rather than taking full responsibility for conducting evaluation activities, the change facilitator can assist by collaborating with a district's assessment office or a local university in creating an effective design. The scope of the change facilitator's role in actual evaluation activities is negotiated during evaluation planning.

SUMMARY

The initiation activities undertaken by change facilitators and their importance have been described in this chapter. Change facilitators learn quickly that these initiation procedures and activities occur at a variety of levels within the school bureaucracy, including central office, building, and classroom. Awareness activities, needs assessments, and commitments to participate on the part of administrators and teachers go hand in hand. Just as the person who invests his money wisely is more likely to benefit from the results of his planning, the change facilitator who invests time informing and educating the various stakeholders during initiation is assured of greater success during the remaining stages of implementation and institutionalization. Most important, change facilitators must recognize that the change process is not linear and that each stage requires constant revisiting. There is, therefore, the expectation that this chapter, and the three that follow, will be reread several times throughout training, implementation, and institutionalization as the business of an earlier stage needs to be revisited. However, successful completion of the initiation stage tasks is a critical precursor to moving forward through the process.

6

Professional Development of IC-Team Skills

The amount of time between the decision to initiate and implement an innovation is often too short to allow sufficient attention to matters of quality. The change facilitator will often be faced with the expectation, whether real or self-generated, to commence implementation of the innovation immediately. However, careful attention must be given to the critical factors influencing successful change. One of the most important of these is ensuring that the skills needed to engage in the processes and procedures of IC-Teams are available to the professionals implementing the innovation package (Fullan, 1991; Hall & Hord, 1987; Miles & Ekholm, 1991). This chapter will outline a reasonable framework for planning and conducting training.

The evolution of IC-Teams has been grounded in the belief that all team members can be effective collaborative problem solvers. However, effective skills, if not in place, require extensive training and support both prior to and during implementation. The process of training individual team members, especially in the role of case manager, is a key ingredient in the implementation of the IC-Team process. The content of training has been elaborated in detail in Chapters 2 and 3, as well as in *Instructional Consultation* (Rosenfield, 1987). The how and when of training is addressed by the change facilitator. This chapter will review general considerations in designing and delivering training to educational professionals and will highlight specific tasks and issues the IC-Team change facilitator will encounter when training teams.

GENERAL CONSIDERATIONS IN DESIGNING AND DELIVERING TRAINING

Research on training in education indicates that 1-day, one-shot trainings are largely ineffective at producing changes in participant behaviors (Hall & Hord, 1987). Considering the complexity of IC-Teams — in which change facilitators train individual team members in the content and process of instructional consultation, while simultaneously facilitating the development and functioning of a team — it is clear that fragmented training will not result in achieving meaningful change.

To ensure ultimate institutionalization, the change facilitator must design and develop training that is comprehensive, covering the core components of IC-Teams, and is tailored to the culture and climate of the individual school in which the innovation will be implemented. Given the individuality of schools, the facilitator's task of integrating many facets of training is no small feat. Over the course of IC-Team implementation, change facilitators have benefited from acquiring certain knowledge related to the design and delivery of training. Specifically, change facilitators require (1) an understanding of general methods of training and of how these methods relate to participant outcomes, (2) knowledge of best practices in adult learning, and (3) a grounding in group development and functioning.

Relationship of Training Methods to Outcomes

An awareness of the impact of training methods on participant learning is necessary in developing an effective IC-Team training program. Joyce and Showers (1980) described several levels of results of training: "The outcomes of training can be classified into several levels of impact: awareness, the acquisition of concepts or organized knowledge, learning of principles and skills, and the ability to apply those principles and skills in problem-solving activities" (p. 380). Hence, the goal for change facilitators is to move IC-Team participants from awareness about the process to actual application of collaborative problem solving within their school settings. Reaching this highest level of impact in training requires careful consideration of training options, and as indicated by Joyce and Showers (1980), change facilitators have the choice of several methods when training the IC-Teams. These include the following:

- Presentation of theory,
- Modeling or demonstration of skills,

- Practice in simulated settings with structured and open-ended feedback about performance, and
- Coaching for application (hands-on, in-room assistance with the transfer of skills and strategies).

Research investigating the various elements and their impact on training outcomes indicate that different training elements are likely to result in particular outcomes (Joyce & Showers, 1980). For example, the presentation of theory, often the sole component of many 1-day workshops, raises awareness and increases conceptual control but results in scant skill acquisition. Modeling or demonstration appears to enhance awareness and increase understanding of theory and knowledge, but is unlikely to result in acquisition and transfer of skills when used alone. Its use, however, appears to be helpful in fine-tuning existing styles or skills.

To build skills that will be useful in practice one must use different methods. Joyce and Showers (1980) found only a few research studies conducted on practice under simulated conditions, but these studies appear to support this type of practice as an effective means of acquiring skills and increasing the likelihood that the skills will transfer into the professional arena. Structured feedback, in which individuals receive feedback either from others or through self-assessment using a predetermined set of criteria, appears to be a good option for fine-tuning existing skills. Open-ended or unstructured feedback, consisting of casual and unsystematic discussion following observation, has shown uneven impact.

An extremely useful training method to help case managers become more skillful at working with teachers is that of coaching for application (Joyce & Showers, 1980). Coaching, as a method of staff development, is described widely in the educational literature (e.g., see Boiarsky, 1985; Joyce & Showers, 1980; Mid-continent Regional Educational Laboratory, 1984–1985; Showers, 1987) and typically refers to the relationship that is established between one professional attempting to utilize newly learned skills and another professional already experienced in that skill. As Showers (1987) points out, "coaching occurs at the point where the trainee attempts to implement the new . . . strategy. . . . Coaches may be peers, supervisors, principals, college instructors, or others who are competent in the utilization of the new approach" (p. 66). Showers (1987) also cites several functions of coaching during the transfer of skills into applied settings. As related to the development of effective case manager functioning in IC-Teams, these include the following:

- The coaching relationship provides support and encouragement to new case managers during a difficult process involving personal and professional risk taking.
- The relationship provides opportunities for increased learning on the part of both the coach and the case manager. Feedback, demonstration, and direct teaching are critical components of coaching, which facilitate further learning.
- Coaching facilitates higher order learning, such as identifying the appropriate times and opportunities to use a newly practiced skill.

Such learning cannot occur within the simulation or didactic arena. In IC-Team training, coaching occurs once preimplementation training has been delivered and the formal implementation phase has begun. The process of coaching employed is described in detail in Chapter 7. When used in combination with the other methods of training, coaching for application appears to be a powerful means of moving team members toward practice and utilization of skills in their daily practice.

Figure 6.1 provides a suggested framework for training selected IC-Team components, based on the work of Joyce and Showers (1980). The grid is organized with four of the major components of IC Teams heading the columns and the desired level of training impact in the rows. The intersecting blocks suggest training methods for the particular skill area that would achieve the corresponding level of impact. For example, if a change facilitator wants participants to gain conceptual control and knowledge about the use of communication skills, the training methods suggested would be "didactic lecture on effective communication skills" and "modeling and demonstration of effective skills by facilitator." Understanding the interdependence between training methods and the level of impact in terms of participant outcomes provides a firm foundation for the change facilitator when designing the training program for IC-Teams.

Understanding Adult Learning

However, there are some additional key considerations that should be incorporated when working with adult learners. Because change facilitators are "adult educators by virtue of their helping adults to learn, they should be aware of the nature of adult learning" (Moore, 1988, p. 2). Moore's (1988) review of the literature on adult learning provides a concise and relevant list of exemplary principles and practices that should be applied to the training of IC-Teams by change facilitators as follows:

Key IC-Team Skill Areas

Level of impact	Problem-solving stages	Effective communication skills	CBA	Data collection procedures
Awareness	Presentation of training components Exercise on cooperative problem solving	Preassessment exercise on participants' current use of communication skills	Review and analysis of current assessment and data collection procedures available Philosophical assumptions of CBA, focusing on mismatch between student functioning and task demands	Review and analysis of current data collection procedures
Concepts and organizational knowledge	Didactic lecture on problem-solving stages Team presentation of model to faculty Readings from *Instructional Consultation* and bibliography	Didactic lecture on effective communication skills Modeling and demonstration of effective skills by facilitator	Presentation of theory and description of skills through didactic lecture and readings	Didactic lecture on graphing and charting
Principles and skills	Individual presentation of problem-solving stages Demonstration/modeling Simulation case studies	Simulated role-plays Written exercise on communication skills Integrating effective communication skills into problem-solving process	Presentation and practice of individual CBA techniques utilizing case studies, modeling, and demonstration combined with open-ended and structured feedback Integration of CBA concepts and skills into problem-solving process	Simulation practice of graphing and charting with modeling and demonstration Open-ended feedback Integration of charting and graphing skills into problem-solving process
Application and problem solving	Training case selected Audio-/videotaping occurs Structured feedback on tapes Coaching on case progress	Facilitated training group focusing on team members' use of effective communication Analysis of written and audiotaped communication through structured feedback	Coaching and modeling in CBA utilizing training case Structured feedback	Coaching on use of charting and graphing skills

FIGURE 6.1. IC-Team components and suggested training methods.

Establishing a climate of respect. Physical environments that convey respect include room arrangements that promote small group interactions and furniture that is comfortable for adults. The interpersonal atmosphere should also convey respect. For example, because the change facilitator and participants are all considered equal in their professionalism, the use of first names or surnames should be consistent across participants and facilitator, and "most important, learners should not be patronized by a domineering facilitator" (Moore, 1988, p. 4).

Establishing a collaborative atmosphere. Participants should be involved in designing, the program, evaluating their learning experiences, and diagnosing their needs. Needs assessments of teams and team members are routine, as are other team maintenance activities.

Capitalizing on participants' experiences. Change facilitators should consider participants' prior knowledge and experience, using it as a foundation for introducing new material. For example, reading teachers on the team have often taken a leadership role in designing CBA procedures in reading.

Ensuring participation. Change facilitators engage participants in the learning experience, including its design.

Fostering reflective thinking. Change facilitators design trainings that provide opportunities for IC-Team members to reflect on current learnings and to examine how such learnings impact their existing assumptions, values, and beliefs relating to their professional functioning.

Fostering problem solving. "As much as possible, information should be related to the real problems of learners" (Moore, 1988, p. 3). Much learning occurs during "teachable" moments, when actual problems in the school provide an opportunity to teach or reinforce a skill.

An Integrative Theory of Group Development

Facilitators are constantly balancing the training of individual team members with facilitating the development of a functioning team. Knowledge of small group process and theories of group development have proven helpful in understanding both team functioning and individual learning within the group context. Wheelan (1990), in reviewing various theories of group development, indicates that groups go through various stages of development: "It is important for trainers to become aware of covert group processes and learn to manage both covert and overt levels of group activity" (p. 15). The first stage, dependency, finds team members typically dependent on the facilitator for structuring the training and the group itself. This initial stage of team functioning is often characterized by everyone being polite and acting

tentatively. Groups who have never worked together often stare blank-
ly, giving little or no feedback as to their understanding of material
presented, whereas groups that have a history of working together often
resort to irrelevant behaviors such as laughter and joking.

The second stage of team development is that of counterdependency or fight. This stage is often characterized by conflict among members and between members and the leader. Wheelan (1990) notes that
"conflict is a necessary part of this process since from divergent points
of view, one relatively unified direction must be achieved if the group
is to be able to work collectively" (p. 19).

The struggle is often about role differentiation and establishing
group norms. An example of this conflict was observed on one team
when the training component of CBA was introduced. The reading
specialist on the team became very defensive and continually questioned
its usefulness and inclusion. Although questions regarding the appropri-
ateness of any training are expected, this team member's concern about
the introduction of CBA was perplexing. After much thought and outside consultation, the facilitator met individually with this team member. It was during this meeting that questions of CBA's impact on his
professional role as reading specialist were raised. The facilitator was
able to answer some of his questions about CBA and ultimately was
able to enlist the team member's expertise in assimilating the training
into the team and the reading program as a whole.

The third stage of team development is marked by the building
of trust and group structure. The team begins to focus on how it will
function and to plan courses of action. At this stage, facilitators function as their name implies. Facilitation requires the ability to "massage"
certain aspects into place and to be patient enough to allow the team
to create some of its own structures. Group needs assessments and goal
setting at this stage are important techniques, which create a focus for
team functioning.

Once trust and team structure begin forming, the team is able to
move into the fourth, or work, stage: "For work to occur, groups must
also be able to use all available resources. Resources include such things
as information, individual expertise, and materials, should these be
necessary to the task" (Wheelan, 1990, pp. 20–21). In IC-Teams, there
are two types of work, (1) the collaborative consultation that occurs between case managers and referring teachers, and (2) the business of
being a functioning team. Teams set goals and expend energy focusing on the referrals received. However, the team must also dedicate
time and effort to maintaining team functioning.

The final stage of group development is task completion. Although
some groups have temporary life spans, others, such as the IC-Teams,

are considered continuous groups. As Wheelan (1990) points out, however, even continuous groups may complete tasks. Ending points may be dictated by reaching the set goals. For example, if a goal is to create and institutionalize additional resources in a school, the team can reach an ending when that goal is achieved. Each ending point may alter the "structure of the group and regression to earlier stages is inevitable" (p. 21).

Understanding the group process prepares IC-Team facilitators to recognize points at which team development is likely to stagnate and to intervene when appropriate. For example, teams that remain in the dependency stage fail to thrive independent of the leader, a characteristic that is recognizable when the leader is not present. At these times, the group often does not function. However, rushing team members too fast into independence may create extended periods of counterdependency, or fight, because of their discomfort with newly acquired skills. Change facilitators should expect some disagreement, for without disagreement the establishment of clear goals and visions is not likely to occur. However, disagreement without resolution is a sign of "stuckness" and requires facilitator intervention.

A final issue often seen in developing groups is overplanning, that is, spending an inordinate amount of time attempting to create foolproof structures. For example, teams may begin creating forms to document for one activity and continue creating forms to document for all possible activities. Teams that spend too much time creating structures often appear to be working very hard, and indeed, they usually are expending great effort. They may, however, be avoiding the real work of the team, which is engaging in case management and collaborative consultation.

CONTENT OF TRAINING

Awareness of the general principles of training, adult learning, and group development allows facilitators to incorporate the critical IC-Team components into a meaningful training program. The remainder of this chapter focuses on specific tasks and issues related to designing an IC-Team training program. It also highlights the key responsibilities and skills change facilitators require to succeed in the delivery of training. It is not our intent to review the specific skills to be incorporated into the training or to discuss how each skill is to be taught. Instead, the chapter will provide guidance, based on our experience in training teams, in how facilitators should (1) sequence the skills of training, (2) group teams for training purposes, and (3) schedule training to ensure participant success during training and subsequent implementation.

Training Sequence

Systematic Problem Solving

At the core of IC-Team training is the systematic process of problem solving (see Rosenfield, 1987; Table 6.1). Combined with the delivery components, the stages of problem solving are the collaborative processes that team members ultimately are required to master. Systematic problem solving is the common thread in how each team member perceives and approaches problems, and so it represents one of the first skills taught. Our experience has been that team members quickly internalize this objective, accountable and proactive approach to problem solving and adopt it as the official language of the team. The facilitator then uses the language of the problem-solving stages to indicate the stages of case manager progress within the consultation process. This common language assists in creating the effective communication essential to team functioning.

By training members in the problem-solving process early, the facilitator builds a scaffold onto which all other training components can be connected. During training, many facilitators begin each session by outlining the problem-solving stages on a blackboard to emphasize the importance of the problem-solving process. As new skills are introduced, the outline is expanded, allowing team members to see where different skills fit into the process. At times, discussion may occur as to whether skills fit one, two, or all stages. Regardless of the sequence of training, it is the facilitator's responsibility to continually help team members to assimilate and tie in new skills to those previously presented. Once a team is trained in the skills of systematic problem solving, the change facilitator can then connect all additional training components to this structure.

Communication Skills

The ability of each participant to establish consultative relationships, to collaborate, and to be a functional member of a team requires strong interpersonal skills. IC-Team members receive training in effective communication strategies, and use of these skills is emphasized throughout training and team functioning. Although many facilitators initially believe that participants already possess such skills, our experience has often shown otherwise. The need for this aspect of development has been documented on more than one occasion through the use of written preassessments, even for team members whose professional background has included some training in effective communication skills (e.g., counselors and psychologists). Individual team members who are skilled in this area can be helpful as coaches to other team members. Considering the different levels of functioning of team members and the fact that we all benefit from continued feedback on our own communication skills, communication skills as applied to the consultation process are always included as a component of training.

CBA

If training is conducted in a short span of time (e.g., 1 week), it makes little difference which content skill follows the introduction of problem-solving and communication skills. However, when training is conducted over an extended period of time, our preference has been to introduce CBA as the next content area. Since the underlying assumptions of CBA are congruent with those of IC-Teams, early training in these skills is beneficial because it reinforces team members' focus on the impact of instruction and curriculum on student functioning. Once the major assumptions and techniques of CBA are introduced, the team then begins to address the critical task of integrating these ideas and strategies with their own school curriculum and materials and introducing CBA to the school faculty.

Other Content Skills

The change facilitator can incorporate the remaining content-related skills listed within Table 6.1 into a training program, based on assessment of team needs and team readiness. Because educational knowledge and technology are continually growing and changing, the change facilitator is free to incorporate other research-based practices that are congruent with overall IC-Team goals so as to support team members in their implementation of the collaborative problem-solving process.

Format for Training

Training design, in large measure, is dependent on the resources accessible, the number of schools participating, and the time available. Training may be delivered in large groups (i.e., several teams brought together for common training) or small groups (typically one team). When more than one school is involved, it makes sense to provide some training within a large group setting, especially at the beginning, thus sharing the cost of trainer consultant fees, if any, and accommodations.

TABLE 6.1. List of IC-Team Training Components and Subskills

Problem-solving skills
    Entry/contract setting
    Problem identification and analysis
    Intervention planning
    Intervention implementation
    Resolution/termination

Effective communication skills
    Pertinent questioning
    Acknowledging
    Perception checking
    Paraphrasing
    Active/reflective listening
    Clarifying
    Elaborating
    Summarizing
    Other

Assessment
    CBA
    Observation-based assessment (OBA)
    Instructional environment assessment
    Task analysis

Interventions
    Best practices in instruction
    Behavior management/modification
    Cognitive behavior management
    Classroom management and organization
    Instructional and curriculum modifications

Data collection techniques
    Charting and graphing

There are additional benefits to bringing teams together for training periodically during implementation. Large group training sessions in which teams sit and work together throughout the activities enhances team building. These sessions also provide each attending team with an expanded view of how implementation works in different schools. Finally, it has been our experience that teams receive a boost of energy and creativity following such large group trainings. Experience has shown that large group training sessions planned late in the first year of implementation also allow each team to compare its progress with other teams. In a sense, these large group trainings provide a basis for comparison for many team members who want to check their facilitators' assessments of their progress.

However, as noted earlier in the chapter in describing differential outcomes of the various training methods, facilitators must be aware that only certain objectives can be accomplished in large group settings. Little actual practice can be provided in such a relatively impersonal format. Large groups provide the opportunity to create awareness and conceptual control over the content. As an example, Table 6.2 provides an agenda for a week of training held for nine teams, which was attended by nearly 90 participants (including district level guests and administrators). As a general rule, large group training is always followed by small group and individual training activities.

Whatever training is delivered in large groups can certainly be delivered in small group settings. In pilot IC-Team implementations involving one or two schools, all training was done in a small group, single team format. Small group training sessions are easy to schedule and usually involve no costs for accommodations. In addition, they may be tailored to individual teams' needs and provide an opportunity to work on higher order outcomes (e.g., the application of skills in natural settings) because more feedback, modeling, and coaching can be provided.

Some training will also occur on an individual level. One-to-one training is, in fact, the basis for individual case coaching, as discussed in Chapter 7. However, it makes intuitive sense that the formation of a team is assisted by small group training, at a minimum, and most training is carried out in teams or groups of teams.

Temporal Aspects of Training

As is true in determining the format of training, the timing and compactness of training are largely determined by the length of time the initiation process takes, the resources available, and number of teams being trained. To fully appreciate at what point in the typical school year training should be conducted, one must look ahead to IC-Team implementation in a school. Implementation, in reality, overlaps training and begins when the team assigns case managers to their first cases, typically considered training cases. The new case manager, while having discrete skills and knowledge, is a neophyte in providing integrated collaborative consultation and requires time to work through a case.

Information obtained from early IC-Team implementations indicated that team members expressed concern regarding the difficulty of receiving training while simultaneously attempting to implement (Gravois et al., 1991). These concerns led to a decision to schedule training late in the spring or in the summer. One team training in the

TABLE 6.2. Example of Week-Long Training Agenda from an IC-Team Implementation

Time	Topic	Time	Topic
	DAY 1 August 9, 1993		DAY 2 August 10, 1993
8:00– 8:30	Welcome	8:00– 8:45	Review of goals
8:30–10:30	Overview	8:45–10:15	Systematic problem solving
10:30–10:45	Break	10:15–10:30	Break
11:00–12:15	Communication skills (small groups)	10:30–12:00	Team problem solving
12:15–12:30	Break	12:00–12:15	Break
12:30– 1:00	Large group evaluation and feedback	12:15–12:50	Temperature taking
		12:50– 1:00	Evaluation and feedback
	DAY 3 August 11, 1993		DAY 4 August 12, 1993
8:00– 8:30	Review of goals	8:30–10:30	CBA
8:30–10:15	OBA		
10:15–10:30	Break	10:30–10:45	Break
10:30–12:00	OBA	10:45–12:15	CBA cont.
12:00–12:15	Break	12:15–12:30	Break
12:15– 1:00	Integration of OBA with systematic problem solving	12:30– 1:00	CBA cont.

	DAY 5 August 13, 1993
8:00–10:00	Integration of week into instructional consultation model
10:00–10:15	Break
10:15–12:00	Delivery system and team planning (small groups)
12:00–12:15	Break
12:15– 1:00	Large group direction setting, evaluation, and feedback for the week

spring solicited a test case and informed the faculty that they were still learning and would not accept cases for consultation until the fall of the following year. In this way the team was able to continue to receive training without the pressure of having to provide full-scale consultation services until adequate skill and knowledge were obtained.

It is obviously advantageous to structure training and subsequent implementation to maximize success for all team members as they become case managers. Implementation in the fall ensures fewer overall case referrals to the team for the first few months, providing some breathing room for the team as a whole. In addition, many cases received early in the school year typically involve less severe concerns, ones that are in their early stages. Spring implementation, on the other hand, often results in a greater number of referrals, many of which have been brewing since September. These referring teachers and their students will have spent several months experiencing failure and frustration. To meet the needs of case managers during the early stages of implementation, it is best to conduct training during the spring or summer (or, sometimes, early fall), which allows for implementation early in the school year.

The compactness of training—that is, the amount of training provided within a given period of time—also depends upon the entry level skills of team members, resources, and number of teams to be trained. Although a large part of the content can be introduced in a relatively short period of time, the initial training phase is conceptualized to extend into the time that the team members are working with their first referrals. Training can occur over a short period of time (as depicted in Table 6.2) or partitioned training can occur over a longer period (as depicted in Chapter 5, Table 5.2). While each training schedule has advantages and disadvantages, team members have expressed the preference that the majority of training be conducted in a block of time rather than occur weekly over several months.

Once the format and timing of training are decided, teams are provided with training schedules. These schedules state that the first cases are considered training cases. In order to avoid unrealistic expectations on the part of classroom teachers regarding the effectiveness of the team, it is also recommended that team members explain to other faculty in the school that training is still occurring and that the initial cases are actually training cases. This provides both team members and facilitators with a realistic climate in which to provide the on-site training and coaching required to build adequate acquisition of skills. Moreover, the open acceptance of a training process for team members establishes a learning and collaborative culture, making it easier for other faculty to learn new ways of doing things when the consultation process is in place.

In addition to the formal training schedule already presented in Chapter 5 (Table 5.2), it is equally important to provide a schedule of activities that will occur during team meetings throughout early implementation. Table 6.3 is a schedule of implementation activities from an IC-Team project, including case consultations, training, and evaluation activities. A schedule of this type further emphasizes to teams that there is a clear plan of operation to guide the early implementa-

TABLE 6.3. Schedule of Implementation Activities

Date[a]	Topic of meeting	Time needed
9/11	Team functioning	1 hr
9/18	Team needs assessment planning	1 hr
9/25	Evaluation of training begins	1 hr
	Case manager consultations begin[b]	
	Referring teachers invited to participate	
	(when? who?)	
10/2	Program evaluation begins	1 hr
	Audiotaping of cases begins	
	Case review	
10/9	Case review	1 hr
	Evaluation of training (cont.)	
	Case manager consultations (cont.)	
10/16	Case review	1 hr
	Training evaluations (cont.)	
	Case manager consultations (cont.)	
10/23	Team business	1 hr
	Case manager consultations (cont.)	
10/30	Case review	1 hr
	Case manager consultations (cont.)	
11/6	No meeting	
	Student achievement testing	
11/13	Team business/case reviews	1 hr
11/20	Case reviews	1 hr
11/27	No meeting	
	Thanksgiving	
12/4	Team business/case reviews	1 hr
12/11	Case reviews	1 hr
12/18	Team business/case reviews	1 hr

[a]Represents actual day of meetings.
[b]Case manager consultations will be arranged individually throughout the week on a rotating basis.

tion phases. Regardless of the format and timing of training, formal cases should not be accepted until the team members have had the opportunity to receive didactic training, practice, and feedback in simulated situations and to establish coaching procedures for when cases are accepted.

Evaluating Training

Evaluation of training includes measuring both the perception of the participants about the training and the actual mastery of the skills. It is not sufficient to evaluate the facilitator's effectiveness in meeting the stated objectives of a workshop and the participants' satisfaction with

EVALUATION

1. The most important thing I learned during this workshop was:

2. As a result of the workshop, I know that I need continuing assistance with:

3. I wish we had spent more time doing:

4. My personal learning goal for the next month will be to:

Name (optional): _____ Date: _____

School: _____   _____

IC-TEAM PROJECT

Date: _____

1. A positive aspect of the project for me is:

2. A concern I have about the project in my school is:

3. An idea about how to address the concern is:

(continued)

FIGURE 6.2. Examples of training evaluations.

FEEDBACK
IC-Team Training

Based on the objectives of this inservice, please rate the overall effectiveness of the session:

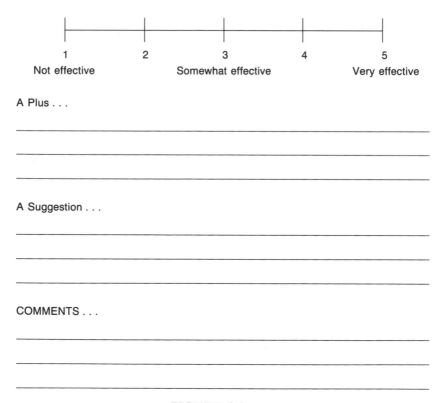

```
|----------|----------|----------|----------|----------|
1          2          3          4          5
Not effective      Somewhat effective      Very effective
```

A Plus . . .

_____

_____

_____

A Suggestion . . .

_____

_____

_____

COMMENTS . . .

_____

_____

_____

FIGURE 6.2. *cont.*

the presentation of material. More importantly, training evaluations should assess team members' conceptual understanding of the IC-Team process and its underlying beliefs, their individual skill acquisition, and their application of these skills in complex situations. Figure 6.2 provides several examples of paper and pencil evaluation forms we have used in previous implementations. Included are several training and workshop evaluation forms that can be easily adapted to assess the clarity and effectiveness of a facilitator's delivery of critical training components. We have also included a simulated referral packet that we have used to assess team members' knowledge of the instructional consultation process. The "Taylor Doe" case study, presented in Appendix C, was completed by team members early in the training process as an informal premeasure. It was readministered after training activities had been conducted and analyzed to gain a better understanding of the team's knowledge of the consultation process.

Recently, Jones (personal communication, 1995) has developed a simulation activity based on assessment center methodology, which consists of having team members conduct a problem identification interview with a trained role player. All activities are videotaped and analyzed using an objective rating system. Such information is both formative and summative in nature, providing a measure of current skill acquisition and use, as well as providing a useful tool for providing feedback to team members. These simulated and videotaped training evaluations afford the change facilitator more information on the quality of training and greater opportunities to maximize the preimplementation training experiences for team members.

SUMMARY

The process of IC-Team training has been built on current assumptions for developing professional competencies in work settings. Careful attention has been given to general considerations about designing and delivering training to adults, as well as the content of training and the process by which that training is incorporated into a comprehensive development program. Although the training program has been separated out from other aspects of implementation, it is impossible to fully describe the training program without overlapping actual implementation. Hence, as facilitators read the next chapter on implementation, it is important to be aware that facilitating implementation and training team members are conceptually connected activities.

7

Implementing IC-Teams

Implementation, the process of putting into action the knowledge and skills of an innovation learned in training, is the second major stage of change and follows successful completion of the initiation stage. IC-Team implementation represents the linking of the team to the personnel within the building in such a way that faculty begin to use the collaborative problem-solving services. Implementation also requires the team to develop skills as a functioning work group, as they build mastery and apply the skills and knowledge learned during pre-implementation training. Recent research (Fudell, 1992) regarding IC-Teams suggests that, although implementing the components of a centralized delivery system is necessary, it is insufficient on its own, and that continued attention to the processes of instructional consultation (Rosenfield, 1987) — such as use of the problem-solving process, effective communication skills, and data gathering procedures — is necessary to ensure effective adoption of the model.

The major tasks of the facilitator during implementation include the following:

1. Facilitating the formation of a functioning team that develops norms of collaborative problem solving, creates a delivery system characterized by easy access for classroom teachers and by effective documentation of services, and is adapted to the individual school's culture and needs;
2. Assisting individual team members to function as case managers, who have mastered the collaborative instructional consultation process in their interactions with referring teachers; and
3. Creating a favorable school environment in which the team and individual team members can function.

To achieve such goals, the change facilitator operates within team meetings, with individual managers, and outside the team structure to positively influence the development of effective IC-Teams and individual case managers. The change facilitator provides leadership and assistance to team members through their first cases, dealing with the ever-increasing pressure on the team to solve all problems and confronting the inevitable stress that results from changing a school's culture.

This chapter describes the activities of a change facilitator during the implementation stage. Unlike the initiation stage, the process of facilitating implementation becomes increasingly idiosyncratic because of school, team, and individual differences. With this in mind, we present a general guide that is based on facilitator experiences with implementing some variation of a consultative support team model in over 60 schools.

As previously emphasized, the efficacy of IC-Teams rests not only in the content and delivery system, but also in assisting teams, and ultimately schools, to create norms of collaborative problem solving. Norms of continuous renewal and collegiality require change in the attitudes, beliefs, and behaviors of the individuals in schools. It requires some people to give up their long-held views that the only mechanism to assist children with learning difficulties is a process that begins with performing batteries of tests to identify the child's inherent weaknesses. It is important to recognize that such views often define people professionally. These beliefs, attitudes, and behaviors exist not only in faculty and support personnel within the school at large, but also within individuals selected to become team members. Although we have never lacked teachers and resource personnel willing to participate, we have found equal numbers who experience great difficulty, discomfort, and pain in actualizing the process on a daily basis. As the facilitator conducts the business of the implementation stage, these personal concerns of the participants should be acknowledged.

FACILITATING TEAM FUNCTIONING

To create effective teams, facilitators must have a general idea of how a well-functioning team works and what activities occur during team meetings. Conceptually, a well-functioning IC-Team has established what Billups (1987) cites as six commonly encountered processes. An adaptation of these processes is presented in Table 7.1. There is considerable overlap between the components of IC-Teams and these processes. For example, the systematic problem-solving process also serves as the common approach to team problem solving.

TABLE 7.1. Six Common Processes of Effective Functioning Teams

1. The team and its members have achieved a sound professional identification. Members understand and agree as to the function of the team and their respective roles on and off the team. Typically this requires time and patience because team member role definitions are changing according to ongoing training and implementation.
2. Team members have addressed and dealt with the team within the larger environmental context. Team members comprehend the influence of the team and its objectives on the environment, and vice versa.
3. The team has established and maintains intercommunication processes for member-to-member exchanges and has processes in place to deal with intra-team conflict that arises.
4. Team members share common approaches in which problems are identified and analyzed, and solutions evaluated, namely the process of instructional consultation.
5. Team members understand that collaborative consultation is carried out by individual team members and that, at times, the team participates in such collaboration. There is a negotiated process by which cases are assigned and team tasks are divided.
6. Feedback and outcome evaluation are incorporated into the team functioning. "Processing is the term [typically] used to designate the activity of gaining perspective and reflecting on the immediate, ongoing transactions of the team even while actively engaged in those transactions" (Billups, 1987, p. 150).

Note. Data from Billups (1987).

As discussed in Chapter 3, there are two basic team functions: team business and team maintenance. It is not uncommon for teams to focus entirely on team business, giving little time to the critical activities that ensure continued team productivity and maintenance. Indeed it is often easier to deal with the referrals presented to the team, or even the teacher making the referral, than it is to provide constructive, nonjudgmental feedback to a fellow team member.

The facilitation process extends to both team maintenance and team business activities. Team members are provided with a description of team functioning activities, listed in Table 7.2, and the goals of team facilitation are continually reviewed during the early stages of team development. Team business activities include developing and implementing the critical delivery system components described in Chapter 3, conducting regularly scheduled meetings, performing routine chores such as taking meeting minutes and ensuring all cases are updated and tracked for progress, as well as problem solving with case managers and referring teachers in the most difficult cases.

Accountability is also built into the procedures. Figure 7.1 provides an example of a simple team meeting recording form. A summary of team meeting activities is followed by a section that delineates future actions and tasks to be completed, the person responsible, and the date due. The system manager is charged with placing copies of the completed minutes in each member's school mailbox and ensuring that previous "future actions" are considered at the next meeting. Not only do such records assist team members in maintaining progress on their own cases, but the records also assist in maintaining effective communica-

TABLE 7.2. Team Functioning Activities

Team business activities

Regularly scheduled meetings — Meetings should be scheduled 1 hour per week at a convenient time for all team members to attend.

Case review and documentation — All team members provide regularly scheduled updates of their cases at which time the system manager and other team members ensure that all necessary documentation is being completed.

Feedback for case managers — The team meeting provides opportunities for members to give specific feedback to case managers regarding case progress and monitoring activities.

Problem solving — Teams engage in creative problem solving to help case managers more effectively manage their cases and offer suggestions as to interventions and resources available. However, team members only offer interventions for well-defined problems.

New case assignments — Each team determines procedures by which new cases are assigned.

Documentation of team meetings — Minutes of each team meeting document activities and future actions and responsibilities.

Team maintenance activities

Temperature taking — Conducted monthly, temperature-taking sessions provide a structured process by which issues and concerns, as well as celebrations and excitement, are shared and discussed.

Collaborative communication skills — Team members model, utilize, and monitor their use of communication during team meetings.

Giving and receiving feedback — Team members are trained in appropriate techniques of giving and receiving feedback. Open, honest, and objective feedback is the foundation for continued team and individual member growth and development.

Needs assessments — Teams conduct needs assessments on an ongoing basis to assist in designing and planning necessary training.

Continued training — Training is provided based on both active involvement of team members and facilitators and the results of needs assessments.

Faculty/parental participation — Team members recognize that the collaborative problem-solving nature of the team requires faculty and parental participation. However, there are times when team meetings provide specific training and feedback for case managers and faculty/parental participation would be unwarranted.

IC-TEAM SUMMARY SHEET

Date: _____

Recorder: _____

SUMMARY OF MEETING

FUTURE ACTIONS

ACTIVITY	PERSON RESPONSIBLE	DATE RUN

FIGURE 7.1. Team minutes recording form.

tion about each meeting's activities. Another technique, which was introduced to IC-Teams by a school nurse, is the "tickler file." Here the system manager automatically places individual team members on the agenda at specified time intervals to ensure regular updates and progress on their cases.

There is one team functioning activity included in Table 7.2 that is considered so critical that it transcends both team business and maintenance: case manager feedback. Although it is certainly a necessary maintenance skill of team members, the ability to give feedback is also considered a critical business activity because accountability and responsibility for successful case management is ultimately the responsibility of the entire team. As such, it is important that team members provide the feedback necessary to ensure that each case is on track and making reasonable progress.

Team maintenance activities are those processes that ensure that everyone on the team is taking an active part and sharing responsibility for the functioning of the team. One regular procedure used by the teams for maintenance, derived from the work of family systems therapy, is *temperature taking* (Schwab et al., 1989), a practical way for teams to "check out and focus on the current life conditions — the what, why, who, when, where, and how — of its members" (p. 106). A monthly temperature taking, following the five steps described in Table 7.3, allows individual members regularly scheduled opportunities to address concerns and complaints regarding any aspect of team functioning, as well as to share information and excitement.

Case Management and the Team Process

The team meeting is a problem-solving environment that focuses on both the tasks of case management and the individual team members' learning and growth. It becomes a setting in which, for example, good communication skills are developed. To model effective communication skills during team meetings, the change facilitator employs paraphrasing and clarifies and checks perceptions as team members interact with each other and present their cases and concerns. At times the change facilitator is explicit in drawing team members' attention to the communication process of the group. As the team continues to develop, other team members can assume the role of process observer for the group, monitoring such things as the team's use of effective communication and member participation.

In addition to promoting the use of effective communication skills, the change facilitator actively demonstrates how the problem-solving process of instructional consultation is applied to cases and to team level concerns and problems. When issues arise (such as cases not making progress or team members arriving late to meetings), the change facilitator places them into the problem-solving framework by modeling how such concerns can be raised at appropriate times and in an

TABLE 7.3. Temperature Taking

STEP 1	Information	Does any team member have any puzzles or need information? Does anyone have information that the group might need?
STEP 2	Complaints	Does any team member have any dilemmas, problems, or complaints?
STEP 3	Recommendations	What do members recommend as solutions to complaints expressed?
STEP 4	Worries and concerns	Does any team member have any worries or concerns to discuss?
STEP 5	Appreciations	Does any team member have any appreciations, excitement, or wishes to share with others or the team?

Note. Adapted from Schwab et al. (1989).

appropriate manner. For example, during an initial temperature taking with one IC-Team, the facilitator raised a complaint about team functioning, specifically about members who always arrived late to the meeting. The change facilitator then took the next step, assessing other members' perceptions of the problem and guiding the entire team through the process of generating solutions.

In another example, the facilitator brought up a concern regarding case managers who were not meeting regularly with their referring teachers. Immediately, other case managers expressed the difficulty they were facing in meeting with their teachers as well. Until that moment, no case manager had ever raised this concern about scheduling case sessions. The change facilitator then guided the team through a problem-solving process by which the team identified the concern as a perceived lack of time on the part of referring teachers. Several solutions were generated so that referring teachers' duties or classes could be covered or that they would be given compensation (in the form of early dismissal) for any after-school time they spent in consultation. (In actual practice, several of these teachers never took advantage of the offers for coverage or compensation, but instead indicated that the recognition of their efforts and the offer itself were most meaningful.)

Although IC-Teams are designed so that the majority of case problem solving occurs outside of the team meetings between the case manager and the teacher requesting assistance, there is a tendency, especially early in the team formation, for team members to attempt to solve cases as a whole team. This tendency is a direct result of years of having Assistance Teams, Support Teams, and other teams that were designed as group problem-solving models (Figure 1.1). Change facilitators should become attuned to signals indicating remnants of this style of group problem solving, which may include a barrage of questions to the case manager and multiple suggestions for implementing interventions, in most cases before the problem is clearly identified, during team updates on cases. During the first months of implementation, the change facilitator helps the team to recognize when inefficient or inappropriate team problem solving occurs and to place the behavior in the perspective of IC-Teams. Team members need to become comfortable with the idea that they, as individual case managers, will problem solve outside of the team meetings with the referring teacher; only when a case manager requests specific input, does the team engage in case-related problem solving.

The following excerpt, taken from the transcript of an IC-Team meeting, provides an example of the inefficient use of team time to conduct case problem solving:

[System manager has requested updates from case managers. The case manager and referring classroom teacher are members of the team — a circumstance not unusual in the early stages of implementation. Both are present and are describing a concern involving a student who has self-injurious behaviors such as picking, biting, and pinching herself.]

SYSTEM MANAGER: Okay, date of first contact?

CASE MANAGER: We've only had informal contact, but have never done a formal interview.

REFERRING TEACHER: We have just met informally.

FACILITATOR: It's kind of interesting, though, because since you're a member of the team you know what the entry contract is.

CASE MANAGER: Well, I wanted to go through the process of doing it. That was something I really wanted to do.

SYSTEM MANAGER: Okay, and what about problem identification?

REFERRING TEACHER: Well, we talked about it informally and I've gone back and forth as to which problem I wanted to deal with. But I think that right now the main problem is the self-abusiveness that she's doing.

CASE MANAGER: And that occurred after she started talking to me about her concerns.

REFERRING TEACHER: Right, because my first concern was the student's overtalking.

CASE MANAGER: The speaking out?

REFERRING TEACHER: Just talking constantly. That was my first concern. Shortly after I contacted [the case manager] the student started self-abusing herself and that became a priority.

TEAM MEMBER 1: What do you mean by self-abusiveness?

REFERRING TEACHER: She picks and bites herself.

(The referring teacher and case manager go on to indicate that they have not done any data collection; however, the discussion among team members continues to evolve.)

REFERRING TEACHER: There were other concerns. I mean, right after that she started stealing things and there were just so many concerns, but . . .

TEAM MEMBER 1: She has many impulsive, and perhaps compulsive, behaviors?

REFERRING TEACHER: And we were thinking obsessive compulsiveness and other medical issues involved.

FACILITATOR: Uh huh. So at this point, what is your plan or where are you at?

REFERRING TEACHER: We're having a staff meeting to hear some testing results and I'm waiting to hear and see where I can go from there as far as intervention goes.

CASE MANAGER: I'm going to attend that staff meeting also.

(Later in the meeting)

REFERRING TEACHER: I actually have started an intervention because every time I see her going toward herself, I just push her hand away.

TEAM MEMBER 1: You give her a signal?

REFERRING TEACHER: I don't say anything. I just put her hand back down.

TEAM MEMBER 1: And she knows that's why you're doing it, 'cause that's what you guys agreed on?

FACILITATOR: So when you said that there hasn't been any data collected, what kind of data would you collect, what's the problem about self-injurious behavior?

REFERRING TEACHER: Probably how often. . .

CASE MANAGER: And when.

There are several issues exemplified in this excerpt. First, regarding the specific issue of having the team assume the role of case problem-solving group, the case manager and teacher on two occasions told the team members that they have not met formally to conduct entry or to identify a problem. The fact that the case manager and referring teacher have not met may or may not be an issue that needs to be addressed by the team. Did the case manager and teacher not meet because of time issues, because the case is relatively new and not much has actually transpired, or because the case manager is hesitant to problem solve alone? These questions were not addressed. Instead the entire team in essence tried to become the referring teacher's case manager and consult with the teacher. The change facilitators' efforts to guide the case manager and referring teacher to consider whether they've identified the problem or collected data are not sufficient to stop the ongoing group problem solving. The integrity of the case management structure of IC-Teams was further violated when, later in the same meeting, the team engages in similar group problem solving around another case. Thus, there are indications that the team as a whole is operating under a misconception about how team functioning and case management are integrated.

In such cases, the change facilitator needs to address the deviation from the appropriate team functioning process described earlier in the chapter. By being directive and explicit, the change facilitator assists in creating the norms of group procedures that will ultimately guide future team functioning. The following alternative to the above excerpt creates a different and more appropriate exchange at the team meeting:

SYSTEM MANAGER: Okay, date of first contact?

CASE MANAGER: We've only had informal contact, but have never done a formal interview.

REFERRING TEACHER: We have just met informally.

FACILITATOR: You're both saying that you've been unable to find a time to meet regarding the case?

CASE MANAGER: We've had lots of snow days and it's been difficult finding a common time to meet.

FACILITATOR: I guess I'm not clear whether there's a problem we, the team, can help with?

CASE MANAGER: The only common time we have is on Thursdays and those have been the snow days.

TEAM MEMBER: Are there any alternatives?

REFERRING TEACHER: We have common times every day, but either one of us is on lunch duty, so we don't match. And I can't stay after school because of classes.

FACILITATOR: So, right now, without more snow, you can begin meeting on Thursdays?

CASE MANAGER/TEACHER: Yes

SYSTEM MANAGER: Then maybe we'll hold off updating the case until you've met this Thursday.

FACILITATOR: (*speaking directly to Case Manager*) Before we leave this, is there anything specific you want help on in terms of your next meeting? Do you feel comfortable doing entry and contracting and beginning the problem-solving process?

CASE MANAGER: I feel real comfortable with the first part. I don't think I'll know about the other until I get into it. I do think I want to meet with you however, and prepare for that meeting.

FACILITATOR: Okay. (*directed toward entire team*) This provides a good opportunity to review what exactly will be happening as [Case Manager] meets with the referring teacher. Remember, one of the goals of problem identification is to define the classroom concern in terms that are measurable and observable, then to decide what data collection procedures are appropriate. If you have any questions or need any help along the way, bring your questions to me or here to the team and we'll discuss them.

The alternative scenario shows how the change facilitator maximizes the use of the team meeting to facilitate the case management process. The goal at the moment is to provide any support necessary so that the case manager and teacher can engage in the collaborative problem-solving process. However, because this is a new case manager, the change facilitator recognizes two possible reasons that the case manager has not met with the teacher. The first reason, time to meet, is resolved for the moment. But the change facilitator also recognizes the uncertainty that new case managers feel in terms of knowing what to do next and allows an opportunity for coaching.

The second issue raised in the original excerpt is how the business of the problem-solving process, as defined in instructional consultation, is being conducted. The desire to move to interventions prior to defining an observable/measurable problem or collecting baseline data is an issue for most newly forming IC-Teams, and was for this team in particular. This may simply reflect the inexperience of the team and case manager. However, the change facilitator can use such teachable moments to reiterate the problem-solving process as depicted in the final statement of the alternative scenario.

There are times, especially during the training phase of team development, when the facilitator will intentionally violate the norm of having case consultations occur only outside of the team. The change facilitator may plan to have a case manager and referring teacher at a team meeting and ask that they engage in the problem-solving process as a model. The other team members can reflect on the process and provide feedback and coaching to the case manager. If this is done, it should be a planned training activity that the change facilitator differentiates from typical case updates by explicitly informing team members of the purpose of such activities.

Case Reviews versus Case Problem Solving versus Group Problem Solving

During team meetings, case managers routinely update the team on the status of their cases, reviewing them in sufficient detail to ensure that the cases are progressing appropriately. There will be times when case managers request assistance with a specific aspect of the case or when they feel stuck, confused about the next step. Case problem solving involves generating the input of team members to assist the case manager in this situation. The key difference between case problem solving and the situation described in the excerpt above is that the team members' efforts are directed to a specific problem-solving situation generated by the status of the case and the case manager's need for input. The following excerpt from a team meeting provides an example of when case problem solving is appropriate: [The case manager has reviewed extensive CBA conducted with the classroom teacher to assess this student's current academic functioning, has developed and implemented an intervention, and has a data collection procedure in place. He has requested ideas for how to proceed over the summer.]

CASE MANAGER: In terms of input from the group, I welcome anything. At the same time, just please understand that it's a very slow process. Now, being the case manager, I can see how you can be overwhelmed sometimes with input. . . . So, that's where we are right now. And, like I said, I welcome any input, whether it's in this format, in this meeting, or just you see me in the teacher's workroom and you say, "Hey I was thinking about this." So . . .

FACILITATOR: One of the things I heard you asking for was maybe something around parents or summer or something? I don't know if folks here have thought about that or that gap in the summer or ways to involve the parents.

TEAM MEMBER 1: I think it would probably be a good idea to maybe meet with [the child's] parents and share that information with them, as far as sharing what you've been doing with her at school and letting them see the progress she has made in her sight words and alphabet.

TEAM MEMBER 2: I know the brother has a tutor in the mornings, maybe the parents would be willing to get a tutor for her.

TEAM MEMBER 3: Last summer, she was involved in a local program, and she may be involved again, as well. But following what was already said, if the parents are aware of what you're doing, perhaps we can get a fifth grader to make up some word cards or something you may be doing, and we could offer it to the mother. It would be really good if she continues this chart system because when she [the mother] came to the meeting a few months ago, she seemed to want information and to be involved.

This excerpt provides an excellent example of a case manager asking for specific input from the team, although typically the teacher would be present when the case manager and teacher are unable to generate their own strategies. The team provides ideas that maintain the integrity of the problem-solving process and at the same time support the case manager in his desire to maintain progress over the summer. Whereas the first team engaged in group problem solving with little input from the case manager or facilitator, in this example, the case management structure is maintained, with the case manager soliciting support and the change facilitator helping to structure the teams' contributions.

There are also times during case reviews or case problem solving, however, that information and feedback must be provided to the case manager without that individual soliciting such information. Providing feedback to others can be a difficult experience and is somewhat rare in education, especially around core issues of instruction and assessment (Rosenholtz, 1989). Yet teams of professionals benefit from learning appropriate ways to dialog about their views, expertise, and experiences regarding the education of children.

The following excerpt provides an example of an IC-Team discussion in which feedback regarding a case is not solicited by the case manager, but is given as part of the team's efforts to support the case manager and ensure that she makes progress and documents the case as expected:

[The case manager and referring teacher have come to the team meeting to update their progress. They have shared some CBAs on the student's letter recognition skills and possible interventions.]

TEAM MEMBER 1: One of the things I was thinking about as far as letting you see the progress, if you say that she doesn't know all her consonants or all of her vowel sounds, if you could concentrate on, like you said, the upper case where she knew 85%.

CASE MANAGER: Right.

TEAM MEMBER 1: And on lower case she knew 81%?

CASE MANAGER: Uh huh.

TEAM MEMBER 1: If she [the student] could see like ... maybe have some data so that we can look at her progress to see what [the student] is doing, if it is helping her as far as her retaining ... and then you'll have something concrete to look at and to talk about the next time you all meet, instead of you saying that you have intervention but maybe some data collection needs to be done. ...

CHANGE FACILITATOR: I thought I heard you say something about the class assistant doing data collection?

CASE MANAGER: Yeah, yeah.

TEAM MEMBER 1: How is she doing that?

CASE MANAGER: She's doing a drill. She'll do one each week where she . . .

TEAM MEMBER 1: But, does she check it off or . . .

CASE MANAGER: No we haven't graphed it in a way that, well, we just have baseline at this point.

TEAM MEMBER 1: Okay.

CASE MANAGER: That's a good suggestion of something we could do to show [the student] that she is making progress.

TEAM MEMBER 2: Maybe the focus should be just on the letter sounds right now?

CASE MANAGER: Uh huh. Right now we're focusing on just recognition at this point.

Although this may not be the most articulate exchange among team members, the excerpt represents one of substance. These team members are providing feedback to the case manager on a critical component of instructional consultation: ensuring that sufficient data are collected to document the student's progress. In this example, although this was a relatively new team, it was willing to broach a delicate area, that of questioning another team member's functioning as case manager. Clearly a sufficient level of trust and comfort had been established to allow such an interchange. Of equal note is the facilitator's minimal, yet important role, in the exchange. Not only does the facilitator's input maintain clear communication, it also serves a more subtle function: it reassures both team members that she is there to intervene if the exchange became too uncomfortable. Such exchanges in team meetings assist in developing the team as a forum for true collegial interaction.

Establishing Ownership of Team Functioning: Enlisting Individual Members' Support

During the initial stages of team development, the facilitator will be a leader in terms of setting the stage for team functioning. However, from the beginning, the change facilitator enlists other members in the team development process, establishing an important norm of group ownership and participation. To enlist others' support in establishing team functioning, the facilitator uses skills in individual diagnosis and trust building to assess which team members display an understanding of team functions and who is willing to contribute during team meetings. There is nothing more powerful during team meetings than when a member, other than the change facilitator, begins to articulate the goals of team functioning and points out when the process is working and when it is not.

IC-Teams have some aspects built in to facilitate taking responsibility for group functioning. For example, the role of the system manager, a core component, ensures that at least one other team member is responsible for certain team activities from the very beginning (e.g., setting agendas, keeping minutes, assigning cases). Several early tasks require active team member participation. Referral and monitoring forms must be adapted to the school culture by team members. In addition, the team is responsible for informing other faculty members about IC-Team processes.

Some team business and maintenance activities listed in Table 7.2 are not so easily assigned or acquired by team members without direct facilitation. For example, giving and receiving feedback, as mentioned previously, is often a difficult skill for new team members. After receiving direct training in what constitutes effective feedback, individual members are guided in structured processes of giving and receiving feedback. Figure 7.2 is a Case Review Feedback Form that all team members complete while listening to case managers review their first training cases. Following the case presentation, each team member is guided in telling the case manager what they heard regarding each of the questions on the form. In essence, the individual team members are giving very structured feedback to the presenting case manager. During early training cases, such review forms and similar structures provide opportunities for each member of the team to experience giving and receiving feedback.

FACILITATING CASE MANAGER FUNCTIONING

The development of a functional IC-Team is linked to the development of individual team members' skills as case managers. The development of the case manager role influences and is influenced by the development of the IC-Team; each must be concurrently facilitated. There will be opportunities for the change facilitator's efforts with the team to result in increased skills or knowledge for particular case managers. For example, if the IC-Team is assisted in the process of giving and receiving feedback, such team skills may be used to assist a case manager in refining similar case-related skills. Likewise, the case manager influences the development of the IC-Team. For example, skills in effective communication are used during a case consultation by individual

Case manager:
Team manager:
Date:
Case:

Problem Identification:
What is the current and desired performance?

_____

_____

_____

What are antecedents and consequences that affect the problem (behavior)? What are the prerequisite skills needed (academic)?

_____

_____

_____

What are the continuing data collection procedures to be used to monitor the intervention? How will mastery be determined?

_____

_____

_____

Intervention Development and Implementation:
What is the intervention?

_____

_____

_____

When and how will intervention be implemented?

_____

_____

_____

Who is responsible for what?

_____

_____

_____

Has a timeline been established (4-week minimum, 6-week maximum)? Are decisions to continue, alter, or terminate based on data/information collected?

_____

_____

_____

FIGURE 7.2. Case Review Feedback Form.

case managers and during team meetings. The key focus for facilitators is to maximize their efforts to increase overall team functioning, while simultaneously increasing the functioning of as many case managers as possible.

Facilitating individual skills in case management requires going beyond the initial training delivered in the preimplementation phase. Change facilitators must diagnose individual team members' current levels of skill, knowledge, and performance within the applied setting, and design a coaching process around their application of those skills in actual cases.

Ongoing Assessment of Individual Needs

A major task is the assessment of individual needs in terms of training and further skill development. Such assessment procedures may be formal, specifically designed to determine team members' knowledge and skills, or informal, conducted during ongoing team and case activities. Figure 7.3 provides an example of a formal needs assessment measure designed to assess individual needs with regard to training and case management. This format gathers information about several aspects, including team member's self-assessment and reflection on the type of training (e.g., theoretical overview, practice in simulated situations, coaching) that would be most appropriate for them to acquire a particular skill. Team members also have the opportunity to rank which skill components are perceived as a priority for training and to reflect on skills and knowledge areas with which they feel comfortable. Not only does such a broadly designed needs assessment provide ample information as to how individual team members perceive their current functioning, it also increases individual team member awareness of the link between training needs and training methods, and of personal ownership of individual growth and development. Information derived from the LOI Scale (Appendix A) can also be used as part of more formalized strategies to gain information on individual team member needs.

Assessments of individual team members' skills and knowledge also may be obtained from informal mechanisms, such as observation and individual case coaching sessions, where the individual team member and change facilitator agree on an area that the team member will focus on for further skill development. Observations, statements, and discussions during weekly team meetings may also enable the change facilitator to pinpoint individual needs.

In addition to assessing knowledge and skills, the change facilitator must also assess individual team members' attitudes and beliefs, evaluating whether they are congruent with those underlying IC-Teams.

Name:
School:
Date:

The following survey is to assess both your individual training needs as well as provide information across team members. Please complete the following survey in order to provide information for future training and planning. The team as a whole will review and plan for addressing the needs assessed.

Of the training I've received in the IC-Team model, I am most comfortable with . . .

Everyone is at a different place with regard to training and at different levels of various skills. Some people continue to need information or knowledge before they practice a skill, whereas others need to practice the skill in simulated or role-play situations. Still others need coaching during the application of skills in training cases. Describe a skill you feel you need at each level:

I need information/knowledge about . . .

I want to practice, in simulated situations, the following skills . . .

I am ready to establish a coaching relationship for the following skills . . .

Overall, my training needs are as follows: (Rank the following 1–7).

_____ CBA
_____ Systematic observations
_____ Collaborative problem solving
_____ Charting/graphing data
_____ Interventions/strategies
_____ Use of communication skills
_____ Other _____

FIGURE 7.3. Needs Assessment of IC-Team members.

This is not a demand for "psychologically" correct beliefs, but it is necessary to facilitate the integrity of implementation. Because incongruent beliefs can and do impact the way in which case managers function and implement the instructional consultation process, it is the facilitator's responsibility to assess and confront beliefs and attitudes that would inhibit confidence or result in ineffective implementation. For example, a commonly encountered belief of new team members is that student behavior, or more specifically misbehavior, is the underlying cause for lack of academic progress. Despite team member training, and growing evidence (e.g., Gickling et al., 1988; Rubinson, 1991) that an instructional and curriculum mismatch frequently underlies lack of student progress, the facilitator will observe that new team members define problems in terms of improving the behavior of the student without ensuring that the student is indeed working at an appropriate instructional level. Another frequently held belief of new team members is that the only way students who have had difficulty in school can experience academic success is by working with a specialist in pull-out programs. This belief conflicts with the assumption that the forum for intervention is between the classroom teacher and the student.

The change facilitator's skills in confrontation, trust and rapport building, and case problem solving are used to support team members working through the difficult task of confronting their own beliefs and attitudes. Some conflicting beliefs, unfortunately, are not easily reconcilable. When team members cannot accommodate the key IC-Team beliefs, they are assisted in making a decision concerning whether they can, or should, continue to remain a team member. Just as psychoanalysts and behaviorists have differing beliefs, school personnel differ in their beliefs about student problems. We have had competent professionals indicate that they could not continue on an IC-Team because they were unable to reconcile their beliefs to those embedded in this approach to school-related problems. A special education teacher on a team, for example, came to the conclusion that her commitment was to working directly with children rather than to working indirectly through adults and cycled off the team. A school psychologist was using his consultation time to catch up on his testing backlog because he could not resolve his strongly held belief that every child should receive a full psychoeducational assessment prior to any classroom intervention (just in case there was a handicapping condition present). After discussion, he was reassigned to a more compatible setting. Doubts and conflicts are more common early in the process before team members and others are able to see outcomes for students, but the paradigm underlying IC-Teams may be untenable for some, and these differences should be respected.

Individual Case Coaching

Improved case manager functioning is achieved throughout the continuum of training methods, but most directly through the process of coaching. An overarching concern expressed by IC-Team change facilitators is how much direction and influence to provide when coaching case managers. The answer, of course, depends on both the skill area being coached and the case manager's current level of functioning with that skill. The change facilitator moves from being highly to less directive as the case manager becomes more skilled in a particular area (see Figure 7.4).

However, because case managers are at varied levels of functioning across many different skills, change facilitators may find themselves adjusting their input across and within coaching sessions. For example, the change facilitator may be highly directive around a newly learned skill, such as use of CBA, and less directive in a skill area in which the case manager is advanced, such as collaborative communication skills. For the newly acquired skill, the facilitator may demonstrate, model, and guide the case manager through the use of CBA techniques during case-related activities, offering plenty of direction in what the case manager should do and how to do it. Alternatively, for the skill of collaborative communication, the change facilitator may observe the case manager and provide specific observations with the

HIGH DIRECT ◄———————— COACHING BEHAVIORS ————————► LOW DIRECT

UNSKILLED / DEPENDENT ————————— TEAM MEMBER LEVEL OF SKILL / DEPENDENCE ————————► SKILLED / AUTONOMOUS

SKILL AREA	EXAMPLE CHARACTERISTICS OF IC-TEAM MEMBERS WITH:		
	BEGINNING ABILITIES	INTERMEDIATE ABILITIES	ADVANCED ABILITIES
USE OF COLLABORATIVE COMMUNICATION SKILLS	Uses irrelevant questioning and advice giving as means of working with teachers.	Overuse of relevant questions to elicit teacher responses, along with some paraphrasing and clarification skills.	Actively listens. Paraphrases, clarifies, and summarizes to fully understand teacher concerns.
USE OF SYSTEMATIC PROBLEM-SOLVING STAGES	Rushes to solutions prior to identifying problem.	Stagnate in problem identification stage, often experiencing difficulty as to when a problem is identified.	Able to identify problem in observable and measurable terms prior to intervention development and implementation.
CBA	Avoids conducting academic assessments.	Performs CBA with students but unable to analyze or interpret findings.	Able to conduct, collect, and analyze CBA information as part of problem-solving process.
ACTIVE TEAM MEMBERSHIP	Rarely participates in team meetings.	Participates in team meetings when presenting case or asked direct questions.	Appropriately participates during team meetings, offering feedback to other team members and requesting clarification and accountability from other members.

FIGURE 7.4. Relationship between coaching behaviors and case manager skill levels.

understanding that the case manager will integrate those observations as necessary. An understanding of the purposes of the coaching relationship, the role and function of the coach, and the issue of directiveness is essential for adopting a coaching process.

The Coaching Process

The coaching process currently practiced by IC-Team change facilitators includes three phases: (1) preconference, (2) data collection, and (3) coaching conference. Each phase is defined by various activities that are accomplished prior to the next phase. Figure 7.5 provides an overview of each phase, the activities involved, and the concerns that have been commonly expressed by change facilitators related to each phase. Change facilitators recognize and share with case managers that the coaching process can be conceptually equated to the problem-solving process articulated by instructional consultation: problem identification occurs during the preconference, data collection is useful for both baseline and evaluation purposes, and the work between the case manager and change facilitator represents strategic interventions.

PHASE	ACTIVITIES	FACILITATOR CONCERNS/ISSUES
Preconference	• Schedule meeting • Select case manager focus area • Review needed skills/modeling • Select data collection procedures • Set next date	• Time to meet • New case manager inexperience with coaching • Change facilitator skills
Data collection (case consultation)	• Case manager meets with referring teacher • Data collection procedure employed	• Meeting not conducted • Data collection not done or incomplete
Coaching conference	• Case manager and facilitator meet • Objective review of data • Open/structured feedback provided on focus area • Preconference for next focus area conducted • Set next date	• Scheduling/time • Incomplete data collection prohibits objective feedback • Providing balanced feedback

FIGURE 7.5. Coaching procedures for IC-Team case managers.

The Preconference. During the preconference the facilitator and case manager reflect upon the impending stage of the instructional consultation process and review the skills that will be necessary to accomplish effectively that stage of the consultation. The change facilitator assists the case manager in selecting a skill area on which to focus. The skill selected is behaviorally and operationally defined so that both the case manager and change facilitator can agree as to its presence or absence, or adequate or inadequate use. Table 7.4 summarizes focus areas that have been identified by case managers in their first 5 months of implementation. Once an area has been selected, the change facilitator and case manager review the skills necessary and conduct an assessment of the case manager's comfort with and use of those skills. If required, the coach may use demonstration, modeling, and simulations to strengthen the skills prior to the case consultation.

Next, the change facilitator and case manager choose an appropriate data collection procedure so that they can review the focus area during an actual case consultation. Because of the interpersonal nature of the instructional consultation process, a common data collection procedure involves the utilization of audiotaping. Case managers record their entire case consultation and later review the tape with the change facilitator, listening for examples of the focus area skill. Videotaping has also been utilized as a data collection process, as has been direct observation of consultation sessions by the change facilitator. During reviews of recorded or directly observed sessions, it is helpful for the change facilitator to note examples of exact wording the case manager used so as to facilitate later feedback. Other possible data collection procedures include review of written output from cases, such as behavior observation coding sheets, CBA formats, and individual Student Documentation Forms (Figure 3.6). Case manager consultation notes and verbal reports can also serve as useful data.

The issues faced by change facilitators in the preconference phase of the coaching process are typically encountered early in implementation and decrease as case managers and change facilitators become more comfortable with the idea of coaching. New case managers typically feel bombarded with new skills and knowledge, and coaching may be seen as another overwhelming or threatening form of assistance. Change facilitators can counter apprehension by reviewing the process of coaching during early team meetings. Sharing Table 7.4 with team members may be helpful to show examples of focus areas new case managers frequently choose.

Change facilitators may be uncomfortable if they themselves do not feel skilled in all IC-Team areas. To provide the appropriate coaching necessary for case manager growth, change facilitators must be well-

TABLE 7.4. Frequently Selected Focus Areas for Coaching within the First 5 Months of IC-Team Implementation

- Cover important components of entry and contracting
- Define problems in observable/measurable terms
- Prioritize/focus on one problem during problem identification
- Target academic functioning and conduct CBA when presenting concern is behavioral in nature
- Avoid "rushing to solutions"
- Set goals (set current and desired performance levels)
- Use data collection procedures
  - Conducting CBA
  - Conducting systematic observations
  - Graphing/charting data
  - Analyzing data
- Collaboratively develop and implement interventions
- Cover components in intervention development/implementation stage (i.e., what? when? how often? who?)
- Use brainstorming strategies during meetings with teachers
- Use collaborative communication skills effectively
  - Paraphrasing
  - Perception checking
  - Clarification statements and questions
  - Active/attentive listening
  - Relevant questions
  - Offering information
- Use time management
- Involve teachers in cases

grounded, experienced, and skilled in the model. If selected focus areas are also areas of skill deficit for change facilitators, several options are available. The change facilitator may use the skills of resource bringing and networking to find others who can coach that particular area for both the case manager and change facilitator. When such persons are not available, the change facilitator can assume a peer coaching model with the case manager, in which both parties develop a coaching plan including a mutual feedback component. Although this may be uncomfortable for the change facilitator, she or he is actually modeling both the coaching process and the need for all team members to engage in continual learning.

The Data Collection Phase. Data are collected during the case consultation between case manager and referring teacher. The case manager secures the permission of the referring teacher to audio- or videotape the session, or to have an outside observer. It is helpful for the case manager to explain the purpose of collecting these data, that is, to assist the case manager in learning the skills of instructional consultation. It is also important in school environments to ensure confidentiality and assure that only the case manager and facilitator will review the materials unless otherwise agreed by all participants.

The major issue encountered by change facilitators at this phase of coaching is that data collection is missing or incomplete. Again, this issue occurs more frequently in early implementation and usually decreases as case managers become accustomed to some of the data collection procedures mentioned. During early implementation of IC-Teams, change facilitators have told stories about how a new case manager was excited and ready to collect data during the preconference, but no data were available for the coaching conference: "The tape recorder did not work." "The teacher did not want to tape." "I was going to write up my notes, but I just didn't have the time." "The teacher and I met briefly and thought this wasn't a good one to tape." These examples of reasons for not collecting data reflect the real apprehension that new case managers typically experience regarding evaluating their own performance. The best place to address issues relating to lack of data is in the coaching conference.

The Coaching Conference. The goal of the coaching conference is to review the data collected in order to provide feedback on the case manager's selected area of focus. The coaching conference begins with a review of the goals set during the preconference, checking to ensure that the case manager still agrees with the purpose of the coaching feedback. The change facilitator and case manager also review the agreed-upon data collection procedures. It is helpful to have case managers make some initial observations of how *they* think they have performed. Inexperienced case managers may only indicate a general feeling about how they have done, whereas case managers with advanced abilities are often more detailed and specific in their observations of their performance.

The change facilitator then provides specific feedback in a nonevaluative manner, while listening, watching for the response to the feedback, and clarifying to ensure that the case manager understands. A helpful tool in the coaching process is the Tape Analysis Form provided in Appendix D, which offers the choice of reviewing the case manager's audiotape for communication skills or covering specific content of the entry/contracting or problem identification phase of problem solving. The Tape Analysis Form also provides a structure for documenting feedback over time and for self-analysis by the case

manager. Upon completing the review of data, the next steps are discussed, including selecting a new area of focus, continuing with the
current one, and discussing which skills will be useful and what data
collection procedures will be collected for the purpose of the next
coaching session.

Giving feedback is the core of the coaching conference and a critical change facilitator skill. Guidelines for giving effective feedback are
listed in Table 7.5 and should be reviewed prior to the first coaching
session. Although it may seem simple enough as presented here, giving feedback has been described by experienced IC-Team change facilitators as one of the most difficult aspects of the role. Being
nonevaluative, being specific, and making sure that the feedback is useful to the case manager have been cited as the most difficult aspects,
and facilitators may want to receive coaching themselves on the skill
areas of giving nonevaluative, specific feedback.

A serious concern associated with the coaching conference phase
is having insufficient data to provide objective feedback. In response,
some change facilitators decide not to hold the coaching conference.
Instead they work with the case manager on alternative ways of collecting data, including having the change facilitator attend and observe
the next case manager/teacher consultation. Other change facilitators
attempt to provide some feedback using alternative data collection procedures (e.g., reviewing the case manager's notes or records).
In one instance, when the conference was to follow the problem-solving
process, the change facilitator had the case manager narrate the story
of what occurred during the entire consultation session. The change
facilitator took notes and then reviewed the notes for accuracy with
the case manager. Feedback was then provided on the process of
problem solving recorded in the notes. It is also important, however,
to address the lack of data collection during the coaching process, a

TABLE 7.5. Guidelines for Providing Effective Feedback

1. Provide feedback about behaviors that the receiver can do something about.
2. Describe, don't evaluate.
3. Be specific rather than general.
4. Time the feedback considering receiver's readiness to hear it and the availability of support afterwards.
5. Solicit rather than impose feedback. Use a preconference to establish the
   expectation feedback.
6. Use clear communication.
7. Ensure that both receiver and giver in a training group have the opportunity to check with others in the group.
8. Take into account needs of both the receiver and the giver of feedback.

task that will require key facilitator skills in confrontation, problem solving, and rapport and trust building.

Group and Team Coaching

Finding adequate time to provide individual coaching is a major issue for change facilitators. Considering the many other tasks involved in implementation, ongoing individual coaching sessions with each team member may not be realistic. However, the need for coaching is critical if case managers are to fully integrate and apply the complex array of skills and knowledge required.

To cope with the constraint of time, change facilitators have developed small-group or whole-team coaching strategies. In one IC-Team implementation, the entire team decided to conduct CBAs of students' written language skills. After learning about the assessment process and practicing within the team meeting, all team members agreed to conduct a written language assessment with a student. The scored writing sample was the agreed-upon data collection procedure. During the next team meeting, time was allotted for a coaching conference, and the change facilitator allowed team members to give feedback to each other in pairs. Such an arrangement can be utilized for many, if not all, of the areas of focus suggested in Table 7.4.

In addition to helping address the issue of time, group and team coaching have unique benefits that cannot be achieved through individual coaching, including the following:

- Having multiple models available to demonstrate particular skills, thereby offering others many examples of the intricacies of applying a skill;
- Increasing ownership of team functioning by having team members take responsibility for each others' learning and growth;
- Increasing learning opportunities by having team members teach and model for others; and
- Creating comfort for team members in conducting team needs assessments and giving and receiving feedback.

A Last Word on Facilitating Case Manager Functioning

Formal training sessions and the coaching process are necessary features used to increase case manager functioning during the implementation stage. However, the change facilitator will also conduct what Hall and Hord (1987) term *incident interventions,* the little, and sometimes not so little, interventions strategically aimed at assisting an individual or group of individuals in implementing critical aspects of IC-Teams. Sometimes small incident interventions provide the biggest payoffs in terms of case manager growth and learning. For example, acknowledging a case manager's contribution during a team meeting, sending memos thanking individuals for their efforts, making sure that case managers are rewarded for their efforts (such as additional coverage at recess or lunch), and using a case manager's documentation as an example for others to follow are just a few small activities that the change facilitator can use to create goodwill and maintain case manager motivation.

Beyond showing appreciation for team members' efforts, change facilitators should demonstrate and model respect for the learning process of others and the difficulty many people face during the change process. As discussed in Chapter 4, the change facilitator develops a view of individual and organizational change that allows all case managers the opportunity to experience change in the most supportive environment possible. To accomplish this, change facilitators monitor their own process of change, reflect on their own functioning, and share, as appropriate, their own learning process. Recently, IC-Team members involved in their first year of implementation told stories of how change facilitators shared their learning process, including their own belief system issues, and indicated that it had positively impacted team members' desire to continue learning. These change facilitators were described by team members as being "human," "open," and "nonjudgmental."

Unfortunately, some team members have had the opposite experience and speak of facilitators who rarely share their own experiences or frustrations and who rarely acknowledge team members' efforts at change. Such change facilitators were described as presenting themselves as "experts" whose skills and knowledge were perceived as being too difficult for others to attain. To be sure, change facilitators should exhibit expertise in educational content and practice, as well as the IC-Team framework, but they must also engage in the key skill of confidence building. To build confidence in others, change facilitators must demonstrate their expertise rather than "be an expert." They provide overviews and insight about how their own expertise is, in fact, composed of knowledge, skills, and experience that can ultimately be achieved by others. In doing so, they enable team members to begin internalizing the idea that the process of collaborative instructional consultation is "do-able." In sum, change facilitators look to themselves first when asking others to change, and in doing so, assist team members to change as well.

CREATING A SCHOOL ENVIRONMENT THAT AIDS IMPLEMENTATION

IC-Teams and case managers function within the larger school environment. During the early implementation phase, the change facilitator works to buffer the team from the pressures that are present as the IC-Team innovation enters the school, and to assist in negotiating the team's acceptance by other faculty. A favorable environment is one in which the team can develop and case managers can begin to implement collaborative instructional consultation processes. Facilitating a favorable context involves working with principal, faculty, district personnel, and parent and community interests.

School Leadership

If the process of initiation was successful, the school principal made a commitment to attend all training sessions with other team members, attend regularly scheduled IC-Team meetings, and take a case as a case manager. Change facilitators must assume that principals and their assistants require the same supports that other new case managers require and undertake all of the activities discussed previously to assist principals to develop skills as effective case managers. In addition, change facilitators must go beyond simply supporting principals as they learn the role of case manager. Change facilitators must also create a trusting relationship in which they can work with principals to address the various issues that will arise regarding the team's and case managers' roles within the school context.

The relationship that is developed between change facilitator and principal begins with, and continues to incorporate, vision building. Miles (1987, cited in Fullan, 1991) stresses that visions include two dimensions: "The first is a sharable, and shared vision of what the *school* could look like. . . . The second type is a shared vision of the *change process* . . . what will be the general game plan or strategy for getting there?" (p. 82). Thus, it is important for the change facilitator to learn about and influence the principal's vision of the school, to assist in the integration of IC-Teams into that vision, and to take the initiative (another key facilitator skill) to propose and receive input on the general change strategy that will be used to implement IC-Teams.

This relationship also allows the change facilitator to address several issues unique to the role of principal, most important of which is the principal's role on the team. The principal is the legitimate authority of the school, and although some principals profess to being "just another team member," their actions and words carry more weight that anyone else's (including the change facilitator's!). Inevitably, the change facilitator will have to confront some action or words on the part of the principal that may negatively influence the IC-Team's development and ultimate implementation.

A frequent issue arises over the principal's attendance at team meetings. Even the most dedicated and supportive principals have missed one or several IC-Team meetings for very legitimate, important reasons. However, when the change facilitator judges that principal's actions, that of not attending, are outweighing their words of support for IC-Teams, they must confront the principal with the issue. Our experience has been that team members look rather than listen for commitment and sense when the principal's actions reflect lack of commitment to IC-Teams. In most instances, when a relationship has been developed, principals respond positively to the change facilitator's requests that they attend meetings.

Sometimes, however, actions of the principal are not so clear cut as to their impact on the team. For example, principals may feel the need to conduct nonrelated business at the IC-Team meeting, they may attempt to utilize the team meeting as a brainstorming session to solve other school problems, or they may use a team meeting to introduce plans for other school-based changes, all of which may disrupt or distract from the team's development. It is up to the change facilitator to assess the impact of such actions and to enter a dialog with the principal concerning how such actions are affecting the team. These dialogs provide the opportunity for the change facilitator to state concerns, for the principal to state intentions and needs, and for both to come to consensus as to how to handle similar situations in the future.

The literature is in agreement that "the principal is central, especially to changes in the culture of the school" (Fullan, 1991, p. 145). Our experience confirms that change facilitators who take principals and their influence for granted will quickly see implementation grind to a halt. However, change facilitators who are perceived by the school leadership as "solving more problems than they create" will be appreciated and their relationship with the principal will deepen.

Faculty Members

The literature on effective schools confirms that the norms of the school community—that is, whether they are collegial and supportive of continued professional learning or they promote isolation and inhibit growth—can shape the success of implementation of a major change such as IC-Teams (Rosenholtz, 1989). Developing, building, and maintaining interest and enthusiasm for the IC-Team starts at the very beginning of the process for both team members and school faculty. Positive momentum grows from effective and clear communication between the team and the school faculty. Faculties of project schools are informed at the very beginning that a team is being trained and what its function will ultimately be.

Change facilitators are typically asked by a team to introduce IC-Teams to the school faculty. However, it is more effective for the team members to make this introduction. This introduction customarily includes an overview of the philosophy, process, and commitments involved in IC-Teams. Information is provided about how team support will be accessed and who on the team will receive all referrals (i.e., the system manager). Other issues to be discussed include the differences between existing and anticipated structures, as well as the time and need for practice that change requires. The newly formed team literally asks their colleagues to support them as they learn a very difficult and complex process, which, it is anticipated, will ultimately benefit the school and the students.

Ongoing support for the team from the faculty is increased and maintained by providing regularly scheduled updates. In previous implementations, team members have made regular, short presentations at faculty meetings; sent newsletters; and individually attended grade-level meetings to provide information concerning the IC-Team's progress and current status. Such updates occur early in the process, while training is still occurring, and continue throughout implementation and institutionalization. During actual implementation, team members are encouraged to share successes with the faculty by reporting progress on current cases. Teachers who have successfully accessed the team are invited to provide feedback about their experiences. One very creative team wrote a rap song and dance routine as part of their presentation.

Perhaps one of the best mechanisms for maintaining clear communication within the school is to invite teachers to attend IC-Team meetings. Teachers who access the team should attend any team meeting in which their referral is discussed in detail, unless the purpose is to update the systems tracking. Teachers who have attended IC-Team meetings have expressed an increased understanding of the team and often comment on how they enjoyed having a total picture of the team process. Nonreferring teachers may also be invited to sit in on team meetings to gain a better understanding of the team process, although these visits will not provide them with a solid understanding of the referral-based problem-solving process that is a major component of IC-Teams.

The ultimate goal of such communication between team and faculty is to ensure clarity of purpose and function. Faculty acceptance of IC-Teams as a service delivery system cannot be guaranteed by the change facilitator. However, efforts to maintain communication with and understanding of the team and its functioning may provide greater assurance that teachers will make an informed decision as to the value of the IC-Teams innovation as it is being operationalized in their school.

District Personnel

With regard to district support, the goal during implementation is to build upon the support established during initiation. The change facilitator and principal collaborate to ensure that essential district level personnel are informed of implementation progress, evaluation procedures, and future planning. An effective and efficient means of communication is to send central office stakeholders copies of memos regarding upcoming trainings, attaching a personal invitation for them to attend. When guests such as central office administrators come to observe, team members usually want to show only positive features. A running joke on one team was that the team was always better dressed on the days guests arrived, and there were always ample refreshments available. Such niceties are certainly important and may help team members feel better prepared. However, it is equally important for guests to see that change is not easy, and that there are difficulties that must be addressed, even when guests are present. Openness and honesty about the process are important in maintaining integrity. As one principal involved in the model stated time and time again: "This is about learning and growing, and they [the guests] get what they see."

Parents and Families

Parents and families should also be provided with information on the development of the IC-Team and its primary function as a vehicle for professional collaboration. Such information may be provided through an overview presentation of the project at a regularly scheduled PTA meeting or in small groups by the change facilitator, principal, and selected team members early in the first year of implementation. As with the faculty, the change facilitator and team members let parents know that the team is involved in a learning process and will be working to develop better problem-solving skills. Subsequent updates to families and parents may be provided via school newsletters sent home with students. In our experience, when parents are provided with information and the opportunity to ask questions and provide input, they respond favorably to the idea that there is support available within the school that ultimately will help all students, and their children in particular.

EVALUATING IMPLEMENTATION

The IC-Team LOI (see Appendix A) provides the basis for evaluating the integrity with which IC-Teams are implemented. A minimum of two administrations of the scale are recommended during the first year to provide benchmarks for the IC-team's functioning and progress. The scale, which is continually being refined, results in a visual presentation of the school's and individual case manager's functioning according to specified critical dimensions (e.g., see Figures 7.6 and 7.7). Such presentation of team and individual functioning provides a concrete marker so that team members can see that their efforts are indeed making an impact.

The information derived from the IC-Team LOI is beneficial in monitoring the progress of implementation, and it alerts change facilitators and team members to critical dimensions that require further training or coaching. Until the IC-Team reaches an acceptable level of implementation (80%), they are less likely to integrate additional functions or duties effectively. For example, in a recent implementation, a strategic plan was proposed to have state-mandated Pupil Services Teams (comprised of guidance counselors, psychologists, nurses, and pupil personnel workers) and IC-Teams merge because they shared common membership. The merger, however, did not occur until the IC-Team achieved acceptable levels of implementation. In this and other instances, having an objective measure of team functioning helped district and school-based personnel recognize the IC-Team's functional level, and avoid introducing new functions that might have overwhelmed the team members.

Finally, as noted in Chapter 3, the IC-Team LOI allows us to gauge when outcome evaluations would be most appropriate. As Rosenfield (1992) suggests, it is premature to evaluate outcomes prior to achieving acceptable levels of implementation. Having a measure of adequate treatment integrity is one, though not the only, necessary precondition to support the causative link between a model's implementation and the outcome variables assessed.

CELEBRATION

Possibly most overlooked during the implementation of an innovation is acknowledging and celebrating the small and large successes experienced by the IC-Team. If, as Lortie (1975) found in his study,

PERCENT OF DIMENSIONS IMPLEMENTED

	10	20	30	40	50	60	70	80	90	100

Collaborative Process

Dimension 1
Use of clear communication

Dimension 2
Entry/contracting

Dimension 3
Problem identification

Dimension 4
Intervention recommendations

Dimension 5
Intervention implementation

Dimension 6
Intervention evaluation

Dimension 7
CBA

	10	20	30	40	50	60	70	80	90	100

Delivery System

Dimension 8
Support team characteristics

Dimension 9
Referral process

Dimension 10
Referring teacher participation

Dimension 11
Systems management

Dimension 12
Organization/monitoring of cases

Dimension 13
Team functioning

Dimension 14
Use of documentation/forms

OVERALL LEVEL OF IMPLEMENTATION

	10	20	30	40	50	60	70	80	90	100

FIGURE 7.6. Example of IC-Team LOI Team Profile.

teachers feel uncertain about their impact and experience only inter-mittent recognition of their efforts in the classroom, then team members will be likely to feel just as uncertain as they proceed through the complex implementation of IC-Teams. The change facilitator must be alert to appropriate opportunities for celebrations of success and progress. Celebrations may be small (such as applause during a team meeting; breakfasts, snacks, or treats brought as a recognition of a team's efforts), or they may be larger, such as an "IC-Team Appreciation Lunch." One change facilitator recently brought stickers (similar to those given to students for good work and behavior) so that team members could acknowledge each other's contributions during a team meeting. Giving certificates for an individual's participation or small prizes and gifts that recognize team members in their case manager functioning are other ideas that have been acceptable in the cultures of IC-Team schools. Whatever is chosen, it is beneficial for principals to participate in the celebration and provide their own acknowledgment of the success to team members.

SUMMARY

This chapter has attempted to provide insight into the IC-Team implementation phase. Facilitating the development of the IC-Team's functioning, team members' skills as case managers, and a favorable school context in which the teams will operate is clearly a complex process that requires the skills of a well-trained and experienced change facilitator. IC-Team implementation can best be compared to juggling, where

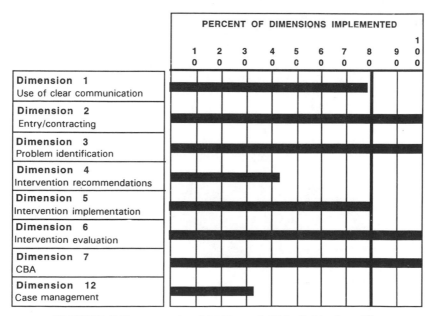

FIGURE 7.7. Example of IC-Team LOI individual profile.

each of these major tasks is equally weighted in terms of importance and must always be addressed in relation to the others. Implementing IC-Teams is not sequential; that is, change facilitators can't develop the team first, then develop the case managers' functioning, and then prepare the school. Instead the change facilitator must have the administrative, organizational, and management skills to coordinate and orchestrate the change process so that many things are occurring at one time. Although such tasks may seem overwhelming, they are not impossible. Just as jugglers drop the ball every now and then, so will change facilitators (we are all human). However, it is the change facilitator's responsibility to ensure that each area is addressed and that there is integrity in the implementation process. In doing so, there is an increased chance of ultimate institutionalization of IC-Teams in the school culture.

8

Institutionalizing IC-Teams

The ultimate goal of all the activities occurring during initiation, training, and implementation is to achieve institutionalization, or the continuation, of IC-Teams. For the change facilitator who is new, inexperienced, and not yet involved with IC-Teams, this concept may seem unimportant when compared with the many tasks and details that have been described in the previous chapters. However, for those change facilitators who have labored to begin the change process with IC-Teams, this stage of change takes on incredible importance, because it represents the culmination of everyone's efforts, ensuring continuation of the outcomes of the change process.

WHAT IS INSTITUTIONALIZATION AND WHY IS IT IMPORTANT?

Over the last three decades, educational researchers have moved from the study of initiating innovations, to investigating the factors that impact implementation, to questioning which practices, activities, and supports are needed to maintain or continue an innovation (Miles & Ekholm, 1991). Attention to this final stage of change emerges from continuing research findings that suggest that even well-implemented innovations often fail to be continued. For example, Berman and McLaughlin (1978, cited in Fullan, 1991) discovered that only a minority of well-implemented projects continued beyond the period of federal funding. Ekholm, Vandenberghe, and Miles (1987) indicate that even deliberate efforts to institutionalize changes succeed less than 50% of the time. Indeed, Miles and Ekholm (1991) suggest that there is little guarantee that new "structures" of schooling, many of them counter to the culture of schools as we know them, will automatically stay in place and survive. The history of most reforms, in fact, suggests the opposite. Schools, like other organizations, have a way of weathering down changes, or subtly ejecting them, unless they are built in to the school, become embedded, a part and parcel of "normal life." (p. 2)

Many terms have been used to label this final stage of change (e.g., institutionalization, routinization, stabilization, continuation, normalization, etc.) by a number of educational change researchers (e.g. Ekholm et al., 1987; Fullan, 1991; Guskey, 1990; Hall & Hord, 1987; Miles, 1983; Miles & Ekholm, 1991). The term that we use to describe this final stage of change is *institutionalization.* Institutionalization, as defined by Miles and Ekholm (1991), "is a developmental process occurring in organizations during and after the implementation of a change. It results in stabilization of the change, and its continuation" (p. 2). Further, it is the way in which organizations and systems go about assimilating and building in new ways of operating so that they continue to exist long after the formal change effort ends (Ekholm et al., 1987).

Conceptually, all activities, from initiation through implementation, are themselves institutionalization activities as well (see Figure 8.1). Figure 8.1, from the work of Miles and Ekholm (1991), reinforces

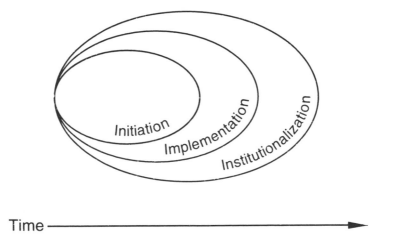

Time ⟶

FIGURE 8.1. The relation of subprocesses of change. From Miles and Ekholm (1991). Reprinted by permission.

how the work of initiating and implementing an innovation relates to and supports institutionalization. However, as depicted, the stage of institutionalization continues beyond the earlier ones; this is also explicit in the educational reform literature. Like the earlier stages of change, institutionalization has its own specific activities and tasks that must be accomplished to ensure an innovation's continuance.

Miles (1983) reviewed institutionalization issues in public organizations and described three components found in institutionalized innovations. First, there is a minimum level of support for the innovation by its users and managers. Secondly, innovations, to become institutionalized, must complete certain passages (e.g., going from soft to hard moneys). Finally, the innovation must survive certain organizational cycles (e.g., initial and subsequent budgets, personnel turnovers, etc.). Hall and Hord (1987) suggest that an innovation is institutionalized, or in routine use, when few changes are being made by participants in its ongoing use and little preparation or attention is given to improving the innovation's use. Miles and Ekholm (1991) suggest the following indications that an innovation is institutionalized:

- There is agreement by major stakeholders as to what the innovation is, as well as its value and its legitimacy within the system.
- The innovation's working is routine and stable.
- The innovation's presence is taken for granted by organizational workers, as is its continuance.
- Provisions for resources necessary for continuance, including time, personnel, materials, and money, are routinely provided.
- Continuance does not depend on any specific individual, but rather is embedded in organizational supports and structures.

This growing consensus in the change literature as to what institutionalization is, the importance of attending to it, and its characteristics when achieved provides the IC-Team change facilitator with direction regarding the activities that will be undertaken during this final stage of change.

CONSIDERATIONS IN INSTITUTIONALIZING IC-TEAMS

The task of institutionalizing IC-Teams is comprised of many activities, both small and large. It assumes that many, if not all, of the activities covered in the previous chapters on initiation, training, and implementation have been undertaken and that the change facilitator has taken the necessary steps to ensure integrity at all levels. It also introduces new activities in which the change facilitator engages to ensure IC-Team continuance. Like the planned and thoughtful activities engaged in during initiation, the change facilitator works proactively with school staff, school leadership, and district personnel to ensure institutionalization of the IC-Team. These facilitator activities, which often overlap with those of previous stages and serve multiple purposes, fall into three general categories: integrating IC-Teams, embedding them, and managing mushrooms, that is, managing the unintended outcomes of certain interventions.

Integrating IC-Teams

Guskey (1990) emphasizes that "what is needed even more than extended support [to achieve institutionalization] is a precise description of how to integrate a system's collection of strategies into some kind of coherent framework" (p. 12). The IC-Team change facilitator, while focusing on the intricacies of developing functional teams, case managers, and a receptive school environment, must not neglect assisting the school at large in integrating IC-Team training and practices with other school strategies and demands. Guskey (1990) suggests the following five guidelines that change facilitators can utilize in aiding school staff to synthesize the many innovations that typically make up a school's improvement programming:

1. The change facilitator works with school leadership to ensure that all innovations initiated share common goals and premises.
2. The change facilitator is mindful, and stresses to others, that no single innovation can do everything. Acceptance of this reality helps school staff to recognize that more than one innovation may be occurring at any one time.
3. Innovation strategies should complement one another, including having similar underlying assumptions about student learning and instructional practices. Commonalties must be constantly emphasized and reinforced for practitioners, and differences acknowledged. When differences are noted, "attention needs to move beyond simple comparative analysis and toward practical synthesis" (Guskey, 1990, p. 14).
4. Because all innovations need to be adapted to classroom and building conditions, the change facilitator assists and supports this process while maintaining IC-Team integrity.

5. When well-conceived combinations of innovative strategies are used, the results are likely to be greater than those attained using any single strategy. The change facilitator assists in determining the optimal combinations of innovative strategies for particular settings and in implementing them in ways that provide the greatest chance to produce effective outcomes.

The change facilitator accomplishes integration activities through presentations, demonstrations, and collaboration with other change agents. At the system level, the change facilitator assists school leadership and district personnel to recognize the fit between the IC-Team's goals and functioning and those of existing and future policies. For example, in a recent implementation of IC-Teams, the school district requested multiple school plans (i.e., a school improvement plan and a pupil services programming plan) describing how schools would address specific school and system goals. The change facilitator recognized the redundancy in submitting two plans, both of which incorporated IC-Teams model as a key initiative for improving school functioning and service to students. He worked closely with the directors of instruction, pupil service providers, and the principal in writing one plan that was acceptable to all. As a result, the school produced, and the directors received, one plan that integrated many key school and district goals, which included IC-Team functioning.

Finally, because of the focus of IC-Teams, there has been a need to help schools and school systems integrate state and federal regulations and mandates regarding the service of students identifiable as handicapped. Change facilitators involved in several implementations of IC-Teams have interacted with state education and special education officials to discuss the necessary integration and fit between existing policies and the IC-Teams' functioning. Where appropriate, waivers were sought to allow the IC-Team process to replace or augment traditional procedures for identifying students with special needs. Often the problem-solving process, documentation, individualized student plans (i.e., Student Documentation Form, Figure 2.8), and creative use of available resources by the IC-Teams, have proven to be more effective at meeting student needs in project schools than the traditional special education processes (see, e.g., Kuralt, 1990).

Embedding IC-Teams

Huberman and Miles (1984) stress the need to embed an innovation into the school and system structure (e.g., policy procedures, budget, school goals, etc.) to ensure its continuance. In the example relating to school planning cited earlier, not only did the change facilitator assist in integrating various school initatives into one school plan, the change facilitator also legitimized the IC-Team's role as a key initiative to meet school goals, ensuring its continuance by embedding it into the overall plan for the school. In addition, regularly scheduled meetings, regular faculty updates, continued training for the team and its members, administrator participation, documentation and accountability for services, and other initiation and implementation activities may also serve to embed the IC-Team into the structures of the school. It is equally urgent to embed the team at the system level, securing a place in the governance and, more importantly, budget structures of the system.

Governance

Governance is the term we use to describe the policy-making processes that typically occur within school systems. IC-Teams must somehow become a part of existing governance and policy structures. That is, it must be recognized on the organizational chart and be clearly linked to activities and policies that are deemed important by the system. Figure 8.2 is a copy of a governance proposal that incorporated both a policy board and a steering, or planning, committee as key governance components. The steering committee, comprised of key school level stakeholders, was responsible for the daily functioning of the project (i.e., designing, implementing, and evaluating IC-Teams) and for making recommendations to the policy board. The policy board, made up of key system stakeholders, was responsible for ensuring necessary supports and making global decisions regarding IC-Teams based on input from the steering committee.

Budget

During the early phases of innovation implementation, the IC-Team, as with most new innovations, has typically been financed through short-term, soft monies (e.g., grants, funds for pilot programs, etc.). However, for institutionalization to occur, the innovation must be supported within the existing budget of the system (Miles, 1983). When planning a budget, consideration should be given to the areas specified in Table 8.1. District personnel tend to focus their design of budgets more on the expansion of IC-teams (No. 1, Table 8.1) rather than continued support for existing schools (Nos. 2 and 3). Recalling that change is a process that requires 3–5 years, the budget should not neglect the neces-

INSTRUCTIONAL CONSULTATION

During the 1994–1995 school year, 13 elementary and 3 middle schools will be involved in instructional consultation as a model of team functioning. The continued expansion of the model provides many opportunities for schools, staff, and students to work collaboratively utilizing systematic problem solving to achieve common goals. Such expansion requires ongoing, systematic planning and organizational considerations in order to effectively maintain the model's integrity while expanding its implementation.

The following proposal is made with regard to the governance of the IC-Teams Project, design of training, implementation, and evaluation.

MISSION

The mission of instructional consultation as a model of team functioning is to link people and resources at all levels whereby general, special education, and pupil services personnel share the responsibility for the education of ALL students through the improved quality of service.

GOALS

- To achieve and maintain collaborative support teams that enable people with diverse expertise to generate creative solutions to mutually defined problems.

- To provide effective and efficient programs by integrating and coordinating support services available to classroom teachers and their students.

IC PROPOSED GOVERNANCE STRUCTURE

Governance

Complex innovations, especially those that are systemic in nature, cross traditional boundaries of functioning. Instructional consultation, as its mission indicates, creates a linkage across departmental lines that requires interdepartmental cooperation, collaboration, and coordination. To maximize the goals of the IC-Teams model, the following governance structure, which includes the formation of an IC-Team policy board and IC-Team steering committee, is proposed:

IC-TEAMS POLICY BOARD

- Is co-chaired by associate superintendent of instruction and project facilitator
- Operates as a decision-making body that approves and provides oversight of the IC-Team's expansion and implementation
- Secures necessary supports for the implementation
- Decides key issues of school selection, quality facilitation, and interdepartmental responsibilities
- Reviews and approves steering committee's implementation and evaluation design
- Meets three times per year

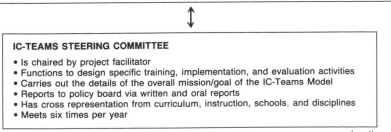

IC-TEAMS STEERING COMMITTEE

- Is chaired by project facilitator
- Functions to design specific training, implementation, and evaluation activities
- Carries out the details of the overall mission/goal of the IC-Teams Model
- Reports to policy board via written and oral reports
- Has cross representation from curriculum, instruction, schools, and disciplines
- Meets six times per year

(continued)

FIGURE 8.2. Sample governance structure for IC-Teams.

IC POLICY BOARD

Function:

- Meets three times per year to provide oversight in the implementation and expansion of the instructional consultation model
- Secures funding to maintain implementation progress and evaluation activities
- Operates as a decision-making body to ensure that the goals for effective implementation of the IC-Team model are achieved

---

GOALS FOR EFFECTIVE IMPLEMENTATION:

- All project teams will reach an acceptable level of implementation (80%) of the critical instructional consultation dimensions as defined by performance on IC-Team LOI
- All project teams will have in place a delivery system by which faculty and staff will access the team.
- Greater than 50% of team members will be active case managers and engage in collaborative instructional consultation as a method of systematic problem solving.
- All project teams will develop and maintain documentation procedures consistent with project criteria that will account for services provided on behalf of specified students.
- All teams will utilize CBA as a method to determine baseline levels of academic performance and to monitor ongoing student performance.

- Selects schools for expansion of IC-Teams based on readiness and established criteria

---

CRITERIA FOR SELECTING EXPANSION SCHOOLS AND GUIDELINES FOR SCHOOL READINESS:

- An informed administration is committed to the collaborative problem-solving model. School administrators understand and agree to support the scope of training required, commit to their own involvement in the IC-Teams model, and are aware of and agree with the underlying principles of instructional consultation.
- School's readiness is demonstrated by providing examples of School Improvement Plans, Project Focus Plans, Pupil Services Plans, etc. that focus on ongoing and targeted staff development in areas that support classroom teachers in servicing students who are considered to be at risk for school failure. Such plans may include staff development activities in data collection, collaborative problem solving, use of best teaching practices, team decision making, etc.
- Schools demonstrate willingness to create a problem-solving culture as a staff response to presentations of the instructional consultation model by project facilitator or IC-Team Steering Committee.
- Schools interested in instructional consultation as a model of problem solving demonstrate the support for weekly team meetings in which classroom teachers are considered integral participants. Such commitment can be demonstrated by the existence of functioning problem-solving teams.

- Selects trained school-based facilitators based on established criteria

---

CRITERIA FOR INSTRUCTIONAL CONSULTATION FACILITATORS:

- Informed and committed to the collaborative problem-solving model. Facilitators understand and agree to support the scope of training required and are aware of and agree with the underlying principles of instructional consultation.
- Trained in the instructional consultation model either as a sitting IC-Team member or through formalized collaborative training programs (e.g., University of Maryland).
- Skilled instructional consultation case manager demonstrated by achieving a high rating on simulation activities and having participated as part of a structured instructional consultation training program utilizing formal feedback mechanisms (e.g., audiotaping and videotaping).
- Demonstrates higher order change agent skills described by Saxl, Liberman, and Miles (1987) including: credibility, initiative taking, trust and rapport building, knowledge of education content and process, knowledge of organizational and individual change, visionary, resource bringer, and collaborator.

FIGURE 8.2. *cont.*

Composition of IC Policy Board:

- Associate superintendent of instruction, co-Chair
- Special projects coordinator
- Directors of special education and pupil services.
- Directors of elementary, middle, and high school instruction (or representative)
- Staff development coordinator
- IC-Team project facilitator, co-Chair
- Others as determined necessary

IC STEERING COMMITTEE

Function:

- Meets six times per year.
- Operates to achieve goals of effective implementation of the IC-Teams model and is responsible to the IC-Teams Policy Board
- Develops and implements a training design that will achieve effective implementation of the IC-Teams model
- Collaborates with various departments in order to achieve system goals of creating "seamless" services for all students and fostering integrated service delivery
- Develops and implements an evaluation design that assures implementation integrity, and documents progress in key outcome variables: student achievement, student referral for special education services, teacher satisfaction with collaborative structures, parental satisfaction with school and home collaborative efforts, etc.

Composition:

- Project facilitator, Chair
- School-based administrator representative
- School-based facilitator representative
- Staff development liaison
- Curriculum representative
- Office of assessment representative
- Related projects representatives
- Office of special education liaison
- Others as selected by Chair

IC-TEAMS GOVERNANCE TIMELINE

IC-TEAMS STEERING COMMITTEE		IC-TEAMS POLICY BOARD
Reviews current design and prepares next fiscal year (FY) project budget proposal	AUGUST	
	SEPTEMBER	
Finalizes FY next budget proposal and submits to policy board		
	OCTOBER	Reviews and gives final approval to next FY project budget
	NOVEMBER	
Prepares next FY training design and solicits application for new expansion schools and facilitators	DECEMBER	

(continued)

FIGURE 8.2. *cont.*

JANUARY

Reviews mid-year implementation
and evaluation progress, continues
next FY design preparation, and   FEBRUARY
submits mid-year review and
schools' applications to policy board   Reviews and finalizes selection of
                                          MARCH   expansion schools and facilitators;
                                                        reviews mid-year progress as
                                                        reported by steering committee

                                          APRIL
Plans with expansion schools'
administrators and facilitators;
selects dates for summer trainings   MAY

                                          JUNE
End of Year Progress Review;
finalized next FY implementation and
evaluation plan submitted to Policy   JULY   End of Year Progress Review;
Board   review of next FY implementation
                                                        and evaluation design
                                          AUGUST

FIGURE 8.2. *cont.*

sary, ongoing supports for existing IC-teams, including on-site facilitation (4), funds for continued training (3), and opportunities to evaluate and reflect on current performance levels (6). In addition, as Fullan (1991) points out, "very few programs plan for the orientation and inservice support for new members who arrive after the program gets started. And arrive they do, chipping away, however unintentionally, at what is already a fragile process" (p. 90). Without proactive planning and budgeting for inservice for newly entering personnel (Table 8.1, No. 2), the efforts of previous stages may be quickly lost to inevitable personnel transitions that occur regularly in schools.

Creating a comprehensive budget to fund the ongoing training and implementation design is important. However, equally important is the change facilitator's access to those in the system's organizational level responsible for funding such budgets. The governance structure cited above (see Figure 8.2) not only provides a process by which IC-Teams will be linked to the decision-making aspects of the system, it also provides an example of the organizational access to the budget process required for that particular distict. In this governance structure, the steering committee would formulate a design to implement IC-Teams in a number of schools and create the accompanying budget. This design and budget would be submitted to the policy board for review and approval. Once approved, authorized members (i.e., associate superintendent) of the policy board would present the budget request to the system superintendent and school board.

TABLE 8.1. Considerations in Designing an IC-Team Budget

1. Introductory training for newly identified school IC-Teams.
2. Training of new team members for existing IC-Teams.
3. Maintenance of and expansion training in new knowledge and skills for existing IC-Teams.
4. Costs associated with training and salary support for school-based change facilitators.
5. Cost of a system change facilitator when expansion goes beyond three or four schools.
6. Support for evaluation activities, including release time for conducting evaluations of training and implementation.
7. Materials and supplies.

Managing the Mushrooms

In Chapter 7, we spoke briefly about critical incident interventions on the part of the change facilitator, times when the change facilitator intervened, in small or large ways, to further the implementation of the team and case management process. Although such interventions typically result in a desired outcome, Hall and Hord (1987) suggest that there may be unintended or unplanned outcomes associated with such interventions, and they introduced the mushroom metaphor to describe these results. In their research, they discovered that, like real mushrooms, these unplanned or unintended outcomes typically develop at the margins of the change process, emerge gradually, and can be either positive or negative in terms of their impact on the innovation.

One example of a negative mushroom with IC-Teams involved a change facilitator's meetings to update a principal on the team's progress. Although the intended outcome was to maintain clear communication with the principal, the unintended outcome was negative feelings from teachers toward the change faciltator and the IC-Team project. Upon closer inspection, it became evident that by meeting with the principal immediately after school, the change facilitator was disrupting a traditional "ceremony" in which teachers lined up at the principal's door and one by one offered brief comments or questions before leaving for the day. One teacher expressed the feeling directly, indicating that she felt "blocked" from seeing and talking with the principal. Once noted, the change facilitator and principal collaboratively agreed to meet later in the day, after teachers had the opportunity to speak with the principal.

As Hall and Hord (1987) note, these mushrooms may also be positive. In one implementation of IC-Teams, the change facilitator regularly invited district level personnel to trainings and team meetings in an effort to further educate them about the complexity of training and the need for continued support and funding. After their visits, team members would often comment how pleased and proud they were that district personnel would come to see their IC-Team. Whereas the intent of inviting guests was initially to secure additional resources for the IC-Team, the mushroom, or unintended outcome, was the team members' feelings of pride and acknowledgment from being visited by district personnel and the ensuing motivation to continue their development. Needless to say, having district personnel greet team members at trainings and visit during team meetings has become a routine aspect of implementing IC-Teams.

Mushrooms occur at the district level as well. As IC-Teams are incorporated, there are unintended outcomes impacting other district personnel and other departments. Positive mushrooms that have occurred include having district personnel and departments offer support via additional funds or training, as well as continuing to offer positive comments regarding the IC-Team's usefulness in meeting overall system goals to key policy makers. Unfortunately, we have also encountered negative mushrooms at the district level, many of which were not orginally seen as negative. For example, as the effectiveness of IC-Teams became more acknowledged within one district, there was a resulting battle as to which department maintained control of the project. Despite the cross-departmental nature of the teaming process and its collaborative focus, key district personnel desired to maintain control, which resulted in confusion. At one point, various district personnel sent multiple memos and directives to schools about IC-Teams, which only added to the confusion. The entire process of battling for control resulted in the undercutting and sabotage of several years of work, threatening the continuance of the project. The system and on-site change faciltiators, in response to the growing confusion, worked with district leaders to define more clearly the roles and responsibilities of key players and to ensure that a clear chain of communication existed between the district and schools.

The point in discussing mushrooms in this chapter is to heighten awareness that the process of change requires attention from start to finish, top to bottom of the system. To achieve institutionalization, change facilitators must be aware of the unintended outcomes associated with their and others' actions, as well as the potentially permanent impacts of such actions. "More effective change facilitators are skilled in early detection of mushrooms and addressing them" (Hall & Hord, 1987, p. 198). If left unchecked, mushrooms may multiply, intensify, and undermine the entire IC-Team process. Further, whereas some mushrooms are easily addressed and removed, others "can only be cut back and will gradually grow again" (Hall & Hord, 1987, p. 199). Although it is difficult to identify particular mushrooms in advance, the change facilitator is responsible to anticipate their growth and manage them when necessary.

SUMMARY

All activities during the initiation and implementation stages of IC-Teams are necessary, but alone they are insufficient to ensure institutionalization. Indeed, although the effects of earlier actions reach fruition during the final stage of change, the change facilitator must engage in additional, specific activities that assimilate the IC-Team into the existing school and system culture so as to assure its continuance. Several key change facilitator tasks—embedding, integrating, and managing—have been discussed as important institutionalization activities.

As we have seen, the research on institutionalization is still in its infancy and researchers find a large number of change initiatives that never reach this critical stage. The information that does exist on institutionalization, and change for that matter, indicates that the activities of the change facilitator (i.e., the "what to do") are equal in importance with the configuration of these activites (i.e., the "how to do it"). There is no "cookbook" to achieve institutionalization of IC-Teams, just as there is no standard manual for achieving lasting change in schools. However, there are many examples, research studies, and experiences suggesting practices that are applicable to initiating, implementing and institutionalizing IC-Teams from which change facilitators can benefit in the process of achieving lasting change.

9

The Future of IC-Teams

The first eight chapters have provided a view of IC-Teams based on past experiences with early versions and current projects in over 60 schools in four states. Both the elements of the innovation package and the adoption process have been detailed as a guide for change facilitators. The concerns and pitfalls that IC-Team change facilitators are likely to confront have been included. The path is not free from hazards, but it can be, and has been, navigated by individuals committed to the development of alternative support services such as IC-Teams and other consultation-based service delivery systems (e.g., Fuchs & Fuchs, 1988; Lennox, Hyman, & Hughes, 1988; Thousand & Villa, 1992; Zins & Illback, 1993). These service systems link people and resources at all levels so that general education, special education, and pupil services personnel are able to share responsibility for the education of *all* students. An alternative service delivery system based on a school support team concept seeks to achieve two goals: (1) to develop and maintain collaborative support teams that both enable and empower people with diverse expertise to generate creative solutions to mutually defined problems, and (2) to provide effective and efficient programs by integrating and coordinating support services available to classroom teachers and their students.

Although much has been accomplished in developing alternative service delivery systems in the past 15 years, the state of the art of consultation-based programs is still at an early stage. As Zins and Illback (1993) state regarding interventions for child-related problems,

> Indeed a plethora of effective treatments are available, most of which can be used in consultation. . . . A major challenge, therefore, is to influence organizations serving children to adopt consultation-based service de-

livery systems. However, surprisingly little has been written about the implementation of consultation methods to bring about systemic change. (p. 204)

We have tried to contribute to closing this gap by providing some guidance for the change process used to achieve institutionalization of one such service delivery alternative, IC-Teams.

FUTURE DIRECTIONS FOR IC-TEAMS

It is important to delineate the challenges and needs for future development. These include (1) providing integrated, seamless services; (2) substantiating critical long-term outcomes through research; and (3) reinventing preservice training of school-based professionals.

Seamless Services

Most of the work described in this book has occurred in elementary schools. Although there have been implementations in both middle and senior high schools, these received less attention in the systems that adopted this type of alternative and have rarely reached the point of institutionalization. There are considerable differences between elementary and secondary schools, both in how they are structured and in their beliefs about and attitudes toward students. In secondary settings, there is a stronger emphasis on subject matter and tendency to focus less on basic student needs; teacher problem solving around individual students is further constrained by the large number of students seen by a typical secondary level teacher. These differences require mutual adaptations of the IC-Team process. In a recent series of introductory trainings with middle school IC-Teams, the concerns and requests from participants paralleled those heard at the elementary level, including the need to create collaborative linkages between grade levels and teachers, to assure continued problem solving for teachers and students, to redistribute resources when needed, and to document and account for student progress. Like their elementary school counterparts, middle school professionals have been open to and enthusiastic about learning, growing, and sharing within the IC-Team process. Likewise, we are learning from and with them the appropriate configurations of IC-Teams, and we look forward to the results of continued collaboration.

The downward extension of consultation-type services to preschool children and their families makes good sense as well (Sheridan, 1993). P.L. 99-457 (Education for Handicapped Amendments) provides incentives for states to deliver services for infants and preschool age children and their families. It has mandates which seek to avoid premature labeling and segregated placements, encouraging collaboration between home, school, and community agencies to the greatest extent possible. Because the emphasis is on comprehensive coordinated and multidisciplinary programs, the IC-Team could provide a useful framework to deliver services to this age group as well. Currently, IC-Teams has been conceptualized as a school-based support system with the school-age population. However, it is feasible to work collaboratively with service providers outside of schools to adopt an IC-Teams model that would incorporate the roles of parents and community agencies.

Both the downward and upward extension of services from the elementary school are steps toward the provision of seamless services for children. The complex process of coordinating and integrating services for all children from birth through the transition to work (which includes the family and community resources, as well as the schools) is a primary task for the next generation of service providers (American Psychological Association Task Force on Comprehensive and Coordinated Services for Children, 1994). With appropriate modifications, IC-Teams, and other, similar consultation programs, could well provide a framework for this process.

Research

As indicated earlier, IC-Teams require three types of evaluation: evaluation of implementation, evaluation of training, and evaluation of outcomes (Rosenfield, 1992). Because many of our collaborations with school systems have had a university connection, it has been possible to embed evaluation projects into the operationalization of IC-Teams. The IC-Team LOI Scale was originally developed as a doctoral study (Fudell, 1992). Much of the research that has been cited here, and much that is currently being conducted, concerns the process of the model itself; examining, for example, modifications to the data collection processes, more extensive assessments of consultant skill mastery, and team development. Moreover, the literature on treatment integrity emphasizes the need to assure that the treatment is actually in place prior to documenting treatment effectiveness (Gresham et al., 1993), so development of a level of implementation measure has been an early priority. These structural types of research are appropriate and necessary for the development of IC-Teams. The IC-Teams model has been inventing and reinventing itself for less than a decade, and much of the emphasis has been on generating an effective and efficient set of procedures and processes.

Although limited, there are a few outcome studies (see, e.g., Kuralt, 1990). As more of the elements of IC-Teams are refined and elaborated, outcome research is the logical next step. Good practice suggests the importance of such research being undertaken by individuals other than the developers themselves, and we look forward to that occurrence. As researchers, we find ourselves increasing our focus on the evaluation of clinical replications of IC-Teams. Recently, there has been increased attention to models for conducting outcome research on consultation-based services (Gresham & Noell, 1993). To the extent possible, evaluation procedures should be built in during the initiation phase of adoption, and school research units should be utilized.

Preservice Training

Most of the school systems which introduced IC-Teams have required extensive inservice training. Research has confirmed the relatively limited opportunities for consultation training provided at the preservice level to school professionals (Hughes, 1994; Stewart, 1985), and there is probably even less availability and sophistication of training in organizational change. However, graduate students in school psychology have been involved in the development of the IC-Teams models and its earlier incarnations, because of the professional affiliations of the authors. Students have served in the role of on-site facilitators and have also conducted research.

More recently, IC-Teams have been part of a professional development school initiative between the Howard County, MD school district and the University of Maryland-College Park College of Education. A two-course consultation sequence in the school psychology program is taught on site in the district, usually including both preservice school psychology students and practicing school psychologists. Practicum experiences are held in district schools that are implementing IC-Teams. Internships from the university have been developed within the district to include IC-Team experience, both as case managers and, for those indicating an interest, change facilitators. Additionally, preservice general and special education teachers are being integrated into the IC-Team process during their student teaching experiences. Doctoral dissertations and masters' theses are providing the research base for IC-Teams. The professional development site provides a structured and supportive setting at the preservice level for students interested in alternative service delivery. They not only receive knowledge and skills in consultation, but also become skilled in the process of assisting a school to change its service delivery system. Increased opportunities for such training are required if alternative services are to become normative.

CONCLUSION

The need for alternatives to current practices in regular and special education were documented in the beginning of this book. One such alternative, IC-Teams, which provides a consultation-based systemic service delivery option, has been presented. It includes service delivery structures, a consultation problem-solving process, and procedures for facilitating adoption at the school and district level. Limitations and research needs have also been delineated.

Deborah Meier (1992), the innovative former principal of Central Park East Secondary School in New York City, has written compellingly of the need to reinvent teaching: "The schools we need require different habits of work and habits of mind on the part of teachers—a kind of professionalism within the classroom few teachers were expected to exhibit before" (p. 594). This call for change needs to be considered for every level of school-based professional. We clearly do not presume that IC-Teams is the only model for indirect service delivery in the schools, but it does provide one alternative for making quality education available for *all* children. Over time we have modified and restructured the process. We assume that the development of IC-Teams will continue, as experience and research accumulates through clinical replications.

The types of change that we are suggesting are more than a description of an alternative service delivery system: "Restructuring for caring and effective education is not an idle wish, but an inescapable obligation" (Wiggins, 1992, p. xi). There is a moral, as well as a professional, obligation to continue to seek effective methods of creating learning communities that benefit students. That is the mission to which this book has been committed, and we urge the reader to continue to seek ways to achieve this goal.

APPENDIX A
IC-Team LOI—Revised[a]

Rosalind Fudell, Todd Gravois, and Sylvia A. Rosenfield

OVERVIEW

The LOI is comprised of several interviews and record reviews that provide information on the collaborative process and delivery system involved in the IC-Team model. Each aspect of the LOI is designed to corroborate the presence of a specific critical dimension indicator (see IC-Team critical dimensions attached). In general each administration of the LOI will consist of the following:

Team Survey
Principal Interview
Case Manager Interview(s)
Referring Teacher Interviews(s)
Documentation/Form Review(s)

The number of Case Manager, Referring Teacher Interviews and Form Reviews conducted varies according to the number of active cases in progress and at the intervention stage.

The LOI provides both formative and summative information regarding the progress each team has made in implementing the model. The scale is formative in that information collected may be utilized to identify future training, specific needs regarding faculty awareness of the team and its process, and needs regarding the collaborative and delivery variables of the model. The scale is summative in that an acceptable level of implementation is desired (80%). This acceptable level is reflected in the overall benchmark resulting from the administration of the LOI Scale.

GENERAL DIRECTIONS FOR ADMINISTRATION

The LOI's interviews should be administered using an objective, conversational approach. To establish rapport, it is helpful to inform team members, case managers and teachers that information is being collected about the "process" of their work rather than success or failure of the intervention strategies.

The following key points are emphasized regarding the general administration and scoring of the LOI.

[a]Reprinted by permission of the authors. Appendix A may be reproduced with written permission of the authors. Please contact Sylvia A. Rosenfield, Benjamin Building, University of Maryland, College Park, MD, 20742.

- It is useful to indicate to respondents that the information collected is confidential and will only be shared as part of an overall team level of functioning. *However, if an individual case manager so desires, an Individual Case Manager Profile will be provided upon request. The Individual Case Manager Profile will only be shared with the involved case manager. No such information will be available for referring teachers.*
- Some items are cross referenced. This means that to receive a positive score, there must be *substantial* agreement between two informants to determine that the critical dimension is present or not. There are no requirements for perfect agreement. Most cross referencing in scoring occurs within the interview of case managers and the respective teachers with whom they are consulting.
- Scoring of the scale should occur after all interviews and record reviews are completed. Many interview questions are cross referenced, and all information must be collected prior to assigning a score.
- Administer the Case Manager and Teacher interviews separately. The Case Manager Interview should be administered prior to the Teacher Interview. When interviewed first, the Case Manager typically provides more detailed responses, which assist in effective prompting during the subsequent Teacher Interview.
- Extra care and time should be taken to build rapport when interviewing referring teachers. Because referring teachers have not been involved in extensive training, and are not necessarily comfortable with the idea of being interviewed, efforts should be made to clarify the purpose of the LOI, its impact on the IC-Team and individual team members.

  In addition, alternative wording and prompting may be required during the teacher interview. Some wording may be unfamiliar or new to teachers (e.g., data, intervention, etc.) and interviewers are encouraged to simplify or choose alternative terms in order to facilitate accurate responses. As an example, interviewers may substitute "information" for "data"; "strategies" or "techniques" for "intervention." Because the teacher may not be as specific or detailed as the case manager in providing responses, at times it may be necessary to ask directly whether or not some aspect of the collaborative process occurred. The use of more direct questions, based on case manager information, may be appropriate when there are indications that the teacher is speaking of similar situations but not offering full descriptions.
- The goal of each question is to investigate whether or not the indicated critical dimension (indicated in parentheses) is present. Begin with general questions (such as those presented within the interviews) and then progress to more specific and directed questioning if necessary. Use alternative wording, prompting, and direct questioning in order to acquire a fuller understanding of the processes employed. Notations in the comments section should be made to indicate the types of prompting or alternative questioning used.

- Certain items are typically not administered directly, but instead are based on other responses or review of records.
- Form checks are indicated throughout interviews to assist the interviewer in assessing availability and accuracy of use of the critical forms associated with the IC-Teams model. Direct review of forms should occur if further information is required to score Forms (F1 through F3).

SPECIFIC DIRECTIONS FOR ADMINISTRATION

A mid-year administration of the LOI provides formative information for the team in terms of their progress and continued training needs. This mid-year administration, combined with an end of the year administration provides summative information regarding the team's overall level of implementation. Hence, it is the end of the year summation of all administrations of the LOI which provides benchmarks as to the IC-Team's level of implementation.

I. Principal Interviews

It is best to administer the Principal Interview prior to the scheduled Team Survey. The Principal Interview may be administered in person or by phone if a face-to-face interaction is difficult to arrange prior to the Team Survey. The Principal Interview must be administered during the mid-year LOI. However, administration of the interview at the end of the year is at the team's and interviewer's discretion. For example, if there are 100% positive scores on the mid-year Principal Interview, an end of the year interview can be foregone. The Principal Interview should be conducted with the building principal as a first choice. An Assistant Principal may participate in the interview process if they have taken primary responsibility as the administrative representation on the team. A notation should be made if the Assistant Principal was the respondent.

II. Team Survey

The Team Survey is administered during a regularly scheduled IC-Team meeting at the mid-year administration of the LOI. Again, an end of the year administration of the Team Survey is at the discretion of the interviewer, facilitator, and team. All team members should be encouraged to participate in answering the questions. Items centered on Delivery System Forms may be presented during the general team meeting or may be conducted with the designated system manager at a separate time.

III. Case Manager, Referring Teacher Interviews, and Review of Forms

1. *Selecting cases to be interviewed* (Early Implementation Phase). During the early implementation phase of the IC-Team process (when all team members have yet to take cases and when the team has not reached 80% implementation), all case managers are to be interviewed provided the following conditions are met:

- Only cases which have reached the Intervention Implementation Stage of problem solving are included.
- Only one interview need be conducted with each case manager. For example, if a team member is case manager for three cases, and of the three cases only two are at the Intervention Implementation Stage, only one of theses two cases need be selected to be interviewed. A random selection process is suggested in determining which case to interview.
- Cases are interviewed only once. However, an exception may be made if the case manager specifically requests that the case be reinterviewed to provide information for continued training or if a case manager requests that a case be reinterviewed because a different problem has been defined since the first interview.

2. *Selecting cases to be interviewed* (Early Institutionalization Phase). During the latter stages of implementation and into early institutionalization of the IC-Team process (when all team members have previously been interviewed at least once, and the team has achieved 80% implementation), a random process may be used in selecting cases to be interviewed. The above cited conditions should continue to be followed. In addition, the following should be considered a guideline:
   - An adequate representation of the team should be interviewed to provide an on-going measure of team functioning. For example, at least 50% of case managers should be included in the random interview process.

3. *Recording responses.* Specific directions for administering and scoring the Case Manager and Teacher Interviews are provided in the following sections. Interviewers should read these sections thoroughly prior to administering the LOI. Because many items are cross referenced between the Case Manager and Referring Teacher Interviews, it is necessary for interviewers to record responses to items for later comparison. Enough information should be recorded in the spaces provided, and in the comments section, to assure adequate interpretation at a later time. It is imperative to record verbatim statements and summarized statements of respondents' responses whenever there is a "blank" provided.

4. *Form checks and form reviews.* A "Form Check" notation is provided in the comment section. Unless otherwise noted in the following scoring guide, "Form Checks" are not used to score the adjacent item, but instead are a prompt of when such forms may be conveniently and naturally reviewed as part of the interview process. If the various forms listed on the attached Form Review section are not reviewed as part of the interview process, the interviewer should directly ask to review the necessary forms prior to concluding the interview. Because each case receives only one score for review of forms, checks and reviews should occur across the Case Manager and Referring Teacher Interviews. For example, if the case manager provides no indication of use of CBA recorded data, the interviewer should allow the teacher the opportunity to present the data prior to scoring F3.

LOI PRINCIPAL INTERVIEW

School: _____ Date: _____

Recorder's name: _____

Process	Delivery		
			Please indicate the **number** of permanent IC Team members by professional role (for example: 2- regular teachers; 1- school counselor, etc.) (8) ____ Guidance counselor(s) ____ Administrators ____ Regular classroom teachers ____ Nurse ____ Special educators ____ Pupil personnel/ ____ School psychologist social workers ____ Others — including _____ _____
P1		Y N	Is there team representation from general and special education as well as support personnel? (8a)
P2		Y N	Is the team comprised of between eight and fourteen permanent members? (8c)
P3		Y N	Is the majority of teacher representation from general education? (8d)
P4		Y N	Do you attend meetings? (8b) YES NO
P5		Y N (Tm1)	When, where, and how often does your team meet? (13c) When? _____ Where? _____ How often? _____

ITEM SCORING

PRINCIPAL INTERVIEW SCORING GUIDE (P1–P5)

P1 through P3 are based on the opening responses of principal to first question regarding team composition.

P1 Score yes if, within principal's description of the team, there is representation from both general and special education classroom teachers.

P2 Score yes if, within principal's description, the team membership is between eight and fourteen members.

P3   Score yes if, within principal's description of the team, the majority of teacher representation is from general education in relation to all other "specialist teachers" on the team.

P4   Score yes if principal attends all team meetings and is an active participant.

P5   Score yes if regular team meetings are indicated and principal's response matches team response (Tm 1).

TEAM SURVEY

School: _____ Date: _____

Recorder's name: _____

The entire team should be interviewed at its regular meeting.

	Process	Delivery	
Tm1		Y N (P5)	When, where, and how often does your team meet? (13c) When? Where? _____ How often?_____
Tm2		Y N	Does your team have a designated System Manager? (11) YES No If yes, who? _____
Tm3		Y N	Who organizes and leads team meetings? (11a) _____
Tm4		Y N	Once a teacher has completed a Referral Form/Request for Assistance Form, what does he/she do with it? (9b; 11b) _____
Tm5		Y N	Are case managers assigned for each referral? (12) YES NO
Tm6		Y N	How is the team kept abreast of the progress on individual cases? (12d) _____ _____
Tm7		Y N	Indicate all training activities that your team engages in: a. ____ Development of (training) needs assessment. (13a) b. ____ Development of team goals. (13b) c. ____ On-site team practice of skills. (13e) d. ____ Participation in workshops, on or off-site. (13e)
Tm8		Y N	Indicate all activities (business and maintenance) that your team engages in: a. ____ Discussion of new referrals. (13d) b. ____ Discussion of case problems. (13d) c. ____ Updates of current cases. (13d) d. ____ Discussion of team process/issues/evaluation of team effectiveness. (13f)

Process	Delivery	Form Availability
Tm9	Y N	**Referral Form: (9a)** ____ Teacher's name ____ Student's name ____ Brief statement of the problem ____ Teacher's availability to meet
Tm 10	Y N	**System Tracking Form: (11c; 14)** ____ Student's name ____ Date of referral ____ Status of each case recorded at no more than 6-week intervals

TEAM SURVEY SCORING GUIDE (Tm1–Tm10)

Tm1 Score yes if regular meeting times are indicated and team response matches principal's response (P5). Regular team meetings should occur not less than once every other week and preferably once per week.

Tm2 Score yes if team members indicate a designated system manager.

Tm3 Score yes if system manager is specified as organizing and leading team meetings. During first year interviews, if principal, facilitator, or system manager are specified as organizing and leading team meetings, score yes.

Tm4 Score yes if system manager is specified as receiving Referral Form/Request for Assistance Form from teachers. In rare cases, schools have divided the duties of the system manager such that another individual different from the designated system manager receives teacher referrals. In such cases, score yes if the person designated to receive referrals is recognized throughout the school as the exclusive entry point to the team.

Tm5 Score yes if a single case manager is assigned for each referral.

Tm6 Score yes if cases are in progress, and team indicates procedure by which members are kept abreast of individual case progress. Terms such as updates, reviews, and discussion are sufficient to score yes.

Tm7 For first interview, score yes if 3 or 4 responses are checked. For subsequent interviews, score yes if 4 of 4 responses are checked.

Tm8 For first interview, score yes if 3 or 4 responses are checked. For subsequent interviews, score yes if 4 of 4 responses are checked.

Tm9 Score yes if Referral Form/Request for Assistance Form is available and includes the indicated information.

Tm10 Score yes if System Tracking Form is available and includes the indicated information.

LOI CASE MANAGER INTERVIEW

School: _____ Date: _____

Case Manager name: _____

Teacher's name: _____

First name of referred child: _____

	Process	Delivery		Comments
C1	Y N (Tr1)		At your first meeting, how did you explain the problem-solving process to _____? (2a) ____ Consultation stages ____ Meaning of collaboration ____ Time to meet ____ Confidentiality ____ _____ _____	
C2	Y N (Tr2)		Did _____ agree willingly to work with the IC-Team? (2b) Yes No	
C3	Y N (Tr3)		Describe the referral concern. How did you and ____ define the discrepancy between _____'s actual performance and what _____ expected in the classroom? (3a) What activities did you and _____ undertake to identify the presenting problem?: (Check the activities described by case manager to identify the academic or behavioral problem - Verbal descriptions)	
			Academic (3b)	FORM CHECK:
C4	Y N		____ Analysis of entry-level skills using CBA.	
C5	Y N		____ Analysis of targeted academic task(s) (e.g., task or error analysis) Specify How?	
C6	Y N		____ Specification of terminal goal. What?	

	Process	Delivery		Comments
			Behavior (3c):	
C7	Y N		____ Analysis of antecedents/consequences. How? _____	
C8	Y N		____ Analysis of setting and situation. How? _____	
C9	Y N		____ Specification of desired behavior. What? _____	
C 10	Y N		____ Possibility of academic problem assessed (3d). What strategies or interventions did you agree to implement? Describe them. Who was responsible for each aspect? When was the intervention to take place? (4b, c) Strategy _____ Who? _____ When? _____ Strategy _____ Who? _____ When? _____	FORM CHECK:
C 11	Y N (Tr4)		There is agreement between case manager and teacher as to which interventions to implement?	
C 12	Y N (Tr5)		There is evidence of specification of who is responsible for what, when in intervention development?	
C 13	Y N (Tr6)		How was the intervention/strategy to be monitored? (4d) _____	
C 14	Y N (Tr7)		At the first follow-up meeting, did you and _____ agree as to how much of the strategy/intervention had been implemented and/or how much correction was needed? (5a) Yes No	

	Process	Delivery		Comments
C 15	Y N (Tr9)		How many times did you have scheduled meetings with _____ to discuss the case and monitor the progress? (5b)	FORM CHECK:
C 16	Y N (Tr11)		How was the decision to modify, continue, or terminate the intervention made? (6b) Yes if based upon data/information No if not based upon data/information	FORM CHECK:
C 17		Y N	Did _____ participate in all meetings (including IC-Team meetings) during which the referral problem was discussed, that is beyond brief updates? (10a) Yes No	
C 18		Y N	Did _____ actively plan and make the decision as to which intervention to implement? (10b) Yes No	
C 19		Y N	How much time passed between _____'s referral and your first meeting? (12a) _____	FORM CHECK:
C 20		Y N	Do you or (teacher) have data generated from this case? (12b) Yes No	FORM CHECK:

CASE MANAGER INTERVIEW SCORING GUIDE (C1–C20)

C1   Score yes if an entry/contracting interview was conducted, all the indicated aspects are checked (4 of 4), and case manager's response generally matches teacher's response (T1). If required, prompt the case manager by asking directly whether an aspect has been reviewed.

Alternative Wording Suggestions: Other prompts or questions include: "Tell me what you told the teacher about the instructional consultation process"; "Tell me how you described the problem-solving process during your first meeting." If the case manager remains unclear, you may address the information that should occur at entry and contracting through more directed questions. For example: "At your first meeting with the teacher, did you talk about how the two of you were to collaborate and what it means?"

C2   Score yes if case manager indicates a mutual agreement to engage in problem solving and case manager's response matches teacher's response (T2).

C3   Score yes if case manager describes the referral concern in terms of a discrepancy between current and desired performance and matches case manager's response with the teacher's response (T3).

Questions C4 through C10 are based on case manager's response to the preceding question. Appropriate prompting should be given to explore each of the C4–C10 items.

C4   (Must always be addressed, regardless of presenting problem).

For an academic or behavioral referral, score yes if case manager indicates that activities were undertaken to determine that the student had adequate entry-level skills to participate in the current curriculum demands. Activities would include conducting running records of current reading material, word search procedures, review of Dolch or vocabulary lists, review of math work samples; assessment of math performance using curriculum material, etc.

Alternative wording suggestions: If the term CBA is not mentioned, ask if any assessments were conducted. "Describe what you did to assess his functioning. What material did you use? What goal did you want the student to reach?"

C5   (May be omitted if referral concern is centered solely on a behavioral concern).

Score omitted if referral concern (indicated in C3) is behavioral in nature. Score yes if case manager indicates that further analysis of student's academic functioning was conducted around targeted areas of concern. A yes score is given if the case manager indicates that task or error analysis were conducted to further identify a specific or targeted area of concern. Examples include: phonic skills analysis, probe of specific math facts or skills, etc.

C6   (May be omitted if referral concern is centered solely on a behavioral concern).

Score omitted if referral concern (indicated in C3) is behavioral in nature. Score yes if case manager describes the terminal goal or desired performance for the academic concern presented.

C7   (May be omitted if referral concern is centered solely on an academic concern).

Score omitted if referral concern (indicated in C3) is academic in nature. Score yes if actions were taken to identify antecedents and consequences relevant to the behavior of concern. These include direct observations of student withing the classroom setting or self monitoring techniques, etc.

C8   (May be omitted if referral concern is centered solely on an academic concern).

Score omitted if referral concern (indicated in C3) is academic in nature. Score yes if actions were taken to identify and isolate the setting or situation in which the behavior occurred. These include direct observations of student within the classroom setting or self monitoring techniques, review of permanent products, or interviews which could be substantiated with any of the above.

C9 (May be omitted if referral concern is centered solely on an academic concern).

Score omitted if referral concern (indicated in C3) is academic in nature. Score yes if desired performance is specified for the behavioral concern indicated.

C10 (May be omitted if referral concern is centered solely on an academic concern).

Score omitted if referral concern (indicated in C3) is academic in nature. Score yes if actions were taken to assure behavior was not a result of academic difficulties or mismatch between student needs and instructional environment.

Questions C11 and C12 are not administered directly, but instead based on case manager's response to preceding question.

C11 Score yes if case manager's description of strategies or interventions matches teacher's description (T4). Form Check: Student Documentation Form should specify intervention aspects.

C12 Score yes if, for each primary strategy there is specification of who, when, and what is involved in the intervention and case manager's response matches the teacher's response (T5).

C13 Score yes if case manager describes the plan to monitor the strategy/intervention and this matches teacher's description (T6).

C14 Score yes if case manager indicates that efforts were made to ensure that the intervention was operationalized as planned and case manager's response matches teacher's response (T7).

Alternative Wording Suggestions: Related back to the previous questions on intervention strategies (C11 and C12). "You've described agreeing on a particular strategy. After it was implemented, did you both meet to discuss how it was being implemented and whether there were any difficulties or changes needed?"

C15 Score yes if case manager indicates regularly scheduled meetings in which monitoring of the intervention/strategy occurred and case manager's response matches teacher's response (T9). Form Check: Case Documentation Form should be available and completed accurately.

C16 Score yes if decision to change, terminate, or continue the intervention was based upon data and case manager's response matches teacher's response (T11). Form Check: Student Documentation Form should be available and used to document data collection.

C17 Score yes if case manager indicates that teacher was included in all IC-Team meetings in which the case was discussed, beyond brief updates.

C18   Score yes if case manager indicates that teacher was an active participant in choosing, developing, and implementing the intervention.

C19   Score yes if 7 or fewer school days passed between the receipt of the referral and first contact with case manager. Form Check: Date from completed referral form and first date on Case Documentation Form provide this information.

C20   Score yes if case manager has data generated from this case or can indicate data are available from the referring teacher. Form Check: Student Documentation Form, Case Documentation Form, and CBA data collection as support.

TEACHER INTERVIEW

School: _____ Date: _____

Case Manager's name: _____

Teacher's name: _____

First name of referred child: _____

	Process	Delivery		Comments
T1	Y N (C1)		What was your understanding of what the IC-Team (collaborative problem-solving) process would be after your first meeting with the case manager? (2a) _____ _____	
T2	Y N (C2)		Did you agree to work on _____'s problem with the case manager and team? (2b) YES NO	
T3	Y N (C3)		Describe the concern that prompted the initial referral. How did you and _____ define the discrepancy between _____'s actual performance and what you expected in the classroom? (3a) _____ _____	
			What strategies or interventions did you agree to implement? Describe them. Who was responsible for each aspect? When was the intervention to take place? (4b, c) Strategy _____ Who? _____ When? _____ Strategy _____ Who? _____ When? _____	
T4	Y N (C6)		Is there agreement between case manager and teacher as to which interventions to implement?	
T5	Y N (C7)		Is there evidence of specification of who is responsible for what, when in intervention development?	

	Process	Delivery		Comments
T6	Y N (C8)		How was the intervention/strategy to be monitored? (4d) _____	
T7	Y N (C9)		At the first follow-up meeting, did you and _____ agree as to how much of the plan had been implemented and/or how much correction was needed? (5a) YES NO	
T8	Y N		Describe what type of information was collected during the intervention. How often was the information collected? (5b) _____ Was information graphed/charted? (5c) _____	FORM CHECK:
T9	Y N (C10)		Did you have scheduled meetings with _____ to discuss _____'s progress? (5b) YES NO	
T 10	Y N		Was the intervention successful? How do you know? (6a) _____	FORM CHECK:
T 11	Y N (C11)		How was the decision to continue, modify, or terminate the strategy/intervention made? (6B) YES NO	FORM CHECK:
T 12		Y N (Tm4)	What did you do with the completed referral form? (9b; 11b)	FORM CHECK:
T 13		Y	Did you feel that you were a contributing member of the problem-solving process? Of the IC-Team? (10a) _____ That your input was valuable? (10b) _____	

TEACHER INTERVIEW SCORING GUIDE (T1–T13)

T1 ˙Score yes if teacher's response indicates that an initial entry and contracting interview was conducted and in general **matches** key aspects checked in case manager question C1. Minimal prompting may occur to substantiate case manager's response.

T2   Score yes if teacher indicates an agreement to work with the case manager and team and teacher's response matches case manager's response (C2).

T3   Score yes if teacher describes the referral concern in terms of a discrepancy between current and desired performance and teacher's response matches case manager's response (C3). Teacher may need prompting and alternative wording.

Alternative Wording Suggestions: Use alternative wording and prompting such as, "Tell me where the student was functioning when you began and where you expect him/her to be functioning as an end result of your work with the IC-Team/case manager."

Questions T4 and T5 are scored based on teacher's response to preceding question and are not asked directly.

T4   Score yes if teacher's description of strategies or interventions matches case manager's description (C6).

T5   Score yes if, for each primary strategy, there is specification of who, when, and what is involved in the intervention and teacher's response matches case manager's response (C7).

T6   Score yes if teacher describes the plan to monitor the strategy/intervention and this matches case manager's description (C8).

T7   Score yes if teacher indicates there was a consensual agreement that the intervention was operationalized as planned and this matches case manager's response (C9).

Alternative Wording Suggestions: Relate back to the previous question on intervention strategies (T4 and T5). "You've described agreeing on a particular strategy. After it was implemented, did you both meet to discuss how it was being implemented and whether there were any difficulties or changes needed?"

T8   Score yes if teacher's descriptions of type of information and collection procedures support that the intervention plan was being monitored as described in T6 **and** that there was frequent graphing/charting of measurement data (no greater than 2-week intervals).

T9   Score yes if teacher verbally indicates regular scheduled meetings and teacher's response generally **matches** case manager's response (C10).

T10   Score yes if teacher's response acknowledges that success or lack of success is judged by the data collection procedures indicated to monitor progress (or other appropriate objective information).

T11   Score yes if decision to change, terminate, or continue the intervention was based on data and teacher's response matches case manager's response (C11).

T12   Score yes if teacher submitted completed referral form to system manager and teacher's response **matches** team response (Tm4).

T13   During first-year interviews, score yes if teacher indicates positive response for 2 of 3 choices. For subsequent interviews, score yes if teacher indicates positive response for 3 of 3 choices.

LOI FORMS

School: _____ Date: _____

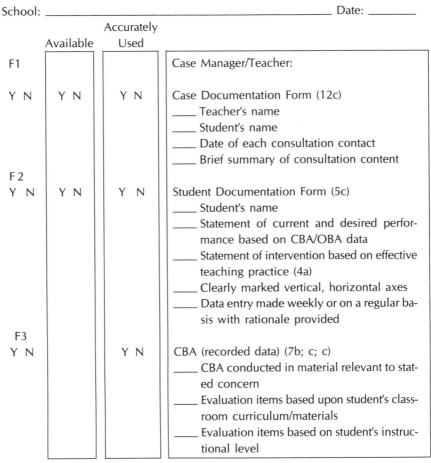

	Available	Accurately Used	
F1			Case Manager/Teacher:
Y N	Y N	Y N	Case Documentation Form (12c) ____ Teacher's name ____ Student's name ____ Date of each consultation contact ____ Brief summary of consultation content
F 2			
Y N	Y N	Y N	Student Documentation Form (5c) ____ Student's name ____ Statement of current and desired perfor-mance based on CBA/OBA data ____ Statement of intervention based on effective teaching practice (4a) ____ Clearly marked vertical, horizontal axes ____ Data entry made weekly or on a regular ba-sis with rationale provided
F3			
Y N		Y N	CBA (recorded data) (7b; c; c) ____ CBA conducted in material relevant to stat-ed concern ____ Evaluation items based upon student's class-room curriculum/materials ____ Evaluation items based on student's instruc-tional level

LOI FORMS SCORING GUIDE (F1–F3)

For each case manager–teacher pair interviewed, the following forms should be reviewed. Review forms throughout interview and ask specifically to see forms to ensure the following:

F1 Case Documentation Form
    Score yes if form is available with the indicated information present and all aspects are accurately used.

F2 Student Documentation Form
    Score yes if form is available with the indicated information and all aspects are accurately used.

F3 Curriculum-based Assessment (recorded data)

This documentation review requests that case managers and teachers demonstrate through forms, charts, notes, student work samples, and so forth, i.e., the various processes which were undertaken to assure an appropriate match between the student's entry level and curriculum/instructional materials. Although not necessarily a standardized form, score yes if indicated information is presented as part of interview. Examples of CBA may include, but are not limited to: reading passages taken from students' readers or novels; informal assessments specifically developed to assess student progress in current curriculum; review of student's work samples; notes and information from diagnostic/prescriptive teaching; and so on.

CRITICAL DIMENSION OF IC-TEAMS

Indicators

Collaborative consultation process—A stage-based method of problem-solving utilizing interactive, nonhierarchical relationships among professionals with diverse areas of expertise is routinely utilized by the staff for classroom-based problems.

1. At all stages, interactions between the case manager and referring teacher are characterized by accurate, clear communication.
   (a) Effective communication is evidenced by teacher and case manager having the same perceptions of issues discussed, or an understanding of the other's perception.

For each case, the following stages are sequentially implemented until the problem is satisfactorily resolved:

2. Contracting:
   (a) An interview between the consultee (teacher) and consultant (case manager) has been conducted in which the following have been discussed: (1) the consultation process; (2) the meaning of collaboration; (3) the time involvement; and (4) confidentiality.
   (b) There is evidence of a mutually agreed-upon contract to engage in the problem-solving process.

3. Problem Identification:
   (a) There is a statement of discrepancy, from the consultee's perspective, between desired and actual performance for the referred child.
   (b) For academic problems, the following activities are completed: (1) analysis of entry level skills using CBA; (2) analysis of targeted academic task; and (3) specification of terminal goal in behaviorally descriptive terms.
   (c) For behavioral problems, the following activities are completed: (1) analysis of immediate antecedents/consequences; (2) analysis of setting and situation; and (3) statement of desired behavior.

4. Intervention Recommendations:
   (a) Intervention recommendations based on effective teaching practices are produced by team members/case managers/teachers.
   (b) A consensual decision is reached on recommendations to implement.
   (c) There is evidence of the specification of who is responsible for what, when.
   (d) A plan for monitoring the effectiveness of the intervention is developed.

5. Implementation of Intervention:
   (a) There is consensual agreement between the consultant and consultee about the extent to which the specified plan has been operationalized.
   (b) The plan is monitored as specified.
   (c) There is evidence of frequent graphing of measurement data.

6. Evaluation and Follow-Up of Intervention:
   (a) Data are used to determine level of progress.
   (b) The decision to terminate, continue, or change the intervention is based on data.

7. CBA is a method to determine baseline levels of academic functioning from the student's own curriculum in order to monitor ongoing performance to determine the success or failure of an intervention.
   (a) The assessment reflects an evaluation of academic behavior in the natural environment.
   (b) The assessment focuses on the individual child rather than on a normative group.
   (c) The child is tested on material from the instructional curriculum.
   (d) The assessment method used is appropriate for continuous monitoring of student progress in order to alter interventions as needed.

Delivery System—The structure by which the collaborative consultation process delivered by a team to a school is developed and maintained.

8. In each building, a permanent support team is specified. It is characterized by:
   (a) Representation from general and special education and pupil support services personnel.
   (b) Presence of building administrator as regular and active team participant.
   (c) Team comprised of between 8 and 14 permanent members.
   (d) The majority of teacher representation is from general education.

9. There is a referral process by which teachers and staff can access the team.
   (a) A referral form (or request for assistance) is readily available that, at a minimum, includes teacher's and student's names, a brief statement of the problem, and the teacher's available time to meet.
   (b) A person to receive the referral form has been designated.

10. The referring teacher becomes a part of the process by participating in all problem-solving activities.
    (a) The referring teacher becomes a temporary team member, participating in all meetings that focus on the referral problem.
    (b) The referring teacher is actively involved in planning and implementing the intervention.

11. A system manager is designated whose role includes:
    (a) Organization of team meetings.
    (b) Receipt of referral form from consultee.
    (c) Monitoring of the status of all cases.

12. For each referral, a case manager is assigned, whose role includes:
    (a) Timely initial contact with consultee (within 7 days).
    (b) Collection and organization of all data.
    (c) Monitoring of all consultation contacts.
    (d) Reporting to team on case progress.

13. The functions of the team are clearly specified and engaged in.
    (a) There is evidence of formal or informal needs assessment to determine the team's own needs.
    (b) A plan to include goals, activities, and consultants is developed each year.
    (c) Regular meeting place and times are specified.
    (d) Team business includes review of new referrals, case updates, case problems, team process.
    (e) There is evidence that the team allots time for practice in specified areas of the consultation process.
    (f) Teams engage in maintenance activities including (1) regular team processing of issues and concerns, and (2) reflection on team's effectiveness through self-assessment and evaluation.

14. A tracking process is in place to ensure systematic record keeping in order to document the delivery system.
    (a) There is an up-to-date System Tracking Form indicating the status of all cases, reported at 4–6 week intervals.
    (b) There are up-to-date monitoring forms for individual cases summarizing all consultation contacts (Case Documentation Form).
    (c) Student Documentation Forms are completed detailing the referral concern stated in discrepancy between current and desired performance, goals, and interventions. Graphic display of data is available for each case.

APPENDIX B
Sample Contract

The Instructional Consultation-Team Project represents a collaborative effort between schools, pupil services, special education and the Division of Instruction to better support teachers and the students they serve. The focus is (1) on establishing a systematic referral process which would incorporate a conceptual and behavioral shift from finding the deficit within the student, to restructuring the setting so that the student can make progress academically, socially, and/or behaviorally; and (2) a restructured management system within the school based on a more collaborative, problem-solving culture, with a school support team as its core.

The undersigned agree that training and appropriate support are of utmost importance in establishing such a collaborative system. As such, all parties are agreeing to commit the necessary time and resources for the purpose of training and implementation:

1. Pupil services agrees to provide training and on-site facilitation of the Instructional Consultation Model. Such services will be performed by designated school psychologists in accordance with the attached training plan.

2. School agrees to establish and commit the necessary time for team training and meeting as outlined on the attached training plan. School also agrees to support the collaborative consultation model by facilitating additional time for team members to consult with school staff who refer to the team.

3. System agrees to support the pilot school however possible and acknowledge the intensity of training and commitment. The system agrees to designate a District Office liaison for the pilot in order to facilitate communication between district and participating schools. The participating schools are held harmless to the extent possible in loss of resources which may result from increased efficiency of delivery of services for a period of 2 years; are held harmless to the extent possible in the implementation of any similar program until level of functioning is established for 2 years. Training stipends will be actively sought.

The importance of evaluating a program's effectiveness is also acknowledged. All agree that such evaluations should be relevant to determining the (1) extent to which the project is actually implemented, and (2) the effectiveness upon predetermined outcome measures. In acknowledgment of the importance of such evaluation:

1. Pupil services agrees to provide maximum support in developing, coordinating, and conducting evaluation procedures. As much as possible, evaluation procedures will be formative, providing relevant information to the on-site facilitator for the purpose of maximizing training. Outcome measures will include those mandated through state requirements, student achievement, referral information, out-

come measures of interest to participating schools, evaluation of team training and implementation of the model, and team and faculty satisfaction.

2. School agrees to provide necessary support to carry out evaluations, including time and dissemination and collection of evaluation materials. An evaluation plan will be provided to all participating schools.

District agrees to review the evaluation plan. Once approved, the district agrees to provide, as much as possible, the needed support and information for an effective evaluation. In addition, the district agrees to facilitate, to the extent possible, the collection of comparison data from predetermined schools.

Additional issues are included below:

Evaluation and implementation materials will be provided for the school.

Signed:

_____

Supervisor

_____

Principal

_____

Director of

APPENDIX C
Simulation Case

IC-Team Request for Assistance

Date <u>10/10/89</u>

Pupil name <u>Taylor Doe</u>   Date of birth <u>11/15/78</u>

I need help with this pupil because <u>He is in a 2-1 reading basal and cannot</u>
<u>handle the skills on this level. He has difficulty decoding words and has</u>
<u>poor comprehension. Math skills are not at 4th grade level. He has</u>
<u>difficulty with basic addition and subtraction facts. Because of his lack</u>
<u>of skills, he is disrupting the class and it interferes with other</u>
<u>children's learning.</u>

Family contact _____

You may contact me on the following days and times:
<u>Monday–Friday, 12:00–1:20</u>

_____

Teacher's name <u>Mr. Fred</u>

Room number <u>410</u>   Grade <u>4th</u>

School <u>Anywhere Elementary</u>

Step 1. Read the above Request for Assistance Form.

What would be the first step in identifying the discrepancy between Taylor's actual performance and the performance expected by the teacher?

Stop. Discuss. Go to step 2.

Step 2. In an initial interview Mr. Fred described Taylor as disruptive. Taylor was often observed hitting, pinching, and kicking other students. This behavior occured on average 5 times a day, most often in the morning.

Taylor was currently reading in the second grade reader, book 2. His teacher indicated that he was placed in this reader according to his performance on the basal series unit tests. Mr. Fred guessed that Taylor was actually functioning below that level.

What other information would you gather to define the discrepancy between current and desired performance?

Stop. Discuss. Go to step 3.

Step 3. Results of CBA on 10/15/89 revealed Taylor to read 27 words per minute
with 12 knowns (56% knowns) in his current reader.

---

*Chart this behavior on the accompanying Student Documentation Form (SDF). Write
an objective for this student on the SDF based on the information provided.*

Stop. Discuss. Go to step 4.

Student Documentation Form

Student name _____ Grade _____ Teacher _____ Date(s) _____ from _____ to

School _____ Case manager _____

Operational definition of
behavior/academic concern: _____

Statement of current functioning:
(based upon above graph) _____

Statement of desired performance:
(specify time period) _____

Describe intervention(s): _____

Step 4. A decision was made to increase Taylor's reading performance within his
current reader.

---

*Based upon the information provided, how would you work collaboratively with
the teacher to develop a strategy with the target student?*

Stop. Discuss. Go to step 5.

Step 5. The following data were obtained after implementing a strategy. *Chart these data on the graph.*

10/14/89	56%
10/21/89	62%
10/29/89	68%
11/5/89	75%
11/15/89	81%

Discuss the effectiveness of the intervention strategy and the decision you would make based on the data.

APPENDIX D
Tape Analysis

Consultant name _____

Consultee name _____ Role _____
(e.g., first grade teacher)

Date of interview _____

Check one:

    ____ Individual analysis
    ____ Transcript analysis
    ____ Peer supervised Peer reviewer _____

At what stage of consultation is this tape being made?
    ____ Entry/contracting
    ____ Problem identification
    ____ Intervention planning
    ____ Intervention evaluation
    ____ Termination

Provide a brief description of goal of interview and perceived outcome related to
that goal _____

_____

_____

_____

_____

_____

Areas addressed by this analysis:
    ____ Use of communication skills
    ____ Component analysis of the specific stage of consultation (Check one below)
        ____ Entry/contracting
        ____ Problem identification
        ____ Intervention planning
        ____ Intervention evaluation
        ____ Termination
    ____ Content

ENTRY/CONTRACTING

Statement of *specific* feedback desired from peer reviewer:

_____

Check all that are covered in interview

Reviewer
comments:

_____ Introduces self as case manager
_____ Reviews process
     _____ Reviews system
     _____ Clarifies team function
     _____ Checks teacher awareness of process

_____ Reviews problem-solving stages
     _____ Entry/contracting
     _____ Problem identification and analysis
     _____ Planning interventions
     _____ Implementing interventions
     _____ Resolution/termination

_____ Clarifies problem of ownership
     _____ Problem owned by consultant and con-
     sultee
     _____ Team involvement in problem

_____ Discusses time involvement
     _____ Need for time
     _____ Amount of time

_____ Explains data collection
     _____ Baseline data
     _____ Kinds of baseline data
     _____ Who will collect data
     _____ Continuing data collection for monitoring

_____ Confidentiality, student's and teacher's
     _____ Not used for teacher evaluation
     _____ School policy on student confidentiality

_____ Gains consultee's agreement to be part of
process

_____ Next meeting date/time established

PROBLEM IDENTIFICATION INTERVIEW

Review tape. (1) Check those components addressed in the interview. (2) Write a brief statement under each component checked indicating *your* perception of what information was presented.

Statement of *specific* feedback desired from peer reviewer:

____ Academic   ____ Behavior   Comments:

____ Referral concern clarified in terms of specific be-
havior/skills.
Indicate clarified concern:

____ Student's current and expected performance specified
(what does the child actually do and what does the
teacher expect of the child as a result of this process)
Indicate specified current and expected performance:

____ Student's current instructional level discussed in inter-
view. Actual instructional level established OR plans
are made to establish student's instructional level. *Indicate student's instructional level or specific steps
agreed to in establishing instructional level:*

____ Conditions under which student does achieve desired
performance specified.
Indicate the conditions clarified in interview.

____ Characteristics of behavioral concern specified OR plans
made to collect further information (e.g., antecedents/con-
sequences; setting, frequency, and duration). *Indicate
characteristics clarified and plans to obtain additional information:*

____ Teacher's efforts to deal with academic/behavioral concern
clarified. *Indicate efforts made by teacher in dealing with
concern:*

COMMUNICATION SKILLS

Tally each type of communication statement heard in review and then total. Provide one example of each type of statement used.

Statement of *specific* feedback desired from peer reviewer:

	Tally of each:	Total:
Requesting clarification:		

Paraphrasing:

Perception checking:

Active listening:

Relevant questions:

Offering information:

Examining child's work:

Irrelevant questions:

Making suggestions/recommendations:

References

Abelson, M. A., & Woodman, R. W. (1983). Review of research on team effectiveness: Implications for teams in schools. *School Psychology Review, 12,* 125–136.

American Psychological Association Task Force on Comprehensive and Coordinated Psychological Services for Children. (1994). *Comprehensive and coordinated psychological services for children: A call for service integration.* Washington, DC: American Psychological Association.

Anders, P. L., & Bos, C. S. (1992). Dimensions of professional development: Weaving teacher beliefs and strategic content. In M. Pressley, K. R. Harris, & J. T. Guthrie (Eds.), *Promoting academic competence and literacy in school* (pp. 457–476). San Diego, CA: Academic Press.

Backer, T. E. (1994). *Readiness for change, educational innovations, and education reform.* Paper prepared for Office of Educational Research and Improvement, Washington, DC.

Baldwin, D. (1994, January/February). As busy as we wanna be. *Utne Reader,* 52–58.

Bardon, J. I. (1983). Psychology applied to education: A specialty in search of an identity. *American Psychologist, 38,* 185–196.

Billups, J. O. (1987). Interprofessional team process. *Theory Into Practice, 26,* 146–152.

Block, P. (1981). *Flawless consulting.* Austin, TX: Learning Concepts.

Bloom, B. S. (1976). *Human characteristics and school learning.* New York: McGraw-Hill.

Boehm, A. E., & Weinberg, R. A. (1977). *The classroom observer: A guide for developing observation skills.* New York: Teachers College Press.

Boiarsky, C. (1985). Changing teachers' attitudes and behaviors through modeling and coaching. *English Education, 17,* 26–31.

Bredo, E. (1977). Collaborative relations among elementary school teachers. *Sociology of Education, 50*(4), 300–309.

Brophy, J. (1986). Research linking teacher behavior to student achievement: Potential implications for instruction of Chapter 1 students. In B. I. Williams, P. A. Richmond, & B. J. Mason (Eds.), *Designs for compensatory education: Conference proceedings and papers* (pp. IV-122–IV-179). Washington, DC: Research and Evaluation Associates.

Campbell, D. T., & Stanley, J. C. (1963). *Experimental and quasi-experimental designs for research.* Chicago: Rand McNally.

Carnegie Forum on Education and the Economy. (1986). *A nation prepared: Teachers for the 21st century.* Washington, DC: Author.

Carner, L. A. (1982). Developing a consultative contract. In J. Alpert (Ed.), *Psychological consultation in educational settings* (pp. 8–32). San Francisco: Jossey-Bass.

Chalfant, J. C., & Pysh, M. (1984). Teacher assistance teams: A model for within-building problem-solving. In L. Liberal (Ed.), *Preventing special education for those who didn't need it* (pp. 16–28). Newton, MA: Gloworm.

Chalfant, J. C., & Pysh, M. (1989). Teacher assistance teams: Five descriptive studies on 96 teams. *Remedial and Special Education, 10*(6), 49–58.

Chalfant, J. C., Pysh, M., & Moultrie, R. (1979). Teacher assistance teams: A model for within-building problem solving. *Learning Disabilities Quarterly, 2,* 85–96.

Cole, E., Siegel, J., & Yau, M. (1990). *The local school team: Goals, roles and functions.* Toronto, Canada: Research Services, Toronto Board of Education.

Cook, T. J., & Poole, W. K. (1982). Treatment implementation and statistical power: A research note. *Evaluation Review, 6,* 425–430.

Dillon, J. T. (1990). *The practice of questioning.* London, England: Routledge.

Doyle, W. J. (1978). A solution in search of a problem: Comprehensive change and the Jefferson Experimental Schools. In D. Mann (Ed.), *Making change happen* (pp. 78–100). New York: Teachers College Press.

Dunn, L. (1968). Special education for the mildly retarded: Is much of it justifiable? *Exceptional Children, 35,* 5–22.

Ekholm, M., Vandenberghe, R., & Miles, M. B. (1987). Conclusions and implications. In M. B. Miles, M. Ekholm, & R. Vandenberghe (Eds.), *Lasting school improvement: Exploring the process of institutionalization* (pp. 243–267). Leuven, Belgium: Acco.

Elmore, R. F., & Associates. (1990). *Restructuring schools: The next generation of educational reform.* San Francisco: Jossey-Bass.

Evans, R. (1990). Making mainstreaming work through prereferral consultation. *Educational Leadership, 47,* 73–77.

Finkelstein, B. (1989). *Governing the young: Teacher behavior in popular primary schools in the Nineteenth-Century United States.* New York: Falmer Press.

Fisher, R., & Brown, S. (1988). *Getting together.* New York: Penguin Books.

Friend, M., & Cook, L. (1992). *Interactions: Collaboration skills for school professionals.* New York: Longman.

Fuchs, L., & Fuchs., D (1986). Effects of systematic formative evaluation: A meta-analysis. *Exceptional Children, 53,* 367–395.

Fuchs, D., & Fuchs, L. (1988). Mainstreaming assistance teams to accommodate difficult-to-teach students in general education. In J. Graden, J. Zins, & M. Curtis (Eds.), *Alternative educational delivery systems: Enhancing instructional options for all students* (pp. 49–70). Washington, DC: National Association of School Psychologists.

Fudell, R. (1992). Level of implementation of teacher support teams and teachers' attitudes toward special needs students. *Dissertation Abstracts International, 53*(05), 1399A. (University Microfilms No. AAC-9227463)

Fudell, R., & Dougherty, K. (1989). *Teacher support teams: State of policy and description of elements.* Unpublished manuscript.

Fullan, M. (1993). *Change forces.* London, England: Falmer Press.

Fullan, M. G. (1991). *The new meaning of educational change.* New York: Teachers College Press.

Fullan, M., & Hargreaves, A. (1991). *What's worth fighting for? Working together for your school.* Andover, MA: Regional Laboratory for Educational Improvement of the Northeast and Islands.

Gartner, A., & Lipsky, D. K. (1987). Beyond special education: Toward a quality system for all students. *Harvard Educational Review, 57,* 367–390.

Gaskins, I. W., Cunicelli, E. A., & Satlow, E. (1992). Implementing an across-the-curriculum strategies program: Teachers' reactions to change. In M. Pressley, K. R. Harris, & J. T. Guthrie (Eds.), *Promoting academic competence and literacy in schoool* (pp. 407–426). San Diego, CA: Academic Press.

Gickling, E. E., & Rosenfield, S. (1995). Best practices in curriculum-based assessment. In A. Thomas & J. Grimes (Eds.), *Best practices in school psychology III* (pp. 587–595). Washington, DC: National Association of School Psychologists.

Gickling, E. E., Shane, R. L., & Croskery, K. M. (1989). Developing mathematics skills in low-achieving high school students through curriculum-based assessment. *School Psychology Review, 18,* 344–355.

Gravois, T. A., Rosenfield, S., & Greenberg, B. (1991). *An analysis of implementation concerns of school support teams.* Unpublished manuscript.

Green-Resnick, B., & Rosenfield, S. (1989, March). *Monitoring student progress in a prereferral system.* Poster session presented at the meeting of the National Association of School Psychologists, Boston, MA.

Gresham, F. M., Gansle, K. A., Noell, G. H., Cohen, S., & Rosenblum, S. (1993). Treatment integrity of school-based behavioral intervention studies: 1980–1990. *School Psychology Review, 22,* 254–272.

Gresham, F. M., & Noell, G. H. (1993). Documenting the effectiveness of consultation outcomes. In J. E. Zins, T. R. Kratochwill, & S. N. Elliott (Eds.), *Handbook of consultation services for children* (pp. 249–273). San Francisco: Jossey-Bass.

Grumet, M. R. (1989, January). Dinner at Abigail's: Nurturing collaboration. *NEA Today, 7*(6), 20–25.

Guskey, T. R. (1990). Integrating innovations. *Educational Leadership, 47*(2), 11–15.

Hall, G. E., & Hord, S. M. (1987). *Change in schools: Facilitating the process.* Albany, NY: State University of New York Press.

Hargis, C. H. (1987). *Curriculum based assessment: A primer.* Springfield, IL: Charles C. Thomas.

Hayek, R. A. (1987). The teacher assistance team: A pre-referral support system. *Focus on Exceptional Children, 20,* 1–7.

Heller, K. A., Holtzman, W. H., & Messick, S. (Eds.). (1982). *Placing children in special education: A strategy for equity.* Washington, DC: National Academy Press.

Hobbs, N. (1975). *The futures of children.* San Francisco: Jossey-Bass.

Holmes Group. (1986). *Tomorrow's teachers.* East Lansing, MI: Author.

Hord, S. M. (1986). A synthesis of research on organizational collaboration. *Educational Leadership, 43*(5), 22–26.

Horvath, M. J., & Baker, L. (1982). Instructional support teams: Their initiation in local school buildings. In S. Stokes (Ed.), *School based staff support teams: A blueprint for action* (pp. 40–46). Reston, VA: Council for Exceptional Children.

Huberman, M. (1983). Recipes for busy kitchens: A situational analysis of routine knowledge use in schools. *Knowledge: Creation, Diffusion, Utilization, 4,* 478–510.

Huberman, M., & Miles, M. B. (1984). *Innovation up close.* New York: Plenum Press.

Huebner, E. S., & Hahn, B. M. (1990). Best practices in coordinating multidisciplinary teams. In A. Thomas & J. Grimes (Eds.), *Best practices in school psychology II* (pp. 235–245). Washington, DC: National Association of School Psychologists.

Hughes, C. A. (1994). A knowledge utilization investigation of the adoption and implementation of a consultation-based indirect service delivery model by multidisciplinary teams. *Dissertation Abstracts International, 54*(07), 2513A. (University Microfilms No. AAC-9328413)

Idol, L., & West, J.F. (1987). Consultation in special education (part II): Training and practice. *Journal of Learning Disabilities, 20,* 474–494.

Jones, G. (1995, August). *Evaluation of training.* Paper presented at the annual meeting of the American Psychological Association, New York, NY.

Joyce, B., & Showers, B. (1980). Improving inservice education: The messages of research. *Educational Leadership, 37,* 379–385.

Kauffman, J. M., Gerber, M. M., & Semmel, M. I. (1988). Arguable assumptions underlying the Regular Education Initiative. *Journal of Learning Disabilities, 21,* 6–11.

Kelly, M. (1994, January/February). You can't always get done what you want. *Utne Reader,* pp. 62–66. (Excerpted from *Business Ethics,* 1993, January/February.)

Kerr, D. H. (1983). Teaching competence and teacher education in the United States. In L. S. Shulman & G. Sykes (Eds.), *Handbook of teaching and policy* (pp. 126–149). New York: Longman.

Kessen, W. (1979). The American child and other cultural inventions. *American Psychologist, 34,* 815–820.

Kline, F. M., Deshler, D. D., & Schumaker, J. B. (1992). Implementing learning strategy instruction in class settings: A research perspective. In M. Pressley, K. R. Harris, & J. T. Guthrie (Eds.), *Promoting academic competence and literacy in school* (pp. 361–406). San Diego, CA: Academic Press.

Kuralt, S. (1990, August). *Classroom collaboration: Implementing consultation-based intervention in five multidisciplinary teams.* Paper presented at the Annual Meeting of the American Psychological Association, Boston.

Lennox, N., Hyman, I. A., & Hughes, C. A. (1988). Institutionalization of a consultation-based service delivery system. In J. L. Graden, J. E. Zins, &

M. J. Curtis (Eds.), *Alternative educational delivery systems: Enhancing instructional options for all students* (pp. 71–89). Washington, DC: National Association of School Psychologists.

Little, J. W. (1990). The persistence of privacy: Autonomy and initiative in teachers' professional relations. *Teachers College Record, 91,* 509–536.

Lortie, D. (1975). *School teacher: A sociological study.* Chicago: University of Chicago Press.

Maeroff, G. I. (1993). *Team building for school change: Equipping teachers for new roles.* New York: Teachers College Press.

Maeroff, G. I. (1988). A blueprint for empowering teachers. *Phi Delta Kappan, 69,* 473–477.

Maher, C. A., & Pfeiffer, S. I. (1983). Multidisciplinary teams in the schools: Perspectives, practices, possibilities. *School Psychology Review, 12,* 123.

McLauglin, M. (1990). The Rand Change Agent Study Revisited: Macroperspectives and Microrealities. *Educational Researcher, 19*(9), 11–16.

McLaughlin, M. W., & Yee, S. M. (1988). School as a place to have a career. In A. Lieberman (Ed.), *Building a professional culture in schools* (pp. 23–44). New York: Teachers College Press.

Meier, D. (1992). Reinventing teaching. *Teachers College Record, 93,* 594–609.

Miles, M. B. (1983). Unraveling the mystery of institutionalization. *Educational Leadership, 40*(11), 14–19.

Miles, M. B., & Ekholm, M. (1991, April). *Will new structures stay restructured?* Paper presented at the annual meeting of the American Educational Research Association, Chicago, IL.

Mid-continent Regional Educational Laboratory, (1984–1985). Coaching: A powerful strategy for improving staff development and inservice education. *Noteworthy, Winter,* 40–46. (ERIC Document Reproduction Service No. ED 272 508).

Moore, J. R. (1988). Guidelines concerning adult learning. *Journal of Staff Development, 9,* 2–5.

National Commission on Excellence in Education. (1983). *A nation at risk: The imperative for educational reform.* Washington, DC: U.S. Government Printing Office.

Nevin, A., & Thousand, J. (1987). Avoiding or limiting special education referrals: Changes and challenges. In M. C. Wang, M. C. Reynolds, & H. J. Walberg (Eds.), *Handbook of special education: Research and practice* (Vol. 1, pp. 273–286). Oxford, England: Pergamon Press.

Oakland, T., & Cunningham, J. L. (1990). Advocates for educational services for all children need improved research and conceptual bases. *School Psychology Quarterly, 5,* 66–77.

Ott, C. A. (1990). *The teacher support team: An organizational approach to enhancing ecologically valid practices in school psychology.* Unpublished manuscript.

Pajares, M. F. (1992). Teachers' beliefs and educational research: Cleaning up a messy construct. *Review of Educational Research, 62,* 307–332.

Parsons, R. D., & Meyers, J. (1984). *Developing consultation skills.* San Francisco: Jossey-Bass.

Plas, J. M. (1992). The development of systems thinking: A historical perspective. In M. J. Fine & C. Carlson (Eds.), *Handbook of family–school intervention: A systems perspective* (pp. 45–56). Boston: Allyn & Bacon.

Pryzwansky, W. B., & Rzepski, B. (1983). School based teams: An untapped resource for consultation technical assistance. *School Psychology Review, 12*, 174–179.

Reschly, D. J. (1993). A review of continuing education programs. In J. E. Zinns, T. R. Kratochwill, & S. N. Elliot (Eds.), *Handbook of consultation services for children* (pp. 394–418). San Francisco: Jossey-Bass.

Reynolds, M. C., Wang, M. C., & Walberg, H. J. (1987). The necessary restructuring of special and regular education. *Exceptional Children, 53*, 391–398.

Rippey, R. M., Geller, L. M., & King, D. W. (1978). Retrospective pretesting in the cognitive domain. *Evaluation Quarterly, 2*, 481–491.

Ristau, J., & Ryan, E. (1994, January/February). Lake Timebegone. *Utne Reader*, pp. 56–57.

Rosenfield, S. (1987). *Instructional consultation.* Hillsdale, NJ: Erlbaum.

Rosenfield, S. (1992). Developing school-based consultation teams: A design for organizational change. *School Psychology Quarterly, 7*, 27–46.

Rosenfield, S., & Feuerberg, M. A. (1987, August). *Supporting child study team change to alternative delivery systems.* Paper presented at the annual meeting of the American Psychological Association, New York, NY.

Rosenfield, S., & Gravois, T. (1992, April). *Training of facilitators for school change: An analysis of problems of implementation.* Roundtable presentation at the annual meeting of the American Educational Research Association, San Francisco, CA.

Rosenfield, S., & Gravois, T. A. (1993). Educating consultants for applied clinical and educational settings. In J. Zins, T. Kratochwill, & S. Elliott (Eds.), *Handbook of consultation services for children* (pp 373–393). San Francisco: Jossey-Bass.

Rosenfield, S., & Kuralt, S. (1990). Best practices in curriculum-based assessment. In A. Thomas & J. Grimes (Eds.), *Best practices in school psychology II* (pp. 275–286). Washington, DC: National Association of School Psychologists.

Rosenfield, S., & Reynolds, M. C. (1990). Mainstreaming school psychology: A proposal to develop and evaluate alternative assessment methods and intervention strategies. *School Psychology Quarterly, 5*, 55–65.

Rosenholtz, S. J. (1989). *Teacher's workplace: The social organization of schools.* New York: Teachers College Press.

Rowan, B. (1990). Applying conceptions of teaching to organizational reform. In R. F. Elmore & Associates (Eds.), *Restructuring schools: The next generation of educational reform* (pp. 31–58). San Francisco: Jossey-Bass.

Rubinson, F. (1991). Instructional matching and its relationship to classroom behavior. *Dissertation Abstracts International, 52*(03), 855A. (University Microfilms No. AAC-9123138)

Rubin, R., Stuck, G., & Revicki, D. (1982). A model for assessing the degree of implementation in field-based educational programs. *Educational Evaluation Policy and Analysis, 4*, 189–196.

Sarason, S. B. (1981). *Psychology misdirected.* New York: Free Press.

Sarason, S. B. (1982). *The culture of the school and the problem of change* (2nd ed.). Boston: Allyn & Bacon.

Sarason, S. B. (1983). *Schooling in America: Scapegoat and salvation.* New York: Free Press.

Sarason, S.B. (1990). *The predictable failure of educational reform.* San Francisco: Jossey-Bass.

Sashkin, M., & Egermeier, J. (1993, October). *School change models and processes: A review and synthesis of research and practice.* Washington, DC: U.S. Department of Education.

Satir, V. (1983). *Conjoint family therapy.* Palo Alto, CA: Science and Behavior Books.

Satir, V. (1988). *The new peoplemaking.* Mountain View, CA: Science and Behavior Books.

Satir, V., & Baldwin, M. (1983). *Satir step by step: A guide to creating change in families.* Palo Alto, CA: Science and Behavior Books.

Saxl, E., Lieberman, A., & Miles, M. (1987). Help is at hand: New knowledge for teachers as staff developers. *Journal of Staff Development, 8,* 7–11.

Schlechty, P. C. (1990). *Schools for the 21st century.* San Francisco: Jossey-Bass.

Schlossberg, N. K. (1989). *Overwhelmed: Coping with life's ups and downs.* Lexington, MA: Lexington Books.

Schon, D. A. (1983). *The reflective practitioner.* New York: Basic Books.

Schwab, J., Baldwin, M., Gerbe, J., Gomori, M., & Satir, V. (1989). *The Satir approach to communication: A workshop manual.* Palo Alto, CA: Science and Behavior Books.

Sheridan, S. M. (1993). Models for working with parents. In J. E. Zins, T. R. Kratochwill, & S. N. Elliott (Eds.), *Handbook of consultation services for children* (pp. 110–133). San Francisco: Jossey-Bass.

Shinn, M. R., Rosenfield, S., & Knutson, N. (1989). Curriculum-based assessment: A comparison of models. *School Psychology Review, 18,* 299–316.

Showers, B. (1987). The role of coaching in the implementation of innovations. *Teacher Education Quarterly, 14,* 59–70.

Skrtic, T. M. (1991). The special education paradox: Equity as the way to excellence. *Harvard Educational Review, 61,* 148–206.

Slavin, R. E., Madden, N. A., & Karweit, N. L. (1990). Effective programs for students at risk: Conclusions for practice and policy. In R. E. Slavin, N. L. Karweit, & N. A. Madden (Eds.), *Effective programs for students at risk* (pp. 355–372). Boston: Allyn & Bacon.

Stewart, K. J. (1985, August). *Academic consultation: Differences in doctoral and non-doctoral training and practice.* Paper presented at the annual meeting of the American Psychological Association, Los Angeles, CA.

Stiggins, R. J., & Conklin, N. F. (1992). *In teachers' hands: Investigating the practices of classroom assessment.* Albany, NY: State University of New York Press.

Stokes, S. (Ed.). (1982). *School based staff support teams: A blueprint for action.* Reston, VA: Council for Exceptional Children.

Stokes, S., & Axelrod, P. (1982). Staff support teams: Critical variables. In S. Stokes (Ed.), *School based staff support teams: A blueprint for action* (pp. 35–38). Reston, VA: Council for Exceptional Children.

Thousand, J. S., & Villa, R. A. (1992). Collaborative teams: A powerful tool in school restructuring. In R. A. Villa, J. S. Thousand, W. Stainback, & S. Stainback (Eds.), *Restructuring for caring and effective education: An administrative guide to creating heterogeneous schools* (pp. 73–108). Baltimore, MD: Paul H. Brookes.

Tombari, M. L., & Bergan, J. R. (1978). Consultant cues and teacher verbalizations, judgments, and expectancies concerning children's adjustment problems. *Journal of School Psychology, 16,* 212–219.

West, J. F., & Idol, L. (1987). School consultation (part I): An interdisciplinary perspective on theory, models, and research. *Journal of Learning Disabilities, 20,* 388–408.

Wheelan, S. A. (1990). *Facilitating training groups: A guide to leadership and verbal intervention skills.* New York: Praeger.

White, L. J., Summerlin, M. L., Loos, V. E., & Epstein, E. S. (1991). School and family consultation: A language-systems approach. In M. J. Fine & C. Carlson (Eds.), *Family–school interaction: A systems perspective* (pp. 347–362). Boston: Allyn & Bacon.

Wiggins, G. P. (1992). Foreword. In R. A. Villa, J. S. Thousand, W. Stainback, & S. Stainback (Eds.), *Restructuring for caring and effective education: An administrative guide to creating heterogeneous schools* (pp. xi–xvi). Baltimore, MD: Paul H. Brookes.

Will, M. (1986). *Educating students with learning problems: A shared responsibility.* Washington, DC: Office of Special Education and Rehabilitation Services.

Yoshida, R. K. (1980). Multidisciplinary decision making in special education: A review of issues. *School Psychology Review, 8,* 221–227.

Ysseldyke, J. (1983). Current practices in making psychoeducational decisions about learning disabled students. *Journal of Learning Disabilities, 16,* 226–233.

Ysseldyke, J., & Christenson, S. (1993). *The instructional environment system — II.* Longmont, CO: Sopris West.

Ysseldyke, J. E., Thurlow, M. L., Graden, J. L.,Wesson, C., Algozzine, B., & Deno, S. L. (1983). Generalizations from five years of research on assessment and decision making. *Exceptional Education Quarterly, 4,* 75–94.

Zins, J. E., Kratochwill, T. R., & Elliott, S. N. (1993). Current status of the field. In J. E. Zins, T. R. Kratochwill, & S. N. Elliott (Eds.), *Handbook of consultation services for children* (pp. 1–12). San Francisco: Jossey-Bass.

Zins, J. E., & Illback, R. J. (1993). Implementing consultation programs in child service systems. In J. E. Zins, T. R. Kratochwill, & S. N. Elliott (Eds.), *Handbook of consultation services for children* (pp. 204–224). San Francisco: Jossey-Bass.

Index

Accountability, 36, 47, 120–121
Administrative support. *See*
    Resources; Stakeholders
Adult learning, 103, 105
Assessment. *See also* Needs assess-
    ments
  classroom-based academic, 31–32
  curriculum-based (CBA), 32–33,
    57, 104, 106, 109
  observation-based, 33
  as training component, 57, 110
Authenticity, 25, 79–80

Backer, T. E., 59
Baldwin, D., 66, 67, 80
Behavior problems, 14–15
Billups, J. O., 119
Block, P., 25, 79
Bloom, B. S., 3, 16
Brown, S., 24
Budget design, 158, 162–163

Carner, L. A., 90
Case Documentation Form, 50, 51,
    53
Case management
  reviews vs. problem solving,
    128–131
  and team process, 123–128
Case managers
  assessing needs of, 134–136
  assignment of, 50

coaching of, 136–143
confidence building with, 144
configuration with IC-Team, 49
as consultants, 22, 23
feedback to and from, 122,
    130–131, 132–133, 142, 143
responsibilities of, 47, 49–50
showing appreciation to, 144
Case Review Feedback Form,
    132–133
Case study (Taylor Doe), 194–199
CBAM (Concerns Based Adoption
    Model), 67–68, 69, 70–71, 78
Change
  assumptions about, 62–63
  chaos theory of, 63–71
  concerns-based approach to,
    67–71
  and facilitator stress, 81–82
  and personal belief system, 61,
    135–136
  readiness for, 67, 88
  Satir's model of, 63, 65, 66, 67
  in schools, 1–2. *See also* School
    reform
  stages of, 19, 60, 153–155. *See also*
    Implementation stage; Initia-
    tion stage; Institutionaliza-
    tion stage
  survival stances during, 65 66
  understanding, 17–18, 59–61,
    81–82

Change facilitators
  activities of, 67, 72, 75, 118–119.
    See also Specific names of ac-
    tivities
  belief system of, 61, 62–63
  developmental progress for, 71
  general concerns of, 78–81
  internal vs. external, 90
  key skills of, 72, 73–74, 75–76, 80,
    142, 143
  need for, 96
  roles of, 59, 62, 71
  selecting and training, 76–78
  self-assessment by, 85
  and stress, 81–82
  support system for, 78, 79, 81
Charting and graphing. *See* Data
  collection procedures
Children, extension of service to
  all, 167–168, 170
Classroom environment, focus on
  instructional match in, 16, 19
Classroom observation, 33
Classroom-based assessment,
  31–32
Coaching. *See also* Professional
  development; Training
  program
  behaviors, skill level and,
    136–138
  focus areas for, 139, 140
  functions of, 102–103, 104
  group and team, 143
  phases of, 138
    conference, 141–143
    data collection, 140–141
    preconference, 139–140
  and Tape Analysis Form,
    141–142, 200–204
Collaboration, costs of, 9–10
Collaborative consultation, 21–37.
  See also Delivery system; Instructional consultation process
  communication strategies in, 24,
    25, 79–80
  conceptual framework for,
    21–22
  documentation, 36–37
  key elements in, 22–23
  relationship, 23, 24–26
  and time concerns, 69–70, 71,
    81–82
  training in, 77–78, 101, 104

Collaborative school culture
  and IC-Teams, 16–17, 19, 24,
    167–168
  importance of, 6–10
  and problem-solving teams,
    10–11, 12, 124
Communication
  dysfunctional patterns of, 65–66
  skills, development of, 123
  strategies, 24, 25, 79–80
  training, 103, 104, 108–109
Concerns Based Adoption Model
  (CBAM), 67–68, 69, 70–71,
    78
Conklin, N. F., 32
Consultant, case worker as, 22, 23
Consultation. *See* Collaborative
  consultation
Consultee, teacher as, 22, 23
Continuous improvement, 6
Contracting, entry and. *See also*
  Initiation stage
  district and school contracts,
    93–94, 192–193
  teacher contracts, 26–28, 36
Cook, T. J., 9
Croskery, K. M., 32
Culture, school, 64
Curriculum-based assessment
  (CBA)
  explanation of, 32–33
  skills in, 57
  training in, 104, 106, 109

Data collection procedures
  during coaching, 139, 140–141
  during problem identification
    and analysis, 31–34
  training in, 104, 110
Delivery system. *See also* Collaborative consultation; Instructional
  consultation process
  assumptions underlying, 38, 44
  case manager
    assignment of, 50
    configuration with IC-Team, 49
    responsibilities of, 47, 49–50
  collaborative team
    characteristics of, 38, 40
    composition of, 40–41, 92, 93;
    functions of, 39, 41–43, 106,
      119–123, 132
  content of, 39

documentation, 36–37, 39, 50–54
  Case Documentation Form, 50, 51, 52
  Student Documentation Form, 50, 51, 52, 53
  request for assistance, 39, 40, 42, 50
  Request for Assistance Form, 43–46
  system manager, 46, 86, 121, 122, 132
  System Tracking Form, 39, 46–47, 48
  underlying premises of, 44, 45
Deshler, D. D., 8
District
  contracts, 93–94, 192–193
  support, 90, 148, 164
Doyle, W. J., 59

Ekholm, M., 153, 154, 155
Entry and contracting stage. *See also* Initiation stage
  district and school contracts, 93–94, 192–193
  teacher contracts, 26–28, 36
Evaluation design
  of implementation, 54–56, 97, 98, 149, 150, 151, 168, 171–189
  of outcomes, 57–58, 97, 98–99, 169
  of training, 57, 97, 98, 114–117, 194–199
Faculty support, 146–148
Feedback, 122, 130–131, 132–133, 142, 143
Feuerberg, M. A., 68, 69
Fisher, R., 24
Friend, M., 9
Frontloading, 88–90
Fudell, R., 54, 55
Fullan, M.
  on initiation stage, 83
  on institutionalization stage, 162
  on role of facilitator, 59, 71, 72
  on role of principal, 145, 146
  on school reform, 6, 17, 18

General education, inclusive model of, 4–6, 170
Gickling, E. E., 32, 33
Goal setting, 106
Governance structures, 158, 159–162

Grade level teams, 10
Graphing and charting. *See* Data collection procedures
Gravois, T. A., 68, 69, 72
Greenberg, B., 68, 69
Guskey, T. R., 156

Hall, G. E.
  on concerns theory, 67–68, 69, 70–71, 78
  on institutionalization stage, 155
  on "mushrooms", 163–165
Handicapped students
  integration of, 4–5
  labeling of, 14–16, 29–30
  programs for, 157
Hargreaves, A., 6
Hord, S. M.
  on concerns theory, 67–68, 69, 70–71, 78
  on institutionalization stage, 155
  on "mushrooms", 163–165

IC-Team LOI scale, 56, 98, 149, 150, 151, 168, 171–189
IC-Team Summary Sheet, 120, 121, 122
IC-Teams. *See also* Collaborative consultation; Delivery system; Evaluation design; Instructional consultation process; Team development; Team functioning; Training program
  adaptations to model, 86
  adoption of, 19, 60, 153–155. *See also* Implementation stage; Initiation stage; Institutionalization stage
  assumptions underlying, 15–17
  budget design for, 158, 162–163
  complexity of, 1, 98
  composition of, 40–41, 92–93
  consultation framework used by, 26
  critical components of, 23
  critical dimensions of, 54–55, 86, 189–191
  development of model for, 21–22, 85
  early implementation sites for, 13
  future of, 166–170
  goals of, 17, 87, 166
  governance structures for, 158, 159–162

IC-Teams (*continued*)
  historical context for, 1–11
  innovation bundle for, 18–19
  key facilitator skills within, 72–76
  research on, 85
Illback, R. J., 166
Implementation stage, 118–152
  celebrations during, 149, 150, 151
  evaluation of, 54–56, 97–99, 149,
      150, 151, 168, 171–189
  facilitator tasks during, 118–119,
      134–136
  favorable school environments
      for, 145–149
  team member concerns during,
      67–71
Incident interventions, 143–144,
      163–165
Initiation stage, 83–99
  adaptations to model during, 86
  critical activities in, 83–84
  definition of, 83
  facilitator self-assessment prior to,
      85
  negotiating wants and needs dur-
      ing, 79, 80
  sharing research results during,
      85
Innovation adoption process, 19,
      60, 153–155. *See also* Imple-
      mentation stage; Initiation
      stage; Institutionalization stage
Innovation quality, 85–86, 156–157
Institutionalization stage, 153–165
  embedding activities during,
      157–163
  importance of, 153–155
  integrating activities during,
      156–157
Instructional Consultation, 26, 100
Instructional consultation process
  integration into school-based
      team model, 13, 21
  outcomes of, 21–22
  as scaffold, 22
  stages of, 26–37
Instructional strategies
  adaptability of, 3
  focus on instructional match,
      15–16, 31, 32
  implementing changes in, 8
  quality of, 35

Interactive professionalism, 6, 38
Intervention
  implementation, 36
  organizational, 42–43
  planning, 34–36
  strategies, 21–22, 110
Interview, problem identification,
      30–31

Joyce, B., 101, 102, 103
Kelly, M., 81
Kerr, D. H., 7
Kessen, W., 15
Kline, F. M., 8

Labels, problems with, 14–16, 29–30
Learning organizations, 8, 17
Learning problems, 4, 14–15. *See
      also* Handicapped students
Level of Implementation Scale. *See*
      IC-Team LOI scale
Lieberman, A., 72
Little, J. W., 9, 10
Lortie, D., 149

Maher, C. A., 11
Meier, D., 77, 170
Miles, M. B., 72, 153, 154, 155
Minority students, in special edu-
      cation, 2
Moore, J. R., 103, 105
Multidisciplinary teams (MDTs), 10,
      11, 12
"Mushrooms"
  examples of, 163–165
  as unplanned outcomes, 163

National Aeronautics and Space
      Administration (NASA), 5–6
Needs Assessment Form, 135
Needs assessments
  of system, 86–88, 89, 94
  by team members, 106, 143
  of team members, 134–136, 139
Nevin, A., 4

Observation techniques, 33
Open classrooms, 10
Outcomes
  evaluation of, 57–58, 97, 98–99,
      169
  and training methods, 101–103, 104

Parents
    needs and resources of, 94
    support from, 148–149
Pfeiffer, S. I., 11
Principal
    impact of, 91
    role of, 145–146
Problem identification and analysis
    stage, 29–34
    completion of, 34
    content of, 31
    data collection during, 31–33
    goal of, 29, 30
    interview process during, 30–31
    role of case manager during, 29,
        30, 34
Problem-solving
    case, 124–128, 128–131
    group, 10–11, 12, 124
    training in, 101, 104, 108,
        123–124
Problem-solving culture
    and collaborative teams, 10–11,
        12
    as condition for school reform,
        5–8
    and IC-Teams, 16–17, 18
Professional development. *See also*
    Coaching; Training program
    at inservice level, 77–78
    need for, 6–7, 17
    at preservice level, 169
Program evaluation. *See* Evaluation
    design
Public Law 94-142, 2, 11, 40, 44
Public Law 99-457, 167

Record keeping. *See* Delivery
    system
Referral process, 43–46
Request for assistance
    forms used, 43–47, 48
    procedures, 39, 40, 42, 43–46, 50
    underlying premises, 44, 45
Resolution. *See* Termination stage
Resources
    accessing, 71, 95–97, 158,
        162–163
    commitment of, 91–92, 93–94, 98,
        192–193
    solutions to lack of, 92
Ristau, J., 80

Rosenfield, S.
    on CBA, 32, 33
    on concerns of team members,
        68, 69
    on facilitator skills, 72
    on program evaluation, 97, 98,
        149
Ryan, E., 80

Sarason, S. B., 7, 13, 14–15
Satir, V., 63, 65, 66, 67
Saxl, E., 72
Schon, D. A., 29
School culture, 64, 65, 69
School psychologists
    data collection by, 14–15
    evaluation standards for, 16
School reform
    current focus in, 7–8, 9, 170
    difficulty of, 1–2, 153–154
    dissatisfaction with special educa-
        tion, 2–3
    failure of, 4, 5, 19
    historical purpose for, 14–15
    need for problem-solving culture,
        5–8
    need for professional develop-
        ment, 6–7, 17
    success factors in, 17–18, 60
    use of problem-solving teams,
        10–11, 12
Schools
    institutionalizing IC-Teams in,
        155–163
    obtaining commitments from,
        93–94, 192–193
    on-site facilitators for, 71, 72, 78,
        79, 82
    proposed adaptations of IC-
        Teams in, 167–168
    as receptive environments, 145–149
    selecting participating, 91–92
Schumaker, J. B., 8
Schwab, J., 122
Shane, R. L., 32
Showers, B., 101, 102, 103
Skrtic, T. M., 5
Special education
    alternatives to, 4–6, 157
    dissatisfaction with, 2–4, 19
    perspective, 3, 14–15
    use of MDTs in, 10, 11, 12

Stakeholders
    changed roles of, 6–7
    desired outcomes of, 98–99
    gaining support of, 79–80, 88–90,
        94, 158
Stiggins, R. J., 32
Student Documentation Form, 50,
    51, 52, 53
System facilitators, 71, 78
System manager, 86, 121, 122, 132,
    146
System Tracking Form, 39, 46–47,
    48
Systemic change, 18, 63

Tape Analysis Form, 141–142,
    200–204
"Taylor Doe" case study, 194–199
Teacher assistance teams, 10, 11
Teachers
    collaboration among, 9, 17, 87–88
    as consultees, 22, 23
    evaluation standards for, 5
    and instructional change, 8
    as interactive professionals, 6
    request for assistance by, 39,
        43–46
    support from, 146–148
Teaching, reinventing, 170
Team development
    and case manager development,
        132–134
    characteristics of effective, 40,
        119–120
    early stages of, 120–131
    participating in process of,
        131–132
    stages in, 105–107
    and team coaching, 143
    training, 128
Team functioning. *See also* Collabo-
    rative consultation; Delivery
    system
    business and maintenance activi-
        ties in, 106, 120–123, 132

as component of delivery system,
    39, 41–43
impact of personal beliefs and
    values on, 61, 135–136
member concerns during im-
    plementation, 67–71
Temperature taking, 122–123
Termination stage, 36–37
Thousand, J. S., 4, 40
Tickler files, 122
Time concerns, 69–70, 71, 80–82
Training program. *See also* Coach-
    ing; Professional development
    content
        format, 109–111
        plans, 42, 94–95, 113
        sample agenda, 112
        schedules, 113–114
        sequence, 108–109
        timing, 111–114
    cost estimates for, 95, 96, 97
    design
        adult learning considerations,
            103, 105
        and group development,
            105–107
        relationship of methods to out-
            comes, 101–103, 104
    evaluation of, 57, 97, 98, 114–117,
        194–199
    preservice, 169

Villa, R. A., 40
Vision building, 145
Wheelan, S. A., 105, 106, 107
White, L. J., 29

Zins, J.E., 166